707

DATE DUE

GAYLORD			PRINTED IN U.S.A.

SANDHILLS BOY

SANDHI

The Winding Trail

ELMER KELTON

LLS BOY

of a Texas Writer

FORGE®

A TOM DOHERTY ASSOCIATES BOOK
NEW YORK

SANDHILLS BOY: THE WINDING TRAIL OF A TEXAS WRITER

Copyright © 2007 by Elmer Kelton

This book is printed on acid-free paper.

A Forge Book
Published by Tom Doherty Associates, LLC
175 Fifth Avenue
New York, NY 10010

www.tor-forge.com

Forge® is a registered trademark of Tom Doherty Associates, LLC.

Library of Congress Cataloging-in-Publication Data

Kelton, Elmer.
    Sandhills boy : the winding trail of a Texas writer / Elmer Kelton—
1st hardcover ed.
    p. cm.
"A Tom Doherty Associates book."
ISBN-13: 978-0-7653-1521-2
ISBN-10: 0-7653-1521-1
    1. Kelton, Elmer. 2. Novelists, American—20th Century—Biography.
3. Western stories—Authorship. 4. Texas, West—Social life and customs.
5. Texas, West—In literature.

PS3561.E3975 Z475 2007
813'.54—dc22
[B]
                                                            2007006539

First Edition: May 2007

Printed in the United States of America

0 9 8 7 6 5 4 3 2 1

Dedicated to the Lipp family of Ebensee, Austria,
who gave me the finest gift they had

SANDHILLS BOY

IN SPANISH IT IS *querencia,* in German *Heimat,* the place of the heart, the homeland. For me, it is that part of Texas west of the ninety-eighth meridian. In particular it is a ranch in Crane and Upton counties, just east of the Pecos River.

Its proper name is the McElroy Ranch, though cowboys of old called it the Jigger Y, or just "the Ys." It is where I grew up, and where I had ambitions to become a cowboy like my father and grandfather. It was where I had to concede, after years of bumps, bruises, and disappointments, that I never would.

This land of my youth lies at the edge of the Chihuahuan Desert. Its earliest inhabitants were migratory hunters and gatherers, seldom remaining long enough in one place to leave much evidence of their passing. The search for food kept them moving, following a sparse offering of game, collecting what edible plants they could find from an arid soil stingy in its gifts. War-painted horsemen down from the high plains hurried across on the Comanche war trail, bent on raiding settlements farther south in Mexico. They swam the Pecos at Horsehead Crossing, only twenty or so miles as the crow flies from where J. T. McElroy established his ranch.

No stranger seeing the land for the first time would describe it as scenic. It is like the ugly child loved only by its mother. For centuries after venturesome Spaniards first set foot there, travelers pushed across the dry stretches of West Texas on their way to somewhere else. Few saw anything that invited them to stay. Water was scarce, grass was sparse. Most forms of flora and fauna were armed with stickers, thorns, horns, or tusks. Roads were few and distances long. Each seemingly barren horizon, when reached, yielded to another much the same. Prolonged droughts were the rule, punctuated by occasional times of healing rains that never seemed to heal quite enough before the next siege of dry years. It was the last part of the state to be settled, and then only because nothing else was left.

Yet, to one who spent his boyhood there, despite the plainness of its surface it had a wild beauty uniquely its own for those who chose to see it. The lonely expanses offered a liberating sense of freedom I never found in crowded towns and cities, in the tyranny of clocks and schedules and production goals. It encouraged quiet contemplation and appreciation for small and transient pleasures like the smell of greasewood after a rain, the distant call of a calf for its mother, even the mournful wail of a coyote on a moonlit night.

Good things had happened there, and bad things as well. On a lonesome stretch of prairie in a McElroy pasture, I felt a chill as more than once I rode by the unmarked grave of a cowboy killed by horse thieves years before. Growing up listening to eyewitness accounts of the open range and long trails, I saw our part of Texas as a living remnant of a fading frontier. I went with cowboys as they saddled their horses and rode out at sunup to work bawling herds of cattle in the manner of their fathers and grandfathers. Nights, out with the chuck wagon, I looked up at stars crisp and bright, almost within reach of my fingers, and was lulled off to sleep by the pleasant aroma of mesquite smoke from a dying campfire. To me, past and present blended. History was still playing out before my eager young eyes.

It was a land of high blue sky, of wind and dust and little rain.

It was a land that constantly tested the fiber of the ever-changing series of people who passed that way. For two generations before my time, it had been the cowboy's domain. Except for fences and a few roads, little had changed from the way the Comanche had seen it during his less than two centuries of dominance.

In the years of my boyhood this land came to know a new breed of pioneers, risk-running wildcat drillers and hard-muscled oilfield roustabouts who punched holes into a resistant earth, seeking energy for a nation beset by depression, then by war. Some were kin of mine.

The discovery of oil brought many changes, some good, some not. It brought work to thousands and riches to a few. Forests of derricks arose across the greasewood flatlands and wind-rippled sandhills, creating a new skyline of wood and steel. New roads cut a cobweb pattern across prairies where only cow trails had been. Black smoke became a constant in skies otherwise blue. All too often the wind brought with it a sulfurous whiff of oil.

Military service carried me to Europe, where in Austria I was fascinated by a vastly different land of towering granite mountains, green alpine valleys, deep blue lakes, and a pretty girl in a dirndl dress. Though that magnificent country won a permanent place in my heart, West Texas was always home. It remains my *querencia*.

True, it is not the stuff of colorful picture postcards, but it was a grand place to grow up, to store away memories that would endure long after the scenes I witnessed as a boy had vanished with the changing winds of time.

The tall derricks are gone now, replaced by unobtrusive pump jacks, often painted in earth tones to blend with the landscape. Production has declined with aging of the fields, many once-rich wells declared dead and permanently sealed by cement. Most of the oilfield towns that pulsed with enthusiasm and clattered with activity are dying by degrees, leaving boarded-up buildings to fall into ruin and abandoned machinery to rust away.

The ranch where I grew up has gone through several changes in ownership. The old headquarters stands silent, its structures neglected and gradually going to the ground. Cattle wander among them, browsing on weeds where flowers once were tended by loving hands and yards raked clean by not-so-willing Kelton boys. The corrals stand empty, their gates open. The big roundups and the bawling herds are gone. The wagon cook's chuck box rests in a museum.

But in memory all is still as it used to be, perhaps bigger and brighter than the reality ever was. I cannot live there again, but I can visit in my mind. I go every day, for a little while.

ONE

OFTEN WHEN I LOOK in the mirror, the face I see is my cowboy father's, the same pinched blue eyes, the same mouth and chin, the same ruddy complexion. Our destinies set us on different pathways. He spent his life within a radius of little more than two hundred miles. The farthest he ever traveled was one visit to his mother's childhood home in Georgia. I have spent time in countries he never saw and gone through experiences he could only imagine, like trudging through the final weeks of a war in Europe, or falling desperately in love with a blue-eyed Fräulein amid the magnificence of the Austrian Alps.

Yet in many ways his influence has continued to shape my life. Despite the long years since his death, he has never seemed far away. My hair is as thin and gray now as his ever was, but often I still pause and ask myself: "What would Dad think?" Usually I know, for his opinions were strong and generally predictable. Like anyone, he could sometimes be wrong, but within the limitations of his times and personal experience he had a good grasp of life's realities.

He never saw an automobile until he was five or six years old. He lived to watch on television as men walked on the moon.

Buck Kelton was a wage-working cowboy most of his life and

**Buck Kelton and baby Elmer at Horse Camp,
on the Five Wells Ranch (1926–1927)**

a cattle owner in a modest way. Ranch-raised on open plains north of Midland, Texas, he came into maturity just in time to be blind-sided by the Great Depression. It inflicted emotional wounds that never healed. The rest of his life he expected the next depression to start this afternoon, or tomorrow at the latest. The worst advice he ever gave me was after the war, when I contemplated buying a house. He said, "You'd better wait until they get cheaper."

I didn't, and they never did.

The *best* advice he ever gave me was to be wary of debt, for he had learned by bitter experience that it could be an intolerable master. He had owned cattle in a small way since he was fourteen. Like most cowboys, beginning with the first who ever raised his foot to a stirrup, he dreamed of having his own ranch. The goal was worthy, but the timing of his first big move could hardly have been worse.

In 1928, three years after marrying my mother, he borrowed money and bought a string of Hereford cows to graze on leased pasture. Prices were strong, and optimists were saying the cattle business would never see another poor day. After the crash of 1929 the cows were worth less than the amount he owed on them. The lender stayed with him, allowing him to hold on through the dark years of the Depression. Some lenders were not so understanding. Many a cattle owner went bankrupt in those bleak times.

During my boyhood, a major part of his hard-earned salary as cowboy and ranch foreman was earmarked toward paying down that debt. In West Texas, spare dollars were as scarce as rain. They were exceedingly rare in the Kelton house. Dad could squeeze a nickel until the Indian rode the buffalo. He had to. His unyielding Victorian sense of ethics told him that a debt had to be honored no matter the sacrifice.

He finally managed to pay off the note just at the brink of World War II. By then the original cows had grown old and had been replaced by their offspring. Fortunately the herd had increased in both numbers and value, finally reaching about five hundred head. The long struggle had been justified despite the pain.

It has been said that his was the last full-time horseback cowboy generation. My brothers and I are fortunate that as youngsters we lived through that era. We were witness to the twilight years of the old-time professional cowboys who lived and worked in much the style of open-range days. For better as well as for worse, we witnessed the slow transition into the mechanized, computerized, and increasingly regulated ranching industry of today.

Our sons and daughters missed most of that. Our grandchildren have missed it all.

Born in 1901, Buck Kelton was a third-generation cowboy. His paternal grandfather, Robert Kelton, moved from the East Texas

Buck Kelton working cattle at the McElroy Ranch (1960)

piney woods to West Texas in 1878, bringing a covered wagon, a string of horses, and a young wife heavy with child. Settling on farm and pasture land in the Belle Plain community of Callahan County, they lived out of the wagon in the beginning, too busy or perhaps too nearly broke to build a house. As my great-grandmother approached her time for delivery, kindly Mrs. Sam Cutbirth offered the hospitality of her home until the baby arrived. Actually, she insisted. Otherwise, my grandfather Bill would have been born in that covered wagon, or beneath it. Instead, he was born in a log house.

Bill Kelton was the first of six children. In 1888, when he was only about ten, his father died suddenly of appendicitis. In rural West Texas, surgery was beyond reach. My grandfather had to drop out of school and work to help support his mother and five siblings. He cowboyed, broke horses and mules, plowed cotton, and did whatever else a youngster could to earn a dollar. As a teenager and young man he worked on ranches from the Pecos River to as far north as the XIT Ranch in the upper Texas Panhandle. He learned his cowboy craft from veterans of trail drives and open range. Later he taught it to my father, who passed it on to us Kelton boys, or in my case, tried to.

I still remember clearly what my grandfather looked like, for he lived until I was eighteen. His face leathery, he had the same blue eyes as my father, pinched by sun and wind. He wore his hat brim low and held his chin high to see out from under it. That gave him a proud and independent appearance. I always thought he looked a little like Will Rogers.

An oddity, which eventually had tragic consequences, was a black birthmark about the size of a quarter on the back of his neck. In time, it would become a lethal melanoma.

Granddad married and started a family, but times were hard in Callahan County in the early 1900s. He wanted to take his brood where he might find more work and opportunity. A younger brother, Frank, had drifted out to Pecos City on horseback about the turn of the century to work as a cowboy. He wrote home that ranch jobs were available there, so Granddad decided to move to the Pecos River. My grandmother had heard stories about the harshness of that dry country and the wildness of Pecos City, notorious for several shootings. She said she would move as far west as Midland, but no farther. Granddad insisted that they would go to Pecos.

My grandmother may have looked thin and frail, but she had a strong will. They went to Midland.

That was in 1906. My father was barely five years old.

Times were no easier around Midland than in Callahan County. Granddad reluctantly worked as a drayman, hauling freight to and from the railroad depot until a ranch job turned up north of town. By this time he and my grandmother had several young mouths to feed. It was customary that ranches furnish groceries for employees and their families in compensation for low wages. Granddad's family was more than the owner counted on. He let Granddad go, then hired him back with the provision that he feed his family himself. Jobs being scarce, Granddad had little choice.

In time he acquired two modest parcels of land a few miles apart. They were not large enough to support the family, which for some years lived on the northernmost place. Granddad worked wherever work was to be had and raised feed crops in a small dry-land field. Home was a plain box-and-strip house like a thousand others on farms and ranches of the time. The siding was one-by-ten pine boards nailed upright against a simple box frame, with one-by-fours applied over the joins to prevent wind and rain from seeping in. As years passed the unpainted lumber would turn an ash gray and the joins would loosen. The only insulation was the wallpaper. Such a house could be miserably cold in winter and insufferably hot in summer. Even so, most people preferred it to the musty dugouts in which many settlers spent the early years. In many ways the dugout was more comfortable, but it was a point of pride to live above the ground rather than under it.

This home place was on a well-beaten trail that led from Midland north to Lamesa. Freighters camped their wagons in a hackberry grove beside a small playa lake east of the house. It would be their first or last night out from Midland, depending upon the direction they were traveling. The lake was brackish or dried up much of the time, so teamsters led their horses and mules up to the house to water them at Granddad's windmill. He would not accept payment, for the water belonged to the Lord. The windmill didn't, so most left hay or grain at the campground as a gesture of gratitude. Dad and his sisters would pull a small wagon down to the site and pick up the leavings to feed the family's own work stock.

Dad marveled at how well trained the freighters' horse and mule teams were. In the evening the harness would be dropped on the ground where the animals stood. The teams would be fed, either in portable wooden troughs or in morrals buckled over their heads. Afterward they would be tethered to a picket line. In the morning the teamster would pop a whip, and each animal would step into its proper place in the harness.

Those hackberry trees still stand, a modest landmark alongside a modern highway that follows the old freighter trail. The lake is still there too, though it rarely has water in it.

Granddad eventually became foreman of the Scharbauer Cattle Company's Five Wells Ranch east of Andrews. There my grandmother cooked for however many cowboys happened to be at headquarters on any given day. There might be one, or there might be a dozen. Many ranch foremen's wives endured this chore. It was an accepted custom of the times but usually carried no extra pay.

Daisy Miller Kelton had never had an easy life. As a small girl she traveled to Texas with her family in a covered wagon. She lived long enough to fly to California in a jet plane to visit a brother.

My grandmother had one luxury at Five Wells and later at the Hackamore N, a party-line telephone. She could learn all the local news by listening in on neighbors' calls. Often she would break in and contribute to the conversation. Callers took for granted that nothing was private on a party line. The rural telephone wires were run above barbed-wire fences at about shoulder height to a man on horseback. A rider could search the line for breaks and repair them without getting out of the saddle.

She expected certain rules of meal-time etiquette to be observed by those who ate at her table, rules still widely observed in ranching country. Cowboys washed their hands and faces and combed their hair before entering the dining room, kitchen, or wherever the meal was to be served. They took off their hats at the door. They carried their plates and utensils to the kitchen cabinet or the sink when they finished eating. To do less was to risk being called sheepherders, an insult of considerable potency.

One did not want to offend the cook, whether male or female, for the penalty was likely to be burned biscuits and rocks in the beans until proper penance was paid.

The Five Wells Ranch was an example of the inaccuracy of local folklore. Old-timers, including my father and his brother Ben, said it acquired the name from an early settler named Wells who had five daughters. But the five wells were designated on Colonel

Ranald Mackenzie's military map of 1872, at a time when Co-manche and Kiowa still held the land. Indians dug shallow wells in the sand in search of water. Hence the name.

White settlement did not begin to any degree on the Texas plains until after Mackenzie's crushing Tule Canyon defeat of the horseback tribes in the fall of 1874. Only when hide hunters had eliminated most of the buffalo did cattlemen like Charles Good-night start bringing in their herds and establishing residence.

Almost from the time he was big enough to sit in a saddle, Dad, like most ranch boys, was expected to pitch in and help the men, whether they were handling cattle on horseback, building fence, or pulling rods from a windmill. Learning the many facets of ranch work was considered as important to a boy's education as reading, writing, and arithmetic. Payment was seldom considered until a youngster was in his teens and ready to take a grown man's full part. In the meantime, the experience he gained was considered re-muneration enough. It was a free education.

Most cowboys in those times grew up on a farm or ranch and from early boyhood were experienced in outdoor work, in han-dling cattle and horses. It was more difficult to train a town-raised boy who lacked that background and the instincts that came with it. Cowboy life entailed hardships and sacrifices most country boys took for granted. These were tough hills to climb for a youngster from a tamer environment, though many managed the transition.

The word "cowboy" has taken on negative connotations in re-cent times, usually denoting rashness and arrogance, especially in a political or military context. In ranch country, however, to be rec-ognized as a cowboy rather than simply a ranch hand was and still is an honor which has to be earned. Hat and boots are not enough. Many a pretender never measures up.

By the time Dad finished the seventh grade in a country school at a now-vanished settlement known as Florey, he was ready to take up a man's load and earn a man's wage. Old photos show him to have grown almost as tall as his father. He day-worked on ranches in the Midland and Odessa area. It later was a point of pride with him that from the time he was seventeen until his mid-sixties, he was never out of a job more than three weeks altogether.

Years later, John D. Holleyman, who worked with him several years in the late 1930s and early 1940s, told me, "I never saw a man who liked hard work as much as Buck Kelton did. The trouble was that he always wanted me to be with him."

Dad's hard experience during the Depression years had much to do with that. He had a strong sense of the value of work and the security it could provide. From the time he took on his first paying job, he was loathe to give up one before he had a firm grip on another. He was hesitant to take a gamble that might bring more hardship to his family than they already had as a natural consequence of the times and his chosen occupation. He counseled that a sparrow in the hand was better than an eagle on the wing. He might reach for the eagle, but he did not turn loose of the sparrow. He could never forget those mortgaged cows that for so long bore down on his shoulders like the weight of the world.

Dad was not a tall man, only about five-eight, but from his twenties through most of his life he carried a lot of weight. He was a hearty eater. He insisted on fresh biscuits, fried steak, and fried potatoes, or at least red beans and corn bread. He loved pies and cakes. In their absence he made his own dessert by pouring a generous amount of blackstrap molasses onto his plate, mixing a glob of butter in it, and swabbing it all up with hot biscuits.

He had worked on ranches where the food was good and on some where it bordered on awful. When he was foreman and later general manager of the McElroy Ranch, he never let his frugal nature affect the buying of groceries for the cowboys. He said workingmen deserved to be fed well, and he saw to it that they were.

He was an early riser. As he left for the milk pen in the dark of the morning, he let the screen door slam hard enough to shake the house. That was a signal for everyone else to get up. Often he led us on horseback to the far side of a pasture long before daybreak. There we waited until it became light enough to see cattle. I thought we could have spent that extra hour or so in bed, but Dad never let daylight catch him asleep. He said he acquired his work habits on ranches where a lantern was of more use than a bed.

He was a year too young for service in World War I. In late fall of 1918 he was cowboying for the Scharbauer family, who had ranched in Midland County since 1887. He was among several hands driving a string of horses about a hundred miles southwestward to a ranch in Pecos County. The wagon boss, Billy Peays, had just received his draft notice. This would be his last ride before he reported for duty. Everyone knew about the horrors of trench warfare, and he deeply dreaded going to France.

The horses were about halfway between Midland and Odessa when some people came along in a touring car and asked if the cowboys had heard the news. An armistice had been signed.

"Billy Peays was the happiest man I ever saw," Dad remembered.

They finished the drive in an early snowstorm, wet and chilled to the bone. The disastrous Spanish influenza epidemic was at its peak. Dad and another cowboy came down with the flu. Clarence Scharbauer Sr. hauled them back to Midland in his car and placed them in the care of Dr. Ed Calloway. The good doctor managed to pull Dad and the other cowboy through, but he lost a rancher who came in shortly after them.

I have often thought on how differently things might have turned out if Scharbauer had not been at the ranch with his car. The trip to Midland would have taken three or four days by wagon, and possibly more because of the snow.

Dad valued physical labor but distrusted indoor work. He did not acknowledge that anyone sitting at a desk was actually working. He liked to see some tangible end product of labor, whether it be cattle for the market, a crop of cotton, a straight fence, a meal on the table, or even a proper shine on a pair of boots. A pile of papers did not count, for these could not be eaten, worn, ridden, or driven.

I often imagined him questioning if the writing I did was really tangible, if the hours I spent at a desk were in any way comparable to a day in the saddle or in a field. What came of it was but words on paper. I always fell short of his expectations as a cowboy. What was to become of a ranch boy who could not rope for sour apples and could not stay aboard a pitching horse past the second jump?

J. R. Williams used to draw a daily syndicated cartoon called *Out Our Way*. One that has stayed with me for sixty years shows a ranch boy in his teens unpacking a typewriter while his rancher father looks on in disgust and says, "A writer? I thought I brought you up better than that." Williams dedicated it to old-time pulp writer Walt Coburn, but it could have been about me.

I can still hear what Dad said when I told him at age sixteen that I wanted to become a writer. He declared, "That's the way with you kids nowadays, you all want to make a living without working for it."

We once passed the Odessa country club, and Dad saw men playing golf on a weekday afternoon. Told that they were there for the exercise, he snorted that if they truly worked they would not need it. "Let them come to the ranch," he said. "I'll show them exercise."

Even after I became a published writer and had steady employment as an agricultural reporter, I felt that he did not trust my choice of occupation. He was all too aware of my limitations as a ranch hand. That gave him reason to be afraid I had other shortcomings that could eventually bring my little make-believe world crashing down around me.

Sometimes when I see Dad in the mirror I wonder about that myself.

TWO

I DISCOVERED AMERICA ON April 29, 1926, at Horse Camp on the Five Wells Ranch a few miles east of Andrews, Texas. My mother recalled that it was a wet, stormy day, which seems ironic. I have spent my life in rain-shy West Texas, where most days we search in vain for a promising rain cloud.

My uncle Ben Kelton, still in his teens, hurried to town to fetch the doctor, for nobody wanted to risk taking my mother out on the slick, muddy road and perhaps have her baby arrive in a car mired in a ditch. Home births were the norm rather than the exception. It was a long way to Odessa and a regular hospital.

Andrews was a small farm and ranch town in the midst of what has been claimed to be the largest oak forest in the United States. The oaks, however, stand only a couple of feet tall, their proper name shin oak. Locally they are known as "shinnery." Little about them provides food for man or beast other than their tiny acorns. When shinnery blooms in the spring it can be toxic to cattle. Its only practical purpose, local people say, is to stabilize the sand. Where shinnery was plowed out long ago in favor of cash crops, and where cover crops are not maintained year by year, the sand moves every time the wind blows. Shin oak regrowth is agonizingly slow.

Later, in the 1930s, Andrews shared in the oil booms and became a force to reckon with in Friday-night high school football.

The Scharbauers raised horses, and Horse Camp was named for those. We left there before I was more than a year old, so I have no personal recollections of the place. I know from old photos and family stories that we lived in a small box-and-strip ranch house, turn-of-the-last-century vintage. A resident bull snake lived beneath the floor, harmless to humans but death on mice. Dad and Mother had eloped to nearby Seminole the previous year, hoping for a private wedding. The minister, with a sense of benign mischief, stalled the service until word could be sent to some of their friends. By the time the ceremony began, a crowd had gathered to witness the embarrassed couple taking their vows.

My mother was known to almost everyone as Bea, though her mother and grandmother insisted on using the full name, Beatrice.

The line camp where they started married life was miles away from Five Wells headquarters. It was Dad's responsibility to watch over its part of the ranch, regularly checking the cattle and horses, keeping the fences up, and seeing that livestock never ran out of water. My birth certificate lists his occupation as "cowpuncher."

Mother had taught school. In those days, with lots of youthful bachelors around, young women teachers usually did not remain single for long. The old story about the cowboy courting the schoolmarm might be considered cliché, but it was real. There were a lot more bachelor cowboys than eligible lady schoolteachers.

At Horse Camp my cowboy career might have been blighted before I was old enough to walk. Mother sat on the fence, holding me as she watched Dad ride a young half-broken horse in circles inside a corral. Dad decided it was time to give me a little cowboy experience, so he took me in front of him on the saddle. The bronc had not been consulted and began to pitch. Dad faced the double challenge of staying on board while hanging on to me. As the bronc pitched around to where Mother was sitting, Dad handed me off to her like a quarterback handing off the football just before getting sacked.

That event may have set the pattern for my later years. I always had a tentative relationship with horses.

It took Dad a while to settle into a permanent job, for ranch work tended to be unstable. For a time he worked for Charlie Goldsmith on a ranch north of Odessa. Our life there left me only a few vague mental pictures which probably owe more to stories I heard than to actual memories. We had a German police dog called Lindy, named after Charles A. Lindbergh, the biggest hero of the time. He once grabbed me by the seat of the britches and pulled me away from a rattlesnake I was trying to pet. I must have had an early attraction to wildlife, for I reached into a cage to pet a bristly javelina someone had roped and brought to the house. A cowboy named Wes Reynolds jerked me away just as the wild peccary snapped his sharp teeth at my fingers.

Wes was one of the old-time cowboys who kept turning up in our lives. A lifetime in the sun had given his face and hands the color and texture of old saddle leather. He could hold his silence for hours, or he could peel the hide with a few gruff words in his raspy voice. A contemporary of my grandfather, he had taught Dad much of what he knew about cattle and horses. He was a lifelong bachelor. It was said that he had had a romance early in his life but lost the girl to another suitor.

He had drifted into the Midland country from New Mexico, where he had been employed on the vast George W. Littlefield ranches. He had known and worked with a legendary black cowboy everybody, in a time and place where the word was commonly used, called "Nigger Add." He said Add was one of the best riders he ever saw, and a substantial body of folklore bears out his observation. Often Littlefield entrusted Add to carry large sums of money on the theory that nobody would bother trying to rob him. Few white cowboys had money, much less a black one. Littlefield often left Add in charge of ranch operations while he was away, which could have created ticklish situations with white employees had Add not been an expert in diplomacy as well as in horsemanship. He had a way of making an order sound like a polite request.

Dad gave orders to the grown cowboys in the same manner: "If you don't mind, would you . . ." or "How about you doing . . ." He was more direct with us boys. We never mistook an order for a polite request.

As we boys became old enough to be of help on horseback, Dad had a ritual every morning before we set out to whatever task we were to undertake. "You boys water out real good," he would tell us. It might be noon before we had a chance for another drink of water, and he did not want to hear us complain about being thirsty. Nobody carried a canteen on a saddle. It wasn't "cowboy."

Years later he told us that when he was a boy he and Wes were driving a small herd down a lane toward Midland. A windmill stood about every two miles along the way. Each time they neared one, Dad would lope up to get a quick drink of water, leaving Wes alone with the cattle. Eventually Wes said, "I believe I'll go with you this time." He watched Dad take a quick sip of water and back away. He said, "I don't believe you've had enough. Drink some more." Every time Dad stopped, Wes made him drink again, until he was ready to throw it all up. Then Wes declared, "Next time, damn you, you'll water out before you leave the house."

"Watering out" became a byword in the Kelton family. Whenever Wes taught a lesson, it stayed taught.

SOME YEARS AGO I visited Horse Camp out of curiosity. I doubt that Mother and Dad would have recognized it. The old box-and-strip house in which I was born had long since been dismantled and a comfortable 1950s-style frame house built in its place. A large complex of steel corrals bespoke modern efficiency.

When Tommy Lee Jones was preparing to film a television movie from my novel, *The Good Old Boys,* I sent a photo of the old Horse Camp house to Carey White, the art director. He used it as a model for the Calloway family homestead on the set. I wished my mother could have seen it, for it was a replica of the home in which she and Dad first set up housekeeping together. Unfortunately, she had passed away a couple of years before.

I gave the Calloway name to my principal characters in honor of the doctor who kept Dad alive during the flu epidemic of 1918–19.

DAD MADE THE MOVE of his life when he hired on with the McElroy Ranch at Crane in 1929. The ranch covered about two hundred and twenty square miles, half of it deeded and half leased from the University of Texas lands system. The university's permanent fund had been granted large areas in sparsely-settled West Texas in the late 1800s. This land was considered nearly worthless semidesert, its grazing and farming potential severely limited by the scarcity of rainfall. No one imagined that vast oil wealth existed beneath the surface, or the university system would never have been handed such a gift. It would almost surely have gone to state politicians and their friends. As it turned out, untold millions of dollars in leases and royalties have gone into the permanent fund of Texas institutions of higher learning.

Large ranches like the McElroy and the Scharbauers maintained outlying camps to reduce travel in the daily routine. The McElroy had two: Sand Camp and the Mayfield place. We went first to Sand Camp, about fourteen miles northwest of headquarters as the crow flew. It was more by road, a challenge for narrow-tired motor vehicles because of deep sand the last couple of miles. An extensive string of sandhills stretches through much of northern and western Crane County, across parts of Ector, Andrews, and Ward counties, and into eastern New Mexico. These are said to have been left by the prehistoric Pecos River, which at one time meandered over an immense area, draining away water from a shrinking inland sea.

Oil discovery had brought a boom to Crane County. Crane

City was born in 1926, the same year I was. My teacher and mentor Paul Patterson used to say they called it Crane City when it was not yet a city, then simply Crane when it became one. I have hazy memories of the town as it was when we first saw it. A testament to the uncertain longevity of boomtowns, most of its original structures were thrown up in haste and as cheaply as possible, for no one knew how long the town might survive. Many such communities born of oil discovery vanished without a trace. Wooden frameworks covered by sheet iron dominated the two-block-long business district. Much of the population lived in tents, the more fortunate citizens having pine flooring and boarded-up sides. Some built "shotgun" houses, long and narrow like a shotgun barrel.

It was not unusual to see a fine automobile parked beside tents and simple wooden or sheet-iron shacks. Workers needed a dependable car to carry them out to the fields. They might have to move on by next week or next month, no longer needing the house or tent. They *would* need the car.

My maternal grandmother, Neta Holland, built a rooming house for oilfield workers and their families in the boomtown of Pyote, then had it partially dismantled and put back together in Grandfalls when Pyote played out. It was a picture of no-frills simplicity, with outdoor toilets and an outdoor shower discreetly enclosed within sheet-iron walls.

Houses built on the cheap were often flimsy, poor protection against the wind. One early-day oilfield woman said she learned to stand almost any hardship, but when wind blew under the house, came up between loose boards in the floor and ruffled the rugs at her feet, she was ready to call it quits.

Newly born Crane had no water system. Water was hauled by truck or wagon and poured into barrels beside the doors of houses and tents. At a time when oil was worth less than twenty cents a barrel, a barrel of water cost a dollar. There was much distress when a passing cow or horse nosed the cover from a water barrel and drank its fill, spoiling what was left unless a family was exceptionally tolerant or could not spare a dollar for a fresh barrel.

People stretched water because of its cost and scarcity. Saturday night bath water was used by the family's youngsters one at a time, then poured on the flowerbed if there was one.

The oilfields resembled a dense forest of wooden and steel derricks. A contemporary book title described the scene: *The Iron Orchard*. Eventually these towering structures were replaced by smaller and simpler pump jacks that blend more easily into the surroundings.

On crisp winter mornings we could hear the grinding and clanking of oilfield machinery from miles away, especially when pipe was being pulled from the hole and stacked inside a steel derrick.

Though rain clouds were scarce, the sky was seldom completely clear. At almost any time, one or two distant columns of black smoke could be seen rising from burning slush pits where waste oil had accumulated. These were a good indicator of barometric pressure, smoke either rising high or rising only a short way, then spreading out horizontally, flat as a tabletop. They were also an indicator of wind direction, though there was seldom any question about that anyway. Cattleman Charles Goodnight said wind was so constant on the plains that natives seldom noticed it unless it stopped. Trees tended to lean permanently northeastward, bowing to the prevailing southwest winds.

Deep sands were a hazard to early oilfield traffic. Primitive roads were marked by the hulks of cars and trucks that had bogged past the hubs, their engines burned out by futile efforts to fight their way out of sand traps. As a boy I found these relics intriguing. It was hard to imagine someone simply abandoning a ruined vehicle half buried in the sand. The relics finally disappeared during the scrap metal drives of World War II.

The solution on heavily traveled roads was to spray waste oil on them, adding density to the sand. This had to be repeated at intervals because oil exposed to the elements would slowly degrade and disappear.

My first clear recollections are of life at Sand Camp. Dad was responsible for the part of the ranch that lay north of the Crane-Odessa highway, then still a graded road subject to wind erosion and rutting. Rain was only an occasional inconvenience.

The house at Sand Camp was typically modest in style and size, with a kitchen, a bedroom, a screened sleeping porch, and no electricity or indoor plumbing. A windmill furnished water, though it had to be carried into the house in a bucket. A surface tank or pond collected the windmill's overflow and served outlying troughs to which horses and cattle came up to drink. The sand had no trees except spindly switch mesquites, so Dad planted a chinaberry sapling in the front yard. Over the years, long after we left, it reached massive proportions.

A small fenced pasture known as a horse trap led into corrals just north of the house. There Dad kept the horses he rode in his daily routine. We did not use our car often because it might sink into a sand trap. The most common solution when this happened was to dig out with a shovel and throw clumps of bear grass in front of the wheels in hope of gaining traction. Dad might let part of the air out to give the tires broader surface contact, though this required airing them again with a hand pump once the automobile was liberated from the sand.

Mark Twain said profanity sometimes has healing powers denied even to prayer. My brother Myrle and I expanded our vocabulary while listening to Dad address the car in blistering terms when it resisted his best efforts to get it unstuck. We also learned not to repeat the words within our parents' hearing.

The ranch company furnished our groceries, but because of the sand these were seldom delivered all the way to the house. A platform was built beside the road on hardpan just at the edge of the sandhills. It was about shoulder-high so animals could not reach the supplies stacked on it. Someone, usually windmiller Cliff Newland, would deliver goods in a truck from headquarters or town and leave them on the platform. Dad would hitch a team to a wagon, which negotiated the sand better than most cars and trucks, and haul the supplies to the house. I enjoyed riding beside him on the wagon seat, but I fell off once. It was a scary experience for a small boy. Dad stopped the team and hoisted me back up to safety. I learned to hang on tighter.

We two little boys were cautioned not to enter a corral with horses or cattle, for they might trample us. Myrle, almost three years younger, was attracted to horses from the first. While still a toddler, he slipped away and crawled under a fence. Mother found him in a corral, playing around and under the horses. These were not pets. Some still pitched on occasion. Even so, they tolerated this curious youngster, taking care not to step on him. Mother was afraid to enter the pen and carry him away, for they might spook and run over him. She called to Myrle to come out, slowly and carefully. After an anxious several minutes, he did.

We had a wooden rocking horse that Mother placed between two beds on the sleeping porch. Myrle would rock that horse until he fell asleep and slumped sideways onto one of the two beds. She would then lift him up and carefully place him where he could not fall off.

He never got over his affinity for horses. In his teens he became a competitive roper, and he remained one well into his seventies.

Except for an occasional cowboy like Doug Medley, sent over from headquarters to break broncs, we were alone at Sand Camp, just Dad, Mother, Myrle, and me. Dad by then was approaching thirty, his ruddy face beginning to flesh out as a result of Mother's cooking. She was a head shorter, strong but not stout, and blue-eyed like Dad.

We had contact with the outside world through a battery-operated Atwater-Kent table radio with a round black dial and a separate speaker shaped like a morning glory. Dad ran an antenna up the windmill tower. The radio picked up a station out of Fort Worth–Dallas and a couple of strong English-language Mexican border stations, which advertised everything from miracle-producing patent medicines to baby chicks and Carter Family songbooks.

Dad enjoyed old-time country music, especially fiddles. Because of that early exposure, I will stop almost anything I am doing to listen to a good fiddle player.

We had a portable windup Victrola and a stack of records. Though I could not yet read, I learned to identify most of the records on sight. Dad's favorite was "Ramona." I would play it for him when he asked me. My favorite was "Springtime in the Rockies," performed by Carson Robison. At age three I knew the lyrics by heart. I could not even imagine what the Rockies looked like. I had seen only sandhills.

The Victrola and the radio gave me an early taste for music of all kinds. Especially enamored of cowboy songs and poetry, I memorized a poem, "Make Me a Cowboy Again for a Day," feeling nostalgic for a lost way of life before I even had a chance to try it.

Cowboy music has always leaned toward the melancholy with songs like "Red River Valley," "Streets of Laredo," and "Cowboy Jack." Mother told of being in a record store where an old cowboy was listening to "When the Work's All Done This Fall." Tears ran down his cheeks as the song lamented a homesick cowboy killed by a falling horse: "Poor boy won't see his mother when the work's all done this fall."

Her own taste ran more to popular and semiclassical music. She could play the piano but did not have one at the time. Nevertheless, she held on to a stack of sheet music acquired when she was in her teens. It was useful when she finally did manage to buy a piano for our home.

An early lesson in humility came as Myrle and I played along the edge of the surface tank just past the yard. Myrle, who had not yet fully mastered the art of walking, lost his footing and slid into the tank. I was three-going-on-four and recognized something funny when I saw it. I got a big laugh out of Myrle's soggy mishap, until my feet slipped from under me and I went into the drink myself. I drew a bigger laugh than Myrle . . . from everybody else. I missed the humor in it.

Lacking electricity, we had no refrigerator. Our "ice box" was an old wooden trunk buried to its lid in cool sand just outside the east door, shielded from the hot afternoon sun. Wet burlap sacks surrounded the trunk and lined its inside for insulation. Anyone who went to town would bring back a block of ice to go into the trunk. We had cold water or iced tea for however long the ice held out.

To keep milk and other perishables reasonably fresh, Mother placed their containers in water in several metal trays stacked on an iron frame. The frame's four legs stood in water-filled cans to ward off the ants that always tried to invade our food. Wet cloths hung like curtains down the sides to keep the milk cool and the flies out.

An idealistic scene indelible in my memory is of my father on horseback, still a young cowboy in his prime, bringing a string of horses over the top of a sandhill and spilling them down its leading edge, pointing them into a wire-fenced corral west of the house. No movie ever seemed to offer its equal. To me, it was in wide screen and full color.

I had my first remembered look at a genuine chuck wagon about that time. This mule-drawn portable outdoor kitchen was of the same general type designed years before by pioneer cattleman Charles Goodnight. It was camped on a flat stretch of ground just below the Sand Camp house. In memory I can still see the wooden chuck box with its hinged lid down, serving as a worktable for the cook. Inside the box were sliding drawers for cups, plates, knives, forks, and spoons. An open space was provided for salt, baking powder, and a large can of flour. Bare wagon hoops were set in place over the bed, ready to be covered by a tarp in case of rain.

The cook placed Dutch ovens in a line on glowing coals beyond the campfire. When he lifted a coal-covered lid to check the high-rise sourdough biscuits, the teasing aroma would set a small boy's stomach to rumbling. Big cowboys', too. After the cook shouted, "Chuck," they lined up to get their plates, cups, and utensils. They walked along the line of Dutch ovens, serving themselves while the heat from live coals rose into their faces.

Breakfast time at the McElroy Ranch chuck wagon (1960)

The cowboys squatted on the ground or sat on tarp-covered bedrolls, eating from tin plates, drinking black coffee from tin cups. The basic fare varied little from day to day: fried steak, fried potatoes, sourdough biscuits, and red beans boiled with strips of bacon to add flavor. Sometimes a cobbler pie contributed a bit of luxury. Otherwise, hot biscuits dipped in molasses served for sweetening.

On larger ranches the wagon might be out on the range a major part of the year. At the Jigger Y it would be out about a week or ten days in late summer and about three weeks late in the fall.

The owner or manager might be boss over the rest of the ranch, but the cook was boss at the wagon. Many of the same mealtime rules applied at the wagon as in the ranch kitchen. Woe unto whosoever might ride a horse close enough to drift dust over the cooking. Unlike in the movies, nobody with a lick of savvy rode right up to the wagon. Nor did one poke around in the pots and pans until the cook hollered, "Chuck," "Come and get it," or similar signal of permission. An exception was the coffeepot. Usually the hands were free to help themselves to coffee at any time. The pot seldom got cold.

It was Dad's unspoken but well-recognized rule that the working hands got their food first while guests waited. When we youngsters were part of the working crew, we ate with the rest. On those few occasions when we were simply visiting, we were last in line. The cook usually waited until everyone else was fed before he filled his own plate.

When the men finished their meal they dropped their tinware into a washtub called the "wreck pan." The cook poured boiling water into the tub and washed everything while the cowboys went back out to work. Sometimes he had a helper at the wagon. If not, somebody like the kid horse jingler might be drafted to help with the cleanup.

I jingled horses a lot once I was old enough. That meant loose-herding them to graze while the main force was out gathering cattle, then bringing the horses to a handy place so the cowboys could catch fresh mounts as they came in off the drive. It also involved moving the remuda from camp to camp.

Now and then a breach of camp etiquette was serious enough to be adjudged a "chaps offense." The transgression might be as minor as quoting someone currently out of favor, especially someone regarded as a braggart or a liar. The usual procedure was to require the culprit to lie belly down over a bedroll while the other cowboys administered corporal punishment, lashing his buttocks with a pair of leather leggings. The recipient was expected to accept this treatment with grace and good humor. Emotional survival depended upon one's ability to endure practical jokes, for cowboys could be merciless to a poor sport. They were only marginally better to a good one.

I remember the cowboys at Sand Camp discussing Jake McClure, a great contest roper of the time. I knew nothing of movie stars or other such celebrities, but I sensed that McClure was someone special for these men to speak of him with such high respect.

He was one of them, but his ability with a rope had carried him to a level of his own.

Cowboys had heroes too.

SEVERAL MILES SOUTHEAST OF Sand Camp was an expanding oilfield. A number of flares, commonly called "torches," burned off excess natural gas produced in the pumping of oil. A giant flare in the Phillips Camp always lighted the night sky and in wintertime attracted cattle as well as a variety of wildlife to bed down nearby, enjoying its warmth.

On one of our infrequent trips to town I was spellbound by the sight of an oil tank blazing furiously, dense black smoke billowing from angry red flames. Even at a distance I could feel the heat. It gave me a reference point whenever a minister warned about the fires of hell.

That was reinforced by a widely circulated photograph clearly showing the devil's face in the smoke of a fatal oilfield fire.

For all I knew at that point in my life, the whole world was cattle ranches and oilfields, and everything ended somewhere not far beyond the McElroy Ranch's outside fence.

Once while helping a neighbor work cattle, Dad came across a huge skeleton of some prehistoric creature where wind had moved the sand. He brought home a shiny piece of tooth, which gradually disintegrated. The sand evidently moved again, re-covering the skeleton. I have never heard of anyone seeing it since.

Another time he visited the remains of a frontier-era wagon train and brought home the forged head of a claw hammer. He said the wheels and parts of the wagons remained more or less intact. It was widely believed then that the train had been wiped out by Indians. A newer theory is that a group of Forty-Niners returning from California let their wagons become hopelessly entrapped in the deep sand and abandoned them. Why they would have attempted to negotiate the sands remains a mystery. They could have gone around.

After a long stint at Sand Camp we moved closer to headquarters, to what was called the Mayfield place.

Around the turn of the century Texas had put up much of its unclaimed state land for homesteading in tracts of up to four square miles. Most of this land had previously been used by cattle ranchers, either on a lease basis or simply free because it was too far from Austin for the state's collectors to come calling. Some of the ranchers, including J. T. McElroy, made a deal to put up the filing fees for their cowboys with a quiet agreement that when they had lived out the required three years and gained title, they would sell the land to their employers. Harve Mayfield was a McElroy foreman, and McElroy obtained Mayfield's homestead through that sort of arrangement. One of the state requirements was that the claimant erect a livable house. Many built them just large enough to meet minimum specifications.

The Mayfield house into which we moved was a simple box-and-strip structure made up of two homesteader houses partially dismantled and joined together. As at Sand Camp, the "convenience" was out in back. One nice touch, however, was a small milk house with a concrete trough through which fresh cool water ran constantly, pumped by an adjacent windmill. This allowed for better cooling of milk, extending its life.

I never had much fear of Hereford range cattle, for they were seldom a threat unless crowded into a tight spot, and then the worst thing they usually did was run over you trying to get away. We had a Jersey bull at the Mayfield place, however, a terror to children and women. Though men could usually handle him, he had a grudge against small people and skirts. My aunt Grace Holland was a tall, strong-willed woman who tolerated foolishness from nobody. She ran her own show and had little fear of man or beast. Nevertheless, that bull ran his bluff on her. At that point in her life, brought up on traditional Southern rules of behavior, she was reluctant to speak the word "bull." She referred to this belligerent animal as a "he-cow." Though she could be a force to reckon with, she stayed out of his way.

I forget who left the Mayfield place first, us or the bull. But as long as he was in the pasture adjacent to the house, we kids never strayed out of the yard.

We were introduced to chores as soon as we were big enough to handle them. By the time I was four, Mother decided I was mature enough to help with the churning, turning milk into butter. I found it monotonous as well as demeaning for a young cowboy meant for more manly activity. One of the worst spankings I ever got happened after I lifted the plunger out and set it on the linoleum floor with butter clinging to it, considering that I was done.

Another came when I nearly killed Myrle. By this time our family had been enlarged by the arrival of brother Bill, still an infant. A little swing had been set up on the porch, supported by springs suspended from the rafters. It was like a deep sack, with holes for the legs so the baby could not fall out. Bill was always of a gentle nature, easily brought to a broad smile. He laughed and cooed as we swung him carefully from side to side.

Myrle decided he ought to enjoy it too, so he climbed in, and I began to bounce him. He was having a jolly time until one of the springs broke loose and slammed down hard on his head. Suddenly he was squalling fiercely and bleeding all over the porch. Mother rushed him to town for emergency treatment. For my part, I had not seen the worst yet. That came when we got home.

From that point on into our teens, Myrle and I had a prickly relationship.

Mother was the real disciplinarian in the family. Dad was short on patience and had an explosive temper. He could curl our hair with caustic criticism. Still, he almost never laid a hand on us. Mother had been brought up by a stern grandmother who had no compunctions against corporal punishment. She did not spare the rod when she thought we needed an adjustment in attitude.

Her grandmother, Martha Barnes, stayed with us a while in the 1930s. Sixty years earlier, she had eloped in an ox cart with John Thomas Barnes. She was a formidable woman who could freeze us boys with a frown and kept us walking wide circles around her. John Barnes had died in 1922 and was buried in Kosse, Texas, near Waco. Great-grandmother lived to be ninety-seven. As she lay dying in Monahans in 1953, she was asked if she wanted to be buried beside John. She said, "These old bones are too tired to travel so far. Just bury me here."

The most painful punishment Mother administered was when she sent us out to bring in a switch, so that we had plenty of time to dread what was coming. Anticipation multiplied the ordeal, illustrating the truth of the adage that the coward dies a thousand deaths, the brave man but one. It was hard to be brave while fetching that switch. I always suspected she learned that technique from Grandmother Barnes.

Though she knew well the necessity for discipline, Mother also had a deep appreciation for the benefits of education. She had attended teachers' college in Denton and had taught in a country school. She encouraged us to study and learn about the world. Before we were able to read, she read to us. I loved stories and wanted to read them for myself. I learned my first letters from a piece of grocery carton nailed up to substitute for a broken window pane: FOLGERS COFFEE. I began to decipher the words on food cans in the pantry. By age five I was reading at a first grade level. That was not as common then as it is today. Crane had no kindergarten.

Mother home-schooled me through the first two grades, though I went to class at intervals to ensure that I was keeping up with the other students. One of my first literary efforts came from an assignment by a second grade teacher, Mrs. Louise Turrentine. She first read to us the old story about the preacher and the bear. In it, the hard-pressed preacher has climbed a spindly tree which seems about to break under his weight. He prays, "Oh, Lord, if you can't help me, for goodness sake, don't you help that bear."

She instructed us to rewrite it in our own words. I misunderstood. Somehow I thought I was supposed to tell the story in rhyme. I labored long and hard to bring it off as a narrative poem.

Flabbergasted, the teacher declared, "Someday, Elmer, we'll see your name up in lights."

I am still waiting.

Mother was responsible for another early inspiration that helped point me toward writing. She often brought home an issue of *Ranch Romances,* a Western pulp magazine. It periodically featured humorous stories by S. Omar Barker about a boy named Mody Hunter, sort of a Western Huck Finn. She once decided to write a story and see if *Ranch Romances* would publish it. She wrote it in pencil on the pages of a ruled tablet. I don't know if she ever mailed it, but the fact that she wrote it helped trigger the idea that I might do the same.

From the time I was eight or nine years old, I was writing stories, though I never had the nerve to put them in an envelope and send them to a magazine. On the contrary, I did them mostly in secret, for writing seemed a sissy activity for a ranch boy when there were chickens to be roped and milk-pen calves to be ridden.

THREE

WE TRANSFERRED TO RANCH headquarters when I was about six. Compared to the loneliness of Sand Camp and the Mayfield place, it was like moving to town. Most of the buildings were new, having been constructed after the ranch came into new ownership. Everything had a fresh and sparkling look. It was home to four families: the Grants, the Newlands, the Smelsers, and us, plus two or three bachelor cowboys and bookkeeper Matt Cleghorn. Lester S. Grant was manager of both the ranch and the company's oil interests. Cliff Newland took care of the ranch's seventy-odd windmills. The Smelsers cooked for the cowboys, and Mr. Smelser did maintenance work around the place.

Dad was advanced to foreman when Fount Armstrong relinquished that position to devote full time to his own ranching interests. I don't know what his starting salary was, but later it remained steady at $150 a month for many years, plus meat and most groceries other than perishables. We were furnished an almost brand-new house, still sporting its first coat of blue-gray paint.

The company had razed most of the old buildings from the earlier McElroy era and kept a crew of carpenters in residence for a year or more constructing residences, an office, a bunkhouse, and a kitchen for the cowboys, and several sheet-iron outbuildings including a barn, a warehouse, and a cow shed. About the only major original structure left standing was the Newland house, J. T. McElroy's personal residence during his stays at the ranch. It was a sprawling turn-of-the-century frame house, impressive in its day. For a time one side room had been used as a school for children from the ranch and neighboring families. Though it no longer served that purpose, a couple of desks and a blackboard remained. The Newlands tolerated us Kelton boys in our frequent visits to the classroom to draw and write on the blackboard.

Headquarters seemed elegant in comparison to other places we had lived. The yard and buildings were kept neat and clean. Unlike the camps it had indoor plumbing and electricity, this furnished by a thirty-two-volt Delco system powered by a gasoline generator and a bank of wet-cell batteries. It produced just enough power to light the buildings and operate a refrigerator at the company kitchen. As a youngster I was frustrated because I could not have electrical toys, for those required 110 volts. But at least I had good light to read by, and I was a voracious reader.

A number of scrubby salt cedar trees furnished what shade there was around the houses. Salt cedars had originally been brought into Texas as decorative plants. Over time they became a serious pest, difficult to control. They spread profusely along rivers and around many of the state's larger lakes, consuming and wasting vast amounts of water resources. They are a sterling example of good intentions gone terribly awry.

The ranch was like a small democratic community. Everyone was on roughly the same economic level except for the Grants, who did not socialize much. Mrs. Grant, a middle-aged wisp of a woman with a perpetual dark frown, lived like a recluse in a house the company furnished. She rarely came out except to walk across the broad, open yard for meals at the company kitchen. She did not ordinarily cook for herself. She showed no liking for children and did not allow dogs on the place. She would occasionally search us youngsters for matches, fearing that we might burn the place down. It was my feeling that she never knew a happy day on that wind-blown, isolated ranch, far from the social amenities she had known. She must have felt as if she had been sent into exile.

Grant spent his days in the office building except when business called upon him to back his long black Packard out of the company's plain sheet-iron garage and travel somewhere. He was a tall, imposing man, balding, well dressed, and wore rimless glasses. He carried himself with the dignity of a college professor, which he once had been. Guardedly cordial, he would have appeared more at home in a bank or a law office than in a ranch corral. Indeed, he rarely entered a corral. That was for the cowboys to do. He had other responsibilities. We youngsters were counseled never to forget that he was the boss and should be treated with quiet respect, with emphasis on the *quiet*.

In the early days of oil discovery, many people involved in Western mining moved easily into the petroleum industry. It was simply another mineral commodity except that it was in liquid rather than solid form. The oil boomtowns were much like the earlier mining towns except that their citizens were more likely to travel in cars and trucks than with horses, mules, and wagons. The boomer spirit was the same, and so were many of the faces.

Grant had a background in South American mining, so he had seen more of the world than anybody on the place, at least until Norwegian bookkeeper Tom Schreiner moved to the ranch, succeeding Cleghorn. Grant had taught at Colorado's School of Mines before being hired to oversee Franco-Wyoming's West Texas oil interests. The ranch itself was incidental to him. The company was far more interested in what lay beneath the ground than in the sparse vegetation on top of it. Day-to-day ranch operations were left to Dad and the cowboys.

Grant had a grasp of range economics, however. When he took over as manager he realized the ranch was overstocked and overgrazed. He sold about half the cattle, easing the grazing load and allowing the grass to increase. He might not have been able to ride and rope, but he saw the larger picture. He was, in short, an early conservationist. A few years after selling the ranch, J. T. McElroy came back to see what had been done with his old place. Grant took him for a tour. McElroy's comment was, "I can see you don't know a thing about ranching. You have two grasses for every cow. I always had two cows for every grass."

This illustrated a common problem among early range operators, an overestimation of carrying capacity. The first settlers came from areas accustomed to higher rainfall than they found in the West. Moreover, hide hunters had eliminated the vast Texas buffalo herds in the 1870s. Ungrazed, the grass made lush growth that misled newcomers into regarding it as limitless. They stocked it at levels today's ranchers would not dream of. Overgrazing caused a decline in the better grasses and an increase in invader species and brush that today's operators must contend with at great cost.

The problem resulted more from ignorance than from greed. Later generations have learned hard lessons about the land's limitations.

By Eastern standards the McElroy Ranch might have been considered huge, but in terms of the cattle it could safely accommodate, it was less than the giant it appeared to be. Each drought that came along—and they did so with discouraging frequency—seemed to leave the land a little poorer than before. It was more fragile than most people realized.

Underground water beneath ranch headquarters was almost undrinkable because of its high mineral content. Cliff Newland usually hauled fresh water a couple of times a week from a deep well in the Humble oil camp. When he came for the barrels, Mother poured up whatever was left of the old water and saved it for her outdoor wash pot. Very little went to waste.

The McElroy bunkhouse was different from most in that each cowboy had his own room, though a small one, with a front door and a rear window. The bunkhouse-kitchen building was L-shaped, the individual rooms facing south. A center lobby gave the hands a place to read, play dominoes, or just loaf and spin yarns. A wind-up console phonograph stood against one wall, along with a stack of records. Most of these were classical, placed there by the Grants. The cowboys did not play them much. A bookshelf held a set of red-backed classics, a couple of books by Will Rogers, and a few magazines. When Dad and Mother finished reading the daily *Fort Worth Star-Telegram,* they took it to the lobby for the cowboys and cook.

Beyond the lobby was the dining room, with one long table where everybody sat together, including the Grants. Past that were the kitchen and the cook's living quarters. A large bell from an old locomotive was mounted on the roof over the kitchen. When the meal was near ready, the cook pulled the bell rope. The clanging could be heard to the farthest set of working corrals. Everybody at headquarters except the Newlands and Keltons ate at the company kitchen. Mother and Mae Newland cooked for their own.

As I became older and was considered responsible enough to wander just about anywhere I wanted—except the office, strictly a place of business—I spent much time in the lobby reading or playing the phonograph, getting an early taste for classical music. But what I enjoyed most was to go over on pleasant evenings when the cowboys were sitting around on the porch. As a class, they and my father were good storytellers. Their conversations often centered around horses they had known and "wrecks" they had been in with horses and cattle. Frequently it was about people they knew or knew about, sometimes going back to the frontier and open-range days.

These stories gave me a deep appreciation for history. They were about real people of flesh and blood like ourselves, not just names in a dry history book. A few of the old men I knew as a boy had been there during the settlement phase of West Texas. They had been up the long trails. The first funeral I remember attending was of a neighboring rancher who was said to have hunted buffalo in his youth at a time when Comanche and Kiowa were still a real and present danger.

South of the ranch headquarters, in the middle of an open pasture, was the grave of a cowboy killed by horse thieves many years before. Riding by that solemn place, I was reminded of the old song, "Bury Me Not on the Lone Prairie." It certainly was lone and lonely.

That grave, and stories the cowboys told, awakened a wonder that stayed with me. They made history come alive. They provided a living connection between past and present, a realization that events of a hundred years ago and more still affect our daily lives, our beliefs and attitudes. They are part of who and what we are. The more we know about them, the better we know ourselves.

My youngest brother, Eugene, came along soon after we moved to Y headquarters. While he was still a toddler, Dad gave him a nickname, Boob, suggested by a comic strip character called Boob Mc-Nutt. He was a towheaded youngster, inquisitive, prone to getting into things and trying to find out what made them work even if his tinkering rendered them unable to work anymore.

One extremely cold winter day when he was still small he ventured out on the ice that formed across a large surface tank beside the main corrals. The ice gave way. Myrle broke ice to reach Gene and rescue him. Their clothes were frozen to their bodies by the time he got Gene to the house. One might think he would be hailed as a hero for saving his little brother's life, but instead he was spanked for letting Gene go out on the ice in the first place. As the old saying has it, no good deed goes unpunished.

Gene contracted rheumatic fever at an early age, slowing his growth for a time. But he outgrew it and became as good a cowhand as Myrle and Bill, and better than his oldest brother.

Family and friends still know him as Boob. Mother was the only one who consistently and defiantly called him Eugene.

In back of our house stood a huge wooden water tank, supported by a heavy platform. Dampness from evaporation cooled the shaded area beneath the tank, so we frequently played there. Like most boys in our time and circumstances, we did not have many bought toys. We made our own. We constructed miniature

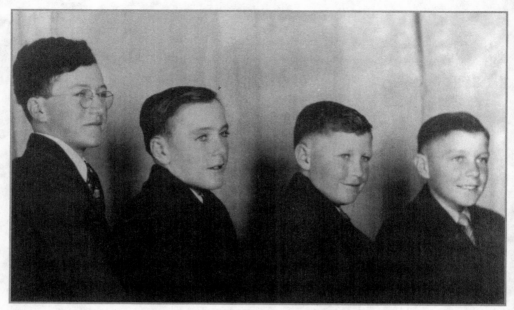
The Kelton boys: Elmer, Myrle, Bill, Gene (1930s)

corrals in the sand beside the house. Marbles became make-believe cattle and horses. Much of our play was modeled after work we saw the grown-ups doing around us.

Almost from the first, Myrle was the number-one cowboy in the family, aside from Dad. Riding, roping, anything having to do with a horse seemed to come naturally and easily to him. Bill was good at it, too, though he seemed accident prone around horses. When he was a toddler, he walked up behind one and was kicked in the stomach. He almost died. Later his hand was lacerated when a horse pulled back just as Bill was tying the bridle reins to a post. Worst of all, on another occasion his foot hung in the stirrup and he was dragged, opening up his scalp. Again, he almost died.

Despite the painful things that happened to him, Bill was probably the most congenial and least temperamental of us boys. Even when he was in a serious mood, he usually looked as if a smile were hiding inside somewhere, struggling to break out.

The Depression had set in. Lots of people were looking for a job. Cowboys drifted across the country as they had done during Dad's youth except now they usually drove a car instead of riding

Buck Kelton and his sons.
From left: **Gene, Bill, Buck Kelton, Elmer, Myrle (1947)**

a horse from ranch to ranch. Some stopped at the Jigger Y, stayed for a meal or two, then moved on if there was no work for them. Some gravitated to the oilfields, where jobs were at least a bit more available than on hard-pressed ranches beset by low cattle prices and, often, drought.

One of Dad's top hands at the time was P. O. "Slim" Vines, a tall, slender fellow with an easy smile and a knack for telling a good story. Slim went away on a trip and came back with a bride, Louetta DeVilbiss. Like so many cowboys who married, he realized he could not get by on ranch wages any longer, so he soon found a job on a Gulf drilling crew. He kept his saddle, though. For years when Dad was working cattle Slim could come out on his off days and pitch in for the pleasure of it. In middle age he took up art and depicted on canvas and in sculptures the cowboy life he had loved and never completely relinquished.

Louetta remained one of my mother's best friends.

Manerd Galer had a laugh we could hear across the big ranch

yard. Like Slim, he was tall and lanky, and he was a maestro with a rope. He did spinning tricks in the Will Rogers tradition. I can see him in memory, spinning a loop with a diameter nearly twice his height, jumping in and out of it in high-topped, high-heeled boots. He reminded me of cowboy star Ken Maynard. A tough competitor in a roping arena, he had a long-legged sorrel roping horse named Socks that more or less fell to me to ride after Manerd left the ranch. He took a long leave once to go to England with Tex Austin's rodeo troupe. Austin had had a successful European tour once before, but this one was a financial disaster. The cowboys came home broke.

Manerd was competing in the Boston Garden rodeo in 1936 when the cowboys went on strike for better treatment and bigger prize money. In those days rodeo promoters kept the entry fees and most of the gate receipts. Contestants were given the short end of the stick. The promoter in Boston tried to replace the striking cowboys with amateurs picked up wherever he could find them. The effort flopped, so he negotiated and got the real cowboys back. Manerd's signature is one of many on the strike list. He became a charter member of the Cowboy's Turtle Association formed in the wake of the Boston event. It was the forerunner of today's Professional Rodeo Cowboys Association that guarantees contestants their rightful share. It is claimed that the "turtle" name came from the notion that cowboys are independent and slow to organize, but in that instance they did.

Manerd acquired a ranch near Nogales, Arizona. I visited him there once in his later years. He still had that vigorous laugh, and rodeo was still part of his life. One of his daughters was married to a champion team roper.

Another longtime McElroy cowboy was Elliott Moore, who grew up in the Midland country. His father, known as Uncle Henry Moore, had a farm not far from my grandparents'. My cousins attended a one-room schoolhouse known as the Moore Hill School. A railroad man in his youth, Uncle Henry liked to reminisce about early West Texas. He resented the fact that the outcasts of frontier society—the outlaws and gunfighters—always drew so much attention. He declared that the only contribution they made was in killing each other off. He regarded them as no more than the freaks in a sideshow. The people who built the West, he declared, were the ranchers and farmers, the freighters and railroad men, the merchants, teachers, and preachers, the homemakers, blacksmiths, and carpenters. He argued that they were the main event, but the sideshow received most of the attention.

Once when he returned home after a stay in the hospital, I asked what they had done to him. "Not much," he said. "They just drained my purse."

Uncle Henry's son Elliott once performed an almost unbelievable feat of strength. He and Dad were hauling a couple of horses in a long homemade trailer behind the pickup when an oilfield worker suddenly pulled in from a dirt road and struck them broadside. Dad was pinned beneath the overturned trailer. Even after the horses had been spilled, it was still so heavy that ordinarily it would have taken at least three men to budge it. But with adrenaline pumping, Elliott managed to lift it enough that Dad could crawl out.

Like Slim and Manerd, Elliott was tall and lanky. He had big, strong hands and a slow way of talking. Gentle with horses, he could do anything in the line of cowboy work. He was a competent carpenter and mechanic, when it came to building trailers or working on ranch vehicles, windmills, and the like.

He had served in the cavalry awhile in the 1930s. He found that his ranch background was more hindrance than help because the cowboy way of riding was not the Army way. "They had to unteach me everything I knew," he said. He was discharged for medical reasons after Army doctors found he had a weak heart. They told him he probably had but a short time to live. He went back to cowboying and stayed with it almost fifty years more, ending up in the Carrizozo, New Mexico, area. Wherever he went, his genial ways cultivated a host of friends in the ranching community.

Cowboys at roundup on the McElroy Ranch (1930)

A similar case, though not a McElroy cowboy, was Louis Brooks, world-champion bronc rider in the early 1940s. After Pearl Harbor he tried to enlist but was turned away because of a dangerous heart condition. Like Elliott, he was given but a short time to live. He told me once that he decided if he was going to die anyway, he had just as well go back to the rodeo arena and enjoy what time he had left. He did, and lived about forty more years.

Some time after we left Sand Camp, the George Teague family settled in there. George was an inveterate roper. If a rodeo or jackpot roping was within reach, he went. In addition he drilled his sons, Earl and Bill, until they became as skilled with the loop as he was, perhaps even better. Often they competed in team roping, two of the three partnering up, then rotating for another run.

Like an avid football father trying to make a star player of his son, George demanded that Earl and Bill practice regularly. I was at Sand Camp one time when a horse threw its head up and struck Earl in the face, bloodying his nose. Earl was ready to quit, but George would not let him. He said there were still calves to be roped, and he would not allow a little blood to stand in the way.

George eventually became county sheriff, Earl a rancher, and Bill a teacher. Bill's son followed the family tradition and became a strong arena contender too.

George lived to a ripe old age, though he had every opportunity to kill himself in an automobile accident. He was a fast driver. One day he and Paul Patterson were on their way to the funeral of Pete TenEyck, a longtime sheriff at Fort Stockton. Paul nervously watched the speedometer inching up and up and up. Finally he asked, "George, whose funeral are we going to, Pete's, or ours?"

As age weakened George's eyes, it became a town joke that somebody had to keep watch on his house. When he climbed into his pickup truck, it was time to sound the siren on top of the water tower, alerting citizens to clear the streets. George was always good-natured and took such hoorawing in stride.

Another cowboy we'll simply call Jones day-worked at the Jigger Y during roundup. Short, stocky, and full of fun, he remained a bachelor until well into middle age, then married a churchgoing woman bent on reforming him and making him give up his reckless ways. She found, however, that the tree had been bent too long to be straightened. One day he tripped up onto the porch in a whiskey haze. She met him at the front door, hands on her hips, and declared, "Mr. Jones, you are drunk."

Swaying a little to starboard, he replied, "Mrs. Jones, you are a splendid judge of character."

One Jigger Y hand used to like to tell about all the ranches on which he had worked. If we added up the years he claimed to have spent with each one, he was considerably more than a hundred years old. He had several eccentricities. For one, he put pepper on his ice cream. He said that way it never gave him a headache.

Bellcord Rutherford day-worked at the McElroy a time or two. Old-timers around Midland and Odessa still smile and shake their heads at the mention of his name. He was notorious in his day. Besides being a good cowhand, he was a con man of no uncommon ability, sort of a horseback W. C. Fields. As Cliff Newland once said about a certain Crane character, "He's a nice feller, but he'll bear watchin'."

Local legend says he acquired the Bellcord name as a boy for stealing the bell rope out of a church steeple and putting it on his saddle.

The main incident I remember took place during fall shipping time. The ranch had a lot of yearlings to work and deliver afoot to the railroad at Odessa, a three-day drive plus a couple or three days of sorting and shipping. Bellcord was one of the day hands. Rather than hire a cook and take the chuck wagon, Dad made arrangements with the proprietress of a café in Odessa to feed the hands while they were there. When the shipping was finished, the full-time hands went back to the ranch, and the day workers went on to other jobs.

After a month or so Dad received a call from the woman in the café. She said, "Mr. Kelton, I thought you should know that Mr. Rutherford's bill is getting a little high." Bellcord had continued to take his meals at the café, charging them to the ranch. Dad assured her he would mail her a check but said she should tell Mr. Rutherford that in the future he would have to buy his own lunch.

Shortly after I returned home from military service I hired out to day-work for H. G. Bedford during roundup on the C Ranch near Midland. Showing the weight of his years, the rangy Bellcord was serving as wagon cook. To avoid losing wallets from their hip pockets while on horseback, most of the hands left them at the wagon, in Bellcord's care. They were not disturbed.

Elliott Moore lamented, "He must be getting old. The Bellcord I used to know would have left for town before the cowboys were out of sight."

The C Ranch had a bunkhouse for its hands. It caught fire one night and was rapidly going up in flames before the cowboys awakened to the danger. Most got out with nothing much more than their underwear. One grabbed a boot. As he stood just out of harm's way, watching the inferno, he realized the futility of what he had done. He said, "I've got two feet. What good is one boot?" and tossed it back into the fire.

Dad's younger brother Ben, nicknamed "Preacher," spent many years on the C Ranch. He was highly regarded as a cowboy. At a relatively young age he managed ranches in the Midland area and at a small town called Tarzan, named for the fictional loincloth hero. He had a long association with Foy Proctor, one of the most highly regarded cattlemen in that part of the country.

One day when Myrle and I were visiting, Uncle Ben brought home a new saddle. For a cowboy, putting the first blemish on a new saddle is akin to other people putting the first scratch on a new automobile. Uncle Ben saw a lone cow in a water lot, closed the gate on her, and put the new saddle on a horse. He pitched a loop over the cow's horns and dallied the rope up short. He then let it play out several times as the cow tugged hard on the line, struggling to get away. The rope left a dark burn on the leather around the saddlehorn.

He said, "Now I won't have to be worrying about it."

He once commented that when he was a kid, people told him he was going to be the best cowpuncher in the country when he got grown. Then, before he knew it, people were saying that he used to be the best cowpuncher in the country when he was in his prime. He was going to be, and then he used to be, but he couldn't remember when he *was*.

He started smoking as a youngster. By late middle age it had done a number on his lungs. Several times he had to be hospitalized and placed under an oxygen tent. He told my mother she should bring all her grandchildren to see him so they would know what a lifetime of smoking could do to them.

Blue-eyed and handsome, he would have been a perfect Marlboro cowboy, but the tobacco company would not have wanted to advertise what cigarettes did to him. It happened to a lot of good people I knew.

In the latter part of his life, Uncle Ben bought a small ranch of his own near Stephenville. One day he saw a cow going the wrong way up a fence and leaped out of his pickup to stop her. The pickup jumped into gear and knocked him down, running over his leg and hip. Though he lived a few more years, he never recovered from the injury.

Ironically, he had ridden literally hundreds of bad horses during his lifetime and had been thrown more times than he would have wanted to admit. It took a mechanical one to do him in.

THE McELROY RANCH HAD two major roundups each year, one at the end of summer to brand the year's crop of calves, and one in early winter. These "works" required extra help beyond the full-time cowboys and the neighbors who came over to lend a hand. The McElroy and many other area ranches depended upon a pool of day-working cowboys clustered around Midland. These drew a higher daily wage than the full-timers, but this helped make up for the many days when they had no work. Day workers like Billy Peays and Bellcord hung out mostly around the Scharbauer Hotel. On pleasant days they often squatted on their heels outside. When the weather was inclement, they loafed around the lobby. Most could not afford to visit the coffee shop often.

Dad could always find a crew in Midland. Having grown up in that area, he knew most of the working hands. He would leave headquarters after breakfast. Toward suppertime he would be back with however many hands he needed, along with their saddles and bedrolls. He would also bring a chuck wagon cook, usually either Tom Grammer or Hub Castleberry.

The two men were worlds apart in temperament. Tom was husky, square-jawed, and had a deep, gruff voice usually either on the offense or the defense. He resembled pictures of the Western painter Charles M. Russell. Tom was an excellent cook but touchy as a sore-footed badger. Usually he would lose his temper a few days into the "works," and the hands had to suffer indifferent cooking until he reverted to a good mood. He could nurse a grudge for days.

A story is told that once while he was cooking for a ranch many miles out from Midland, one of the cowboys said or did something that set him off. He had not started supper when he declared that he was quitting. He dragged his bedroll out some distance from the wagon, sat down on it and sulked. The cowboys had to pitch in and fix their own supper. The next morning he was still in an ill mood and made no move to cook, so the cowboys got their own breakfast. When time came to move camp, a cowboy and the cook's helper loaded the wagons. There were usually two, the chuck wagon and a "hoodlum" wagon that carried bedrolls and supplies. As they started to leave, Tom ran up, carrying his bedroll, and pitched it onto the chuck wagon. The cowboy driver threw it back down and told him, "You quit yesterday." They left him standing there afoot in the middle of a large pasture, miles from town.

By the time somebody went back to get him, he had gotten over his "mad." Chastened, he fixed supper for the crew.

Tom kept a keg or a crock jar of sourdough starter for his biscuits. He mixed the starter with flour and water or milk for each batch, saving back enough that it was self-perpetuating. In cold weather he protected the sourdough starter as if it were a baby, taking it to bed with him if necessary to prevent it from freezing. He kept the starter alive between jobs.

Hub Castleberry, of slighter build and calm temperament, was a former cowboy who had been a boyhood friend of Dad's, a partner in mischief. He was missing one thumb, probably pinched off between a rope and a saddlehorn, not unusual for cowboys. Unlike Tom, he never seemed to lose his cool, but for some reason he kept a six-shooter in the chuck box. I never heard of him using it for anything more than killing a rattlesnake or a beef, but it was there. Most cowboys I knew never owned a pistol and couldn't hit a barn from the inside if they had one. One morning when I was "jingling" horses and came to Hub's wagon for a cold biscuit, he let me fire that pistol. It was the first I ever had in my hands, and I was not prepared for the recoil. It jerked my arm straight up and drove the pistol back over my shoulder. I never have cared for pistols since.

Hub later became manager of a large ranch in the Davis Mountains of far West Texas. Near the end of his life he suffered a stroke

Hub Castleberry, chuck wagon cook

that completely altered his personality. I went to see him in a Fort Stockton nursing home and found that they had to keep him in the lockup wing because of his tendency to wander. He mumbled incoherently and did not know me. The other patients seemed afraid of this old cowboy who had always been so gentle. The next time I went by the nursing home, they told me he had passed away.

Not all wagon cooking was good. Sometimes the chore was turned over to a stove-up cowboy who couldn't boil water without scorching it. Dad told about one cook who mixed canned tomatoes into almost everything except the bread.

Once when Dad was in his teens and on the Scharbauer payroll,

Uncle Chris Scharbauer picked up a big bargain after a train wreck. The family's financial manager, he bought a large supply of Mary Jane molasses salvaged by the railroad. He sent cans of it out to ranch headquarters and all the camps, expecting to cut back on the sugar bill. Dad ordinarily liked molasses, but he said this was the worst he ever tasted. Morning, noon, and night, the cook managed to work it into the menu. The cowboys became sick of it, but orders were to use up the molasses. The cook carried several large cans in the bed of the chuck wagon.

Dad and Billy Peays were taking a nap in the shade beneath the wagon before moving camp. Weather was dry, and boards in the wagon bed had shrunk so that sizable cracks showed between them. Through those cracks Billy could see the bottoms of the molasses cans.

He asked, "Buck, is your knife sharp?"

It was. They took turns pushing the blade point through the cracks and puncturing the cans. Afterward, Dad followed the wagon, bringing up the horse herd. In the wagon's wake, several thin trails of molasses stretched halfway to the next camp. It was "Good-bye, Mary Jane."

The best the cook could figure, jostling back and forth in the bed of the wagon must have worn holes in the cans. At least, that is what he told Uncle Chris. Before long the cowboys were enjoying a better brand of molasses.

The cook climbed out of his blankets extra early each morning, starting breakfast while the hands slept a little longer. Usually the first thing that went on the fire was the coffeepot. The next man to arise, when he was part of the crew, would be an old cowboy named George Lee, who went back to open-range days of the 1880s and 1890s. Like many cowboys, George could subsist for long periods on cigarettes and coffee if he had to. He would hover over the coffeepot, waiting for it to come to a boil, then pour in a cup of water to settle the grounds. He could drink coffee just one step down from a full boil.

George and his brother, Young Lee, were reputed to be the best branding-pen ropers in that part of the country. George rarely missed when he cast his loop at a calf 's heels. Young was said to be even better, though I never got to watch him work. Around Midland they used to tell incredible stories about how many loops he threw without missing one. These men were not contest ropers. They were working cowboys who did their roping for wages, not for prize money.

Once in later years I was sitting beside Young at an Odessa rodeo. Buster Welch was one of the nation's top cutting horse trainers. After the regular contest, Buster's son, Ken, came out for an exhibition ride. He was about five years old and already an accomplished horseman.

"Poor kid," Young declared. "He's ruined for life."

The size of the McElroy Ranch required that only a fraction of it be worked at a time. The chuck wagon would move from one campsite to another as the operation shifted. Several pastures were so large that the crew worked them piecemeal, each day overlapping some of the previous day's coverage to be sure no cattle were missed.

The ranch in those days kept well over a hundred horses. Each cowboy was assigned several as his "mount." Usually one horse would be ridden on the morning drive, then unsaddled and another taken for the working of the gathered herd. Some campsites had no pens, so when it came time to change horses they would be bunched inside a temporary rope corral formed by cowboys standing around them in a circle, holding extended ropes about waist-high. Though they could easily have overrun such a flimsy barrier, most ranch horses had learned such respect for a rope that they seldom challenged it.

The cowboys called out the names of the horses they wanted to ride. Dad and sometimes one other man would rope them. It was always a pleasure to see them cast a loop across a sea of horses' heads and make it drop over the one they aimed for. This was a special art. Even some cowboys otherwise expert with the rope never were competent at catching a horse out of a remuda.

I was filming Dad once with a movie camera and caught his loop falling short. He asked me to cut that scene. He was ashamed for anyone to see him miss.

We frequently witnessed a brief rodeo when cowboys first mounted up, especially on early mornings when the air was fresh and the horses frisky. More often than not, one or two would pitch out across the pasture. Once they got the "buck" out of their systems, they were usually ready for a morning's work. Young broncs were given on-the-job training. So were young cowboys.

When Dad became foreman he decided the old mule-drawn wagon was slow and inefficient. Before each "works" he bolted the chuck box onto the back of a flatbed truck large enough to haul all the bedrolls, the pots, pans, and groceries. This made a second wagon unnecessary. Moving camp was faster with the truck. Purists might contend that eliminating the wagon took away some of the romance, but Dad was a realist. He never let romance get in the way of economy or efficiency. Romance was for the movies, which he did not attend anyway.

At the end of each roundup the chuck box was dismounted from the truck and placed in the warehouse building. The pots and cast-iron Dutch ovens were washed, then greased with lard or shortening to prevent their rusting. As time neared for the next roundup, the chuck box would be washed again and the Dutch ovens thoroughly cleansed with soap and hot water to remove the grease. We youngsters often helped with this cleanup job. It was one of the less attractive aspects of cowboy life, like digging post-holes and pulling up a windmill's wet, slick sucker rods, which moved up and down in the pipe to pump water.

Dad was a proponent of horse trailers before they became com-monplace. In our early years at the ranch we often found ourselves on horseback before daylight, riding miles to reach a pasture where we were to work cattle. We might put in a couple of hours traveling before we even started the job we went for. Dad favored the idea of hauling horses to the work instead of riding them there. He began building trailers to pull behind a pickup. He would build a boxlike lumber framework on top of an old truck chassis. The result was not pretty, but it was practical. "Pretty" didn't get the job done.

Horses were led in from the rear and tied with their heads to the right so they did not look squarely into oncoming traffic and perhaps be spooked by it. Besides, if they hung their heads over the left side, passing traffic could possibly sideswipe them. An oilfield contractor once lost a truckload of mules when the truck driver misjudged the clearance beneath an overpass. Most horses soon learned the trailer routine, though now and then one resisted. A rope stretched across its rump, then pulled from both sides, would force-lift the animal into the trailer.

Dad's use of trailers eliminated most of the time lost getting to and from the job. This allowed us to work one pasture in the morning and another in the afternoon. Getting twice as much done appealed to his frugal nature.

Once we entered a pasture, however, we usually operated the drive about the same way Granddad and his contemporaries had. Dad would drop us off at intervals, then we would move forward in a more or less straight line, pushing ahead of us any cattle we found. In brushy pastures we had to work closer together than in the more open ones where we could see farther. The cattle would be thrown together at the far side, where in most cases there would be a set of working pens. If there was not, we drove them to one.

Most often we worked the herd in the open before penning them. Usually this consisted of cutting out the "dry" cows, those that did not have calves. They might be placed in a separate pasture afterward. Those that consistently failed to calve were shipped to market, for fertility was a heritable trait. A slow breeder was likely to pass her poor fertility on to any offspring she might produce. The cow-and-calf pairs would be driven into a pen, where the calves would be branded.

A frequent "kid" job assigned to me was holding the "cut," those cattle removed from the rest of the herd. Typically one or two men, Dad and perhaps one cowboy who had a good cutting horse, would work through the main bunch and ease these animals out. My job would be to see that they joined the cut and did not run back into the larger herd, their natural tendency. I also had to see that the cut cattle did not stray off. For the most part it was an easy job, though now and then a determined cow would test my mettle and my vocabulary. Usually I did this job alone. If the cut grew large, one of my younger brothers might be sent out to join me.

Frequently bulls would be sent to the cut. It was always entertaining to watch them, for being thrown together aroused their competitive nature and caused them to fight. They would paw dirt and bellow, then run together with a great clacking of hoofs and horns. These fights did not last long, for usually the larger and stronger quickly prevailed. The vanquished would turn tail and run. His escape could be hazardous to man, horse, cow, or calf that happened to be in the way. A beaten bull being pursued would run into and over anything in his path. We learned to watch these sparring matches from a safe distance.

I had a hard time keeping up on drive because too often I could not see the men on either side of me. I would fall behind or, worse, get ahead of the others so the cattle they scared up would cut in back of me. Nobody realized that I was seriously nearsighted until a fifth grade teacher suspected it and had me sent for an examination. I endured a lot of ribbing and grief over my tendency to "get lost" and mess up the drive. This ridicule caused me to develop a serious inferiority complex that added to the handicap of poor vision. I dreaded doing anything that might make me the butt of yet another joke, so I held back and tried to play it safe on any horseback job. The desire was there, but even stronger was the reluctance to face more criticism.

By the time I acquired glasses and could see better, this tendency toward drawing back was deeply ingrained. Ridicule can have a poisonous effect on a youngster trying to find his way. I considered myself a failure, at least as a cowboy. Though this was a negative attitude, it might have had one positive feature. I worked doubly hard at those things I *could* do.

Reading was a refuge. It carried me away to other places, other times, where for a while I could put aside the shortcomings that gave me so much anxiety. With access to the school library, I devoured the standard childhood classics such as *The Wizard of Oz, Hans Brinker, The Bobbsey Twins,* and *The Dog of Flanders,* though *Alice in Wonderland* left me puzzled. Grade school teachers conducted a reading hour each day in which they read aloud books we might not be advanced enough to read for ourselves. When one started reading *Treasure Island* a bit at a time, I became so enraptured that I badgered Mother into buying me a copy so I could read ahead. It was the first book I ever owned. I still have it.

I discovered Texas folklorist J. Frank Dobie, the finely illustrated cowboy-and-horse books by Will James, and the colorful Western adventure novels of Zane Grey. These became a strong influence on the direction my career would take.

BECAUSE OF MY AVID reading, I developed a knack for writing. By the time I was eight or nine years old, I fantasized about someday writing the Great American Novel. It would be a Western, naturally. I had also discovered an artistic streak. I filled a tablet with drawings of horses and cattle and cowboys. Just as my writing instincts owed much to my mother, some of my artistic talent was probably inherited from Dad. He could draw a pretty good horse.

Writing and drawing were another escape mechanism.

My love for stories led me to a fascination with films. Because we lived nine miles from town, going to the movies was a special occasion. Sometimes Dad had business in Crane and would drop us boys off for a Saturday matinee. He did not go himself. I can remember only three times that he went into a movie theater, and he was more or less shanghaied into all of them. The only one he ever talked about afterward was *State Fair,* with Will Rogers. He could relate to Will and his prize hog, Blue Boy. He did not relate to movie cowboys who always rode their horses in a run and seldom if ever worked cattle.

Mother enjoyed films, however. She was fond of Nelson Eddy and Jeanette MacDonald musicals. She liked romances and nature films like Frank Buck's and those of Martin and Osa Johnson. She took us to the Tarzan pictures to see the wildlife. One of her brothers told her he had just seen a cute animal picture and urged her to go. He had to stay out of her sight for a while after she followed his advice and took us to see *King Kong*.

The Crane Theater was nothing more than a plain frame building with sheet-iron siding and burlap padding on the inner walls to help the acoustics. But with the lights off and images moving on the screen, it was a mystical palace, like a magic carpet that carried me away to places I would otherwise never see and to witness adventures I would never have. I liked anything that was on the screen and moved, talked, or sang. My special favorites, however, were Westerns. Some of the first I saw featured Buck Jones and Ken Maynard, both expert horsemen. The Saturday B Westerns usually ended with a big shoot-out. I would play these over in my mind, puzzling out how I would describe the scene on paper. About the best I could come up with was: *And then the fireworks started*. I have avoided prolonged shoot-outs in my stories ever since.

Because we had just one theater, we were limited in the variety of Western stars we could see. Up-and-comers like John Wayne and Bob Steele, and old-timers like Hoot Gibson, did not get to show their stuff in Crane. As time went by I enjoyed Hopalong Cassidy, Gene Autry, and Roy Rogers, who did.

I was aware of the wide difference between movie cowboys and the real working cowboys I knew, but it did not bother me. I realized early that Hollywood was one thing and reality was another. I saw enough reality around me every day. While it had its moments of excitement, these were all too often overshadowed by the boring and gritty. Hollywood was neater. Movie cowboys rarely dug postholes, never doctored cattle for screwworms, or waded into the deep mud to rescue a bogged-down cow that would thank you by trying to ram a sharp horn through your hip pocket.

Movie cowboys did a lot of shooting. I can remember only once in my boyhood seeing my father with a gun. It was a rifle, and he was trying to kill a coyote that had been raiding our chickens at Sand Camp. I don't think he hit it.

One of the best cowboys I ever knew borrowed Hub Castleberry's pistol to kill a beef for the chuck wagon. Firing at point-blank range, he missed three shots. It was not like the movies, where in his very first film Hoppy shot the bad guy with a pistol at what appeared to be at least fifty yards, and from horseback. That did not diminish the movies in my eyes. I saw them as a pleasant alternate reality, life as it should have been, not as it was.

I tried not to miss the big-budget Westerns featuring the likes of Gary Cooper, or adventure films starring anybody. One that especially impressed me was John Ford's *Drums Along the Mohawk,* starring Henry Fonda and Claudette Colbert in a story of colonial America. A splendid example of bringing history to life through fiction, it inspired me to keep writing my own stories.

Growing up, I knew one real cowboy who had had a fling with the movies. During prohibition, Happy Smith met silent movie hero Jack Hoxie at a show in Odessa. Hoxie had a thirst, and Happy knew the bootleggers. Hoxie hired him to go to Hollywood, where he did stunts and played bit parts for a while. He became tired of the artificial Western life, however. He was ready to quit after he was called upon to double for Hoxie in a scene where he was to jump a mule off into deep water and be rescued by a pair of dogs in whose sharp teeth he had no trust. When Hoxie got into a fight with his manager, Happy sensed that the star's career was in descent, and he came home to be a real cowboy again. He endured some good-natured hoorawing over having been a movie cowboy, but he was the genuine article.

Happy promoted the first rodeo I can remember seeing, an impromptu local affair in the middle of a large pasture near Odessa.

There was no arena fence. Spectators lined their automobiles along the sides as a barrier of sorts. The far end was wide open except for a couple of cowboys standing by on horseback. Sometimes the bucking stock kept on going. Now and then one would find an opening between the cars. Ropers who missed the first loop might have to pursue their quarry "plumb out of sight." It was a far cry from the well-organized rodeos of today, but it was probably more fun. Certainly it was less predictable.

Happy had known J. T. McElroy, founder of the ranch, and told me a story about him. McElroy had a packinghouse in El Paso and owned several ranches that he depended on to furnish cattle for his plant. He would ride the train out from El Paso, rent a buggy from an Odessa livery stable, and drive it thirty miles south to the Jigger Y. On one occasion he stopped at the Dawson windmills to water his team and found a couple of Y cowboys roping and "fairgrounding" cows for fun, tripping and throwing them down. They were new hands and did not know him.

He said, "Don't you think the owner of these cows might object to you mistreating them this way?"

One of the cowboys said, "He's a rich old son of a bitch who lives in El Paso. He'll never know."

McElroy drove on down to headquarters. When the cowboys rode in later, he had their checks waiting for them. He told them, "That rich old son of a bitch from El Paso says you're fired."

Though I considered Crane my hometown, Dad always looked upon Midland as his. He had grown up on ranches north of there. When we had heavy shopping to do, we usually went to Midland. Odessa and Midland were twin cities, but each had a personality of its own. Midland was staid and conservative, home for well-to-do ranchers and, later, oil company offices and executives. Odessa was a working-class town, in the early days a cowboy hangout and cattle-shipping point, in later times home to oil-patch workers, tool companies, and the like. Midland was comfortable and quiet, Odessa rough and ready.

The difference is illustrated in a story I heard from historian

J. Evetts Haley. He said that an Odessa bank decided to move its operations to Midland, where financial prospects were better. At the same time, a Midland madam gathered her girls and moved her operation to Odessa, where there was more action. A Midlander lamented, "Every time we trade with those gentlemen from Odessa, they skin us on the deal."

"Gentleman from Odessa" was a term cowboys sometimes gave to a chuck-wagon concoction otherwise known as son of a bitch stew. Paul Patterson said, "I always wondered why they called it that, until I met a gentleman from Odessa."

FOUR

BRANDING WAS HOT, HARD work, but it could often yield a certain amount of fun, usually at someone's expense. Occasionally one of our neighbors branded calves in the open pasture, but the Ys branded in fenced corrals where cattle could be controlled better. Usually there would be one or two ropers, depending upon the number of calves to be branded. It was an honor to be selected to do this, for not all cowboys were skilled enough with the loop to keep the flankers busy.

The roper usually tried to catch a calf by its heels and drag it up to the two-man flanking team. With a rope around both hind feet, it could not put up much of a fight. One flanker would grab the tail, the other the rope from the opposite side. A well-coordinated yank brought the calf down on its side. The man who pulled the tail dropped one knee onto the neck and grabbed a foreleg. The man on the rope grabbed the topmost hind leg with both hands and held the other leg snugly against his boot heel.

If a roper felt playful, or perhaps became miffed at the flankers, he might purposely rope a large calf around the neck instead of the heels. It usually bellowed and pitched and with a little luck could place a hoof where it hurt the most. Like the cook, the heeler was not a man to mess with.

One man applied the branding iron, which stamped the ranch's modified figure Y on each calf. In the early days the irons were heated in a conventional wood fire. In time Dad acquired a steel heater that operated on kerosene. Eventually kerosene gave way to butane, which made a hotter and more dependable flame.

A second man carried a sharp knife to cut the earmarks and to castrate the bull calves. Still another carried a syringe to vaccinate the calves against blackleg and whatever other diseases might be a threat.

As a youngster I was at first too light in weight to flank calves, so I usually was assigned to carry the "dope" can. It was filled with a thick, black, smelly liquid meant to repel blowflies. I mopped it on open wounds, mainly on castrated bull calves. I might also carry a can of linseed oil to apply to the fresh brand. This cooled the burn and helped the brand to peel properly.

After seventy-odd years I can still conjure up the pungent sulfurous smell of burning hair.

If the calves were not separated from the cows beforehand, the cows took an anxious interest in what was happening to their offspring. Often a cow would follow her calf as it was dragged ignominiously to the edge of the bunch, both bawling all the way. Occasionally a cow would paw sand and charge the flankers, her head down and her horns poised to administer punishment. In extreme cases the cowboys ran for the fence, but usually they could discourage her by hollering and slapping her across the nose with a hat.

The branded calves were sometimes counted out the gate, but often they were tallied by counting the little pieces of ear the knife man placed in a pile.

Unless we were pressed for time, Dad usually kept the cows and calves in the pen awhile after branding was finished, or we pushed them out the gate, then loose-herded them. This calmed them and allowed mothers and offspring to pair up. The calves could get some milk into their bellies before they drifted back into the pasture. Often we simply opened the corral gate and rode away quietly, letting the cattle find their way out in their own good time, without pressure.

Young cowboys sometimes had to be cautioned about handling them too roughly and looking for an excuse to use their ropes. Older hands knew that the less the cattle were stressed, the less difficult it would be to handle them the next time. Range cows had a long memory when it came to mistreatment.

There used to be an expression, "Matadoring" the cattle, which meant handling them fast and rough. The term came from the Matador Ranch in the Texas Panhandle. Dad never liked to see cattle roped in the pasture unless it was absolutely necessary. It tended to make them wild. That might suit adventuresome young cowboys, but it was bad for the ranch's bottom line.

He had an ambivalent attitude toward ropes. He saw them as a necessity, yet recognized that in their own way they could be as dangerous as a gun. When I was small, his friend Gabe Beauchamp became entangled in his own rope and was dragged to death. The tragedy shook Dad all the way down to his boots. For years he would not allow his sons to carry a rope on a saddle. When he finally changed his mind, the change was abrupt. One day I reported to him that I had found a dead cow beside a water trough, and he asked if I had dragged her away. I said no, I had nothing to drag her with. He said, "Don't ever let me catch you away from the house again without a rope."

Thus my brothers began using ropes at a younger age than I did, and I never caught up to them in skill.

Myrle in particular was always ready to cast a loop over anything that moved, or anything he could cause to move. Paul Patterson tells a story about Wes Reynolds, who was batching at the Lea Ranch while Dad had it leased for his own herd of cattle. One day Wes found his pet tomcat sleeping peacefully on a chair. He said, "You'd better get your rest while you can, you poor little son of a bitch, because those Kelton boys will be here tomorrow."

Once while Wes was away on a summer visit to kinfolks, Myrle and I were holding down the Lea Ranch in his stead. Dad brought over four little Mexican mules, wilder than jackrabbits. He warned, "Whatever you boys do, don't you rope any of these mules." The dust had not settled behind his pickup before Myrle tossed a loop over a mule's neck. For a while it looked as if he never was going to get his rope back. That mule tore up enough ground to plant a garden.

Once while we were on horseback in what we called the Beef Pasture, Ralph Scott spurred after a badger. Roping a badger is only a little less difficult than roping a coyote, but he made a catch. That turned out to be the easy part. Getting his rope back was far harder, for badgers are notoriously ill tempered. The little animal abruptly went on the offense, going up the rope toward Ralph and his startled horse. For a while it was all he and the horse could do to stay out of its way. In such a situation it is usually best to let the badger keep the rope.

Louis Brooks told me that when he was an aspiring young rodeo cowboy he was working for the noted Albert Mitchell in New Mexico. Mitchell had a strict rule against unnecessary roping. Louis, however, could not resist practicing on the ranch's calves. One day Mitchell rode up on him unexpectedly. Regretfully, he said Louis was a good hand, and he did not want to lose him. He offered to keep him on the payroll if he would promise never to do it again.

Louis said, "Mr. Mitchell, I won't make you a promise that I know I can't keep." He resigned and went on to become a rodeo champion.

The area around Crane and Rankin produced many good contest ropers in the 1930s through the 1950s. One was Bill Nix, a cowboy in his younger years and a barber later on, though he never gave up his favorite pastime. He became so stove up with arthritis that he sometimes had to be helped into the saddle. Once there, though, he was a serious team-roping opponent. In those days the header roped the head and the heeler caught the hind feet, stretching the animal out. The header then jumped to the ground and tied the hind feet with a pigging string while the heeler held his rope taut. Bill was too crippled to work on the ground any-more, but he became known as one of the best heelers in West Texas.

Late in life his heart began troubling him. His doctor kept try-ing to persuade him to quit his strenuous activities. At last, in des-peration, he pleaded, "You're going to die in the middle of some arena if you don't stop, and I don't want to feel responsible for it."

Bill said, "I did the only thing an honorable man could do. I changed doctors."

Another old-time roper from Rankin was Harry Howard. Near the end of his life I saw him at a benefit steer roping on the OS Ranch near Post, Texas. By that time he had palsy. His gray head and his hands shook constantly, and his creased face bore a pallor. Nevertheless, he showed up to compete. His friends worried aloud that "poor old Harry" had no business in that arena. In his condition he could die out there.

When it came time for him to rope, Harry prepared his loop and backed his horse into the box. His head and hands went still, and he sat steady in the saddle. He nodded to the chute man to re-lease the steer. "Poor old Harry" spurred out into the arena and won the roping.

John D. Holleyman was a McElroy cowboy for several years in his late teens and early twenties, before he answered the nation's call and went into the Air Corps just before the onset of World War II. He won a lot of matched calf ropings and "jackpots" around West Texas, along with regular rodeo events. Like so many, he practiced wherever he had the chance. One year while I was in high school I fed a steer for the 4-H Club show in Odessa. For some reason the steer wasn't gaining the weight that it should. I found out John D. was roping him. We have laughed about it several times over the years, but I didn't find the humor in it at the time.

Myrle and I joined the 4-H Club, but in our case it was nothing more than a name. Our county agent, H. L. Atkins, served three counties, Ector, Andrews, and Crane. He had little time to get around to all the youngsters and advise them. He may have seen our prospective show steers twice in all the months we fed them. We had none of today's scientific approach. Mostly we fed them the same mix that went to the ranch's milk cows.

That March, when the Odessa show came around, we took our steers in for the contest. Neither of us had ever been to a stock show before and had no real idea what to expect. We lined them up for preliminary inspection, and my steer was promptly "sifted," eliminated before the competition ever started. That took me by surprise. I didn't even know what the word "sift" meant in relation to show animals. Myrle's steer went on to win a place in the sale.

I had another shock coming. Dad gave each of us a little money, perhaps five dollars, for meals. At that time, five dollars was enough. A carnival was set up just across from the show barn. I walked over out of curiosity and saw a game in which a set of numbered table tennis balls floated on a cushion of air. You paid a dime to reach in with a small net and try to fish one out. If you caught the right number, you won money.

I was a freckle-faced country boy, green as a gourd, a sheep ready to be sheared. The man running the game let me win several times, working up my confidence. Then suddenly I wasn't winning anymore. Before I realized it, my meal money was gone, and I still had a couple of days to spend in Odessa. I was too ashamed to tell anybody about my plight. I kept tightening my belt until the two days were over. The double disappointment of my steer being rejected and my money taken away was almost too much. Remembering how hungry I was, I have been averse to gambling ever since.

I never fed another show steer, though Myrle did.

An annual highlight for us boys was a trip to the July 4 rodeo in Pecos, once we became old enough to go by ourselves. Myrle would enter the calf roping. The best I could do was to hold his horse. It was the custom for one cowboy to rent a room in the Brandon Hotel, then several others to sneak in, carrying their bedrolls, and sleep on the floor. It was amazing how many cowboys could crowd into one room.

Pecos has always advertised that it had the first real rodeo, though Prescott, Arizona, makes the same claim. Pecos seemed to attract the perfect combination of local talent and professional rodeo hands. Even the great Toots Mansfield, one of the best ropers who ever lived, could occasionally be beaten by a working cowboy off some ranch on the Pecos River. There was an unusual openness and friendliness, a feeling of community.

Toots showed up at the McElroy Ranch on a few Sunday afternoons to practice with other ropers from the area, though he was in a championship class by himself. He was unassuming and down-to-earth, a gentleman and a gentle man. We boys would put calves into the chute and turn them out for him and the other ropers. Toots always had a pleasant "thank you" for us. In later years we got to be good friends, and he always had something positive to say about my writing. We never brought up my mediocre record as a cowboy.

It is common today for rodeo champions to conduct schools for beginners in their individual specialties, be it roping, bronc riding, bull riding, or whatever. Toots started that in the 1950s, conducting a calf-roping school at his ranch near Big Spring. He was one of the first rodeo professionals to train like an athlete, doing roadwork to build his strength and endurance. Most of the serious ones do it today.

BECAUSE MY MOTHER HAD taught me at home, when I reached seven and started school in town full-time, I was given a test and placed in the third grade. I was a year to two years younger than almost anyone else in class as well as being too small to match the other boys in athletics. I never could see a ball until it hit me, which should have been a tipoff that I was nearsighted. Before long, when they chose up sides to play touch football, it was, "We had Elmer yesterday. You take him today."

This, along with my inadequacies as a cowboy, compounded my problems with self-esteem. The only area in which I found that I could excel was in English, which included writing. I could usually even beat the girls when we had spelling bees, which in a tough oil-patch town like Crane made me a little suspect.

Nevertheless, I had a circle of friends like Ted Hogan, Bill Lovelace, and Gail Roy Melton who didn't care whether I could play football or not. Most of them had lived in other oil towns before Crane, and they broadened my horizons. They were from working families of similar economic backgrounds. Few had much money to spend, so we did not expect much and were not often disappointed. We took pleasure in small things, like a double-dip ice cream cone for a nickel at Keltner's Drug, or a hamburger for a dime at Pat Passur's grill, next door to his domino parlor. School kids were welcome in the tiny café, but they were forbidden under threat of corporal punishment to stick a head in the door of his other establishment.

Oil-patch people took a strong interest in their children's education. Their usual explanation was that they wanted their sons and daughters to have an easier life than their own had been. The town was still brand new when it put up a sprawling school building, substantial for its time. It was of frame construction, stuccoed and painted a dull yellow. In its center was a Mexican style patio, flanked by high school classrooms and a large auditorium and decorated with flowerbeds. The patio helped the circulation of fresh air in rooms adjoining it. Air conditioning was not even a consideration.

We had no school cafeteria. Mother usually packed lunches for us, but sometimes she let us eat instead at a café next to the school grounds where we could get a soft drink, a plate lunch, and a candy bar for a quarter. Or we could walk uptown to Pat Passur's for the greatest hamburger in the world.

An old man eventually set up a competing hamburger joint closer to the school and sold his for a nickel apiece. They were not as good as Pat's, but he offered two for the price of one. There has always been a contest between quality and quantity. When I was really hungry, quantity won out, but quality was more satisfying.

The ranch headquarters were in the extreme northern part of Upton County, thirty miles from school in Rankin. Rather than run a bus all the way out there, the school paid Dad a small subsidy to find his own transportation and send us across the county line to Crane. For the first year or so the Newlands' son Jack, a high school student, took me to town with him. After that Dad would contract with someone in the area who had schoolchildren and let them take us with their own.

When I was about twelve, I started driving myself and my brothers in, though I was too young to have a driver's license and had to sit on a pad to see over the steering wheel. To avoid a highway or town street where I might get in trouble with the law, I would park the car at the Plate family dairy, against a barbed-wire fence that marked the city limits. We would walk the final half mile or so up to school. I obtained a provisional license at about age fourteen.

All of us learned to drive on the ranch, of course. Gene, the youngest and always eager to experiment, learned how to start a pickup but could not reach the brake pedal to stop it. He plowed into a corral fence. This did no damage to the vehicle's looks. Dad's ranch pickups usually bore deep dents and scratches and occasionally lost a side mirror from plunging through mesquite thickets and across deep ditches in pursuit of cattle or horses. He would risk a thousand-dollar pickup in an effort to catch a thirty-dollar horse. It was one contradiction to his normally frugal nature.

MY FIRST FULL-TIME TEACHER, in the third grade, was Lois Ann Hicks. Because I was a naive ranch kid with little experience that didn't have to do with horses or cattle, the more worldly town boys could pull practical jokes on me that might not have worked on anyone more savvy. One chalked a forbidden sexual term on the school wall and waited until Mrs. Hicks approached, then said, "Elmer, you're good at spelling. What does that word say?"

I had never heard or read the word before, so I sounded it off just as it looked to me. Several boys in on the joke ran away giggling. Mrs. Hicks must have understood how green I was, for she never gave a sign that she had heard anything.

A friend who was not part of the joke explained to me what the word meant. "It's something all married people do," he said.

I had watched cattle enough that I got the picture, and it was disturbing. Not *my* parents, I told him.

I was aware that Crane had a small area in the northeast corner of town which people said was the red-light district, but I had no idea what went on there. Beer drinking, I supposed. In Mother's view that was a mortal sin.

Leland L. Martin came to take over as school superintendent and to teach mathematics. He was tall and lank, a little like Abraham Lincoln without the beard. He spoke in stentorian tones that I often imagined would have been Lincoln's. His deep voice, combined with the boring nature of his subject, was a strong invitation to sleep in class. But that voice could also awaken students like a gunshot when he noticed that they had nodded off. A veteran of World War I, he enjoyed talking about his experiences in Europe. We discovered that if we could get him to expounding on those, we could distract him from mathematics for the rest of the period. Consequently we learned more about war and European geography than about geometry.

Though many teachers had an influence, Paul Patterson had a profound effect on my life. He had grown up in Upton County, his father a farmer, a rancher, a jailer, and eventually a county judge. His older brothers were cowboys, and Paul's ambition was to become a cowboy too. By the time he finished high school he was sick of education. He just wanted to work as a cowboy, so he got a job with the Hoover Ranch on the Pecos River and put academia behind him. The Hoover horses were notorious for being some of the saltiest in the country. Paul was thrown off many times that summer. One horse in particular had his number and kept trying to pound Paul's head into the ground.

"That old horse gave me a burning yearning for learning," he said. That fall he went to college and eventually became a teacher.

Bilingual, Paul served a stint teaching mostly Mexican-American youngsters in Sanderson. He was then hired by the Crane school system and arrived a couple of weeks before the fall semester. To fill the time, he signed on for day-work at the McElroy Ranch, where his brother John had been employed for several years. Thus I got to know him first as Paul the cowboy.

School started, and there was no more Paul the cowboy. He was *Mr. Patterson*. No student called a teacher by his or her given name.

Wes Reynolds watched him on horseback and declared, "He's too good a cowboy to waste his time teaching school."

Paul was never one to stand on ceremony. He was always friendly, usually could tell a witty story to illustrate a point, and became a great favorite as a teacher for more than fifty years.

Mother was protective about the ranch's cowboys and did not take it kindly when anyone made a disparaging remark. Once when the hands, including neighbors, were branding cattle in a corral, some women visiting from the East were perched on the fence, watching. Like so many, they assumed that cowboys were an uneducated lot. One of the women noticed Harold Smith's college ring and declared, "I wish you'd look. That cowboy has been to college!"

Mother's temper flared. She pointed to Paul Patterson, who was holding down a calf and awaiting the branding iron. "That's nothing," she said. "That one is a professor!"

Paul was a lovable teacher but not an easy one. He never gave students a grade that they had not earned. He saw that they worked for what they got. He taught journalism and Spanish, and I took both. He, more than anyone, pointed me in the direction of newspaperwork as a way to get into writing as a profession. My Spanish mostly faded away in later years, but the journalism stuck.

So has my friendship with Paul, who eventually became a noted storyteller and a favorite of the Texas Folklore Society. He celebrated his ninetieth birthday at a folklore meeting. They prepared a large birthday cake with ninety lighted candles and a local fireman in full uniform standing by with a fire extinguisher.

One year several of us were rehearsing for a school play. We were up against a test we were sure was going to be a tough one. We knew also that the teacher had prepared the questions and had run them off on a mimeograph machine in the school office. After rehearsal, when no one else remained in the building, our little circle of conspirators decided to see if we could find where the test copies were hidden. We rummaged around, watching and listening, in fear of being caught at any moment. We knew Double L Martin would drop the hammer on us. We finally found what we were looking for—we thought. We studied it until we were sure we could score a hundred.

And we might have, except that we had found a leftover copy of the previous year's test. We decided crime did not pay, and besides, it was too scary.

One student showed up frequently in school with bruises and abrasions. The suspicion was that his father was beating him up. A couple of the bigger boys took it upon themselves to mete out justice. They roughed up the father and warned him that it would be worse the next time his son came to class showing signs of a beating.

It turned out that the mother was the guilty party. She beat up not only the son but the father as well.

Not having much skill at athletics, I decided I would like to play in the band, so I studied clarinet. Our band master was an easygoing sort, who never pushed much, promoting members on the basis of seniority more than skill. He left, and we found ourselves facing a wrinkle-browed little firecracker of a man, who immediately turned the band upside down. Jacques "Jack" Nonce was a professional musician; he'd worked in European symphony orchestras and could hear a sour note in a thunderstorm. He gave every student an individual audition, then placed them according to skill, not by how long they had been in the band. To say the least, he left several egos deeply bruised. But soon he had us sounding like pros, playing classical and semiclassical music. His hero and role model was the autocratic conductor Arturo Toscanini, who tolerated nothing short of perfection. Nonce was a hard taskmaster, much like Dad, but he made us accomplish more than we thought we could. I learned that the tougher the teacher, the better the lesson.

He gave me a taste for classical music and taught me that even a cowboy can enjoy Beethoven, Bach, and Brahms.

Band trips were a highlight, especially to exotic locations such as Waco and Lubbock for contests. We also carried our instruments to out-of-town football games and marched in formation at halftime. The bus driver would caution us to behave ourselves and add, "Did you hear that, Guy Eddy?" Guy Eddy Bosworth was the most usual suspect when something went awry, though the truth was that he took many a bum rap for someone else.

There were thirty in my senior class. Knowing that several of the young men were eager to join the military, the teachers were determined to see every one of us graduate. That presented a problem when three or four of us failed our final chemistry exam. We were given a chance to take it over, an unusual concession probably in violation of Texas Education Agency policies. Willie Stroud, the chemistry teacher, would walk along and watch us writing answers to the questions. A short, sturdy woman whose bearing bespoke authority, she periodically stopped and nodded in the affirmative or shook her head. Without saying a word, she got all of us up to a passing grade, and the whole class graduated.

Crane in its early years was overwhelmingly Protestant. In time it had churches of just about every known Protestant denomination. However, it had neither a Catholic church nor a Jewish synagogue. For many years, the relatively few citizens of those faiths had to travel to Odessa or Fort Stockton for services.

Dad belonged to no church until late in his life. Even then I suspect his joining owed more to Mother's urging than to his own wish. He had grown up far out in the country where distance made churchgoing difficult. He was a believer, though he frequently invoked the Lord's name in ways not sanctioned by any church.

Mother put up a strong argument on those Sundays when Dad felt that he needed us boys for work more than she needed us for church. She had grown up Methodist and remained steadfastly so all her life. Her parents had divorced when she was a small girl, so she was brought up by sternly religious grandparents in southern Oklahoma. She had only occasional contact with her father, Bert Parker. He had worked as a cowboy in New Mexico, went adventuring to Alaska, and returned to labor in the Texas oilfields. He died in early middle age, when I was a baby. I never knew him, and she was never able to tell me much about him.

Nobody felt obliged to apologize for the church's strong influence on Crane's official life and in education. Almost any school event began with a group prayer. Teachers spoke of their faith and lectured about morality and values even as they coached us in English, math, and history. Paintings of Jesus hung in many classrooms, right alongside Washington, Lincoln, and Franklin D. Roosevelt. School regulations as well as local laws were heavily rooted in the Ten Commandments.

Our Methodist minister, H. L. McAlister, did not restrict his services to the church sanctuary. Besides ministering to the ill and infirm wherever they might be, he visited oil-patch workers in the fields. Several times when the McElroy Ranch was working cattle he came out to visit with the cowboys. He did not hammer people over the head about religion but tried to teach by example and by simply being there. Dad liked and respected him though he heard him preach only at funerals.

Politics was another area which offered little diversity in the 1930s. The oil patch was strongly Democratic, as was all of Texas at the time. It was a heritage from the Civil War and the bitter decade of reconstruction that followed. However, the rapidly growing oil industry brought workers and executives from other parts of the country, and Republicans began to infiltrate the once-solid ranks. The McElroy Ranch office was the polling place for the Upton County precinct in which we lived. Election days were like a small festival, candidates offering cigars and setting out tubs of iced-down soft drinks for voters and their offspring. The precinct had only two registered Republicans, ranch manager Grant and Mrs. Grant.

Bill Allman had brought his Republican views down from Kansas, but for years his voice was lost amid the tumult. Things did not begin to swing his way until after World War II, when Dwight D. Eisenhower broke the traditional Democratic hold on the state. It was no longer considered an act of treason to vote for someone other than a Democrat. Today the area is almost solidly Republican. A recent joke has been that Crane had only two Democrats left until a former resident moved back from Odessa and increased the ranks by 50 percent.

FIVE

MOST OF THE MEN in my father's family were involved in ranching or stock farming. On my mother's side, most worked in the oilfields, including her brothers Paul and Charles Holland, already teenagers when I was a small boy. Growing up, I was exposed to both backgrounds. Crane was a center of ambitious oil exploration in a huge area of West Texas known as the Permian Basin, more than two hundred miles across in one dimension, three hundred and fifty in the other. Geologists found that the basin had been at the bottom of a Permian-era inland sea and was rich in oil and gas. The fathers of most of my schoolmates were directly involved in the oilfield or catered to those who were.

Crane was a working-class town with no frills and no pretensions. Oil company executives chose to live in more amenable surroundings like Midland, Fort Worth, Dallas, or Houston. Most of the people we knew were on an economic level similar to ours, not exactly poor but far from prosperous. It was years before Crane even had a bank of its own. Local people usually banked in Odessa or Midland if they had use for a bank at all. Many simply cashed their paychecks at the grocery store and hoped the money would stretch to next payday.

Because we rarely saw anyone to envy, we youngsters were not as aware of the ongoing Depression as we might have been in a more cosmopolitan setting. We did not see anyone much better off than we were. Oilfield workers tended to be transient. If they had a steady job with one company, they were always subject to being transferred to other fields. If they were shuffling from one company to another, they were even more likely to be up and gone with little or no notice, seeking jobs wherever they could find drilling activity. Only a few of my classmates were with me all the way through school. I was constantly losing friends and making new ones as their families moved around between Crane and Odessa, Wink, Monahans, McCamey, Iraan, Borger, Ranger, and some towns now all but forgotten, like Best and Texon.

Because no one had reason to feel either superior or inferior, there was a strong sense of togetherness in the oil-patch community, a feeling that *we're all in this together*. Anybody's good fortune was everybody's good fortune, and anybody's bad luck was shared, in spirit at least. It was *our* football team, *our* band, *our* town.

The oilfield economy was up and down, much like the cattle market. It was a standing joke during one of the down times that Crane had become a noted rest resort, though by circumstance, not design. The amount of one's salary was less important than the fact that he had a salary at all. Many did not.

One day an old bus pulled into a service station while we were filling up our car. It had been converted into a traveling home, with a small kerosene-burning stove for cooking and fold-down bunks for the family members. Naive, I thought how wonderful it must be for these people to take their home with them wherever the father worked. In later years I began to appreciate their poverty and desperation. That old bus came to symbolize the Depression years for me.

For untold centuries, people had been traveling across that area on their way to somewhere else. The countryside offered little to make them want to stay. Average annual rainfall was only about twelve inches, and lots of years the actual amount was half that.

Grass was short. Much of the land was covered by a scrubby cre-osote growth known as greasewood, of little use to man or beast. To the southwest lay a huge salt lake, usually dry, where hunter-gatherer Indians had come for salt centuries before Comanche in-vaders took over the land. It was known as the Juan Cordona Lake.

The Pecos River was the county's western boundary. In frontier times it ran swiftly and deep, dangerous to cross except at a few sites where the banks were gentle on both sides instead of sharply up and down. One of these "safe" spots was Horsehead Crossing, named for the many horse bones that once lay along the bank, vic-tims of drowning or of drinking too much of the river's bitter wa-ter after a long trip across the desert.

To the east a dozen or so miles was a pass in King Mountain through which Gold Rush travelers and Butterfield stages had beaten out a trail. It was known as Castle Gap. One of J. Frank Dobie's many stories told of outlaws having robbed the Emperor Maximilian's treasure as the doomed archduke tried to get it out of Mexico by wagon train ahead of the Juaristas. The thieves were supposed to have buried it in Castle Gap. They intended to come back but were set upon by Indians, leaving just one survivor to tell the tale.

Most great treasure stories were told by a lone survivor who ei-ther died soon afterward or spent the rest of his life in a vain search for what he had lost.

From our back porch I could see that cleft in the mountains less than twenty miles away. I often wondered if Dobie's story had any truth behind it. Cliff Newland was convinced it did, for over the years he spent a tremendous amount of time searching the gap, looking for signs, digging holes. He would occasionally find relics of the past and be certain he was right on top of the treasure. I always thought it was probably just as well that he never found it, because he lived for the search. Life might have been empty for him had there no longer been anything to search for.

Cliff was one of those old-timers always full of stories about the so-called good old days. He once declared, "Things just ain't like they used to be. And I don't think they ever was."

The mighty Pecos River was gradually reduced to a nasty trickle by upriver dams and oilfield pollution. A person today is more likely to be poisoned by it than drowned in it.

LIKE THE RANCHING INDUSTRY, the oilfields produced a rich legacy of folklore and great stories of luck, good and bad, especially from the early wildcatter days. Much depended on where the spudder took the first bite of earth. A few feet one way or the other could decide whether the driller became a rich man or a pauper.

Bill Allman had gotten oil in his blood in Kansas before he came south into Texas, following the booms to Odessa, McCamey, and Crane. He was one of the best-liked men in town, though he could be stern when the occasion demanded it. The oilfield was not a place for the timid. Usually he disarmed strangers with a smile that could light a room and thrust out his hand with an enthusiastic "Put 'er there, pal."

He remained a cable-tool driller even after that type of relatively simple equipment was largely replaced by the faster but more complicated and dangerous rotary drill. The cable tool raised the bit in the bottom of the hole, then dropped it hard, chipping its way down by inches. The rotary was a power drill, grinding steadily through sand, rock, shale, or whatever was in its way. When Bill was ninety years old he spent a whole summer day standing on a derrick floor in the blazing sun at an Odessa oil show, demonstrating the cable tool to younger generations, who had never seen it operate. He loved that rig.

"The cable tool was slower," he admitted, "but it got there."

Bill and Ardeth Allman had a son, Billy, and a daughter, Joyce, both classmates of mine. Billy piloted a P-38 and was killed in World War II. He was the first of my close friends to die in that conflict. I heard the news and wept.

Bill had a vast knowledge of the history of the Permian Basin fields, for he had been a part of it almost from its beginning. He told me about the Crane discovery well. A wildcatter named B. F. Weekley drilled it just a few hundred yards from the Upton County line and a few miles east from where the town would be established soon afterward. It was February 1926, and he was almost exhausted both physically and financially. Not certain he could pay his bills, he was about to give up the project and declare it a dry hole. He owed $500 to one of his drillers and offered an offset eighty acres in lieu of the money. The driller held out for cash.

After eating supper, Weekley decided to take his crew back to make one more run before dark. That last forlorn effort, those last few feet into the earth, struck oil and set off the Crane County boom. Bill went to work for Weekley shortly afterward. He said the offset eighty acres, once offered to settle a $500 debt, were sold for $80,000.

Weekley had owed $2,500 to a rig builder named Jones and talked Jones into taking a 160-acre lease in payment. Jones sold that lease for $100,000.

Often when a wildcatter struck it big, he invested the money in more wells. He could then become immensely wealthy or hopelessly broke. For many it was steak today, hash tomorrow.

At the time of the Crane strike, Weekley had two other wildcat operations going, one at Vernon, Texas, the other south of San Angelo. Both were failures. The Crane well saved him.

His discovery was one of a series that followed the original Santa Rita No. 1 west of Big Lake. An attorney named Rupert P. Ricker suspected that most geologists were wrong when they declared there was no oil in Reagan County or the area around it. He obtained a permit to drill a wildcat well on university land but encountered much difficulty in raising money. Among the investors were a group of New York Catholic women. In their honor, Frank Pickrell climbed to the top of the derrick to scatter petals from a rose the New York ladies had given him and to christen the well the Santa Rita, after the saint of the impossible.

On January 8, 1921, the last day the permit was valid, Pickrell spudded in the well. That was enough to hold the lease. An experienced driller named Carl Cromwell took over the rig. He was a Pennsylvanian known as "the big Swede." He and his wife lived in an unpainted shack on site. There for twenty-one slow months she raised chickens and grew a garden while a cantankerous cable-tool rig gradually hammered its way down a little more than three thousand feet. The crews came and went, largely cowboys who disliked the job and did not stay long.

On the morning of May 28, 1923, oil roared up and over the top of the derrick. Though Santa Rita No. 1 turned out to be only a mediocre producer, it opened Pandora's box. The rush was on, and drilling crews were soon busy all over that area of West Texas.

WHEN LESTER S. GRANT CAME down to Crane from Colorado to manage the McElroy Ranch and the Franco-Wyoming oil interests, he brought with him a new retractable steel tape measure for survey work. It was used to lay out the Crane town site and divide it into individual lots. After a major part of the survey work was done, it was discovered that the tape had a flaw of several inches. All the lots were a bit smaller than they were supposed to be. By the time the survey had reached across the town site, the small error had compounded into a major discrepancy. The entire job had to be redone.

There had been a previous attempt to establish a town in the county, that time because of water rather than oil. An effort was made to start a major irrigation project along the Pecos River, employing river water to make the desert bloom like a rose. The promoters built a dam, reservoir, and irrigation ditches, and planned a celebration the day the first water was to be turned into the field. The ceremony drew a considerable crowd to see history made.

The excitement quickly turned flat. At the big moment, the promoters turned on the pump and started water down the first row. *Down* was the right word, for the water went straight down into the thirsty desert ground. It never reached the end of the row.

A townsite had been laid out ten miles west of the later Crane. It was stillborn. Crane's only farming boom was over before it began.

No one in those days had ever heard the term *air pollution,* but Crane had it, thanks to the gas that invariably escaped from the oil operations. At night we could see dozens of flares across the fields, burning off excess gas. The largest, at the Humble camp, went out at least a couple of times, killing animals that had gathered for warmth. I heard but do not know it for a fact that several people died during one of these mishaps. Bill told me that twenty-five mules were gassed in a corral one night. He told me also of a woman who fed a set of turkey poults, figuring they would fetch a good price in town. About the time they were ready for the table, they all died from gas poisoning.

Because of the gas, an effort was made to start a competing town south of Crane, away from the oilfield. A sign was erected: "Out of the Gas, into the Ozone, Building a Town Where the Town Belongs."

Like the other townsite, it did not survive past the promotion stage.

Though it made no effort to become a town, a beer joint and bootleg-whiskey place got a foothold for a while north of Crane, partway to Odessa. It was a convenient spot for oilfield workers on their way between the two towns. Dad found that some of the ranch's cowboys made up reasons to work on the ranch's north side. He was pleased when the establishment closed, probably moving to Odessa where there were more thirsty people.

By the time Crane was a year old, its citizens decided to organize the county. It had been platted on paper as far back as 1887, but until the oil boom it did not have enough population to organize.

A story has been told that should be true, even if it isn't. It is claimed that one precinct in the county had only fifteen voters. Two men were running for the commissioner's court. One knew all the voters and was confident he could depend on eight of them. When the votes were tallied, however, he had only seven. His opponent had eight. Sure he had been defrauded, he paid for a recount and found that his mother-in-law had voted against him.

When time came for election of the first county officials, polls were set up in a floorless tabernacle, Crane's first and only church at the time. Unfortunately the town received one of its infrequent rains, making a loblolly of the dirt floor. The polls had to be moved to a business building that had a floor of wood.

It was an early example of the separation of church and state.

Some of the lawless element, bootleggers and gamblers, were not in favor of organization. Early attorney J. P. Cotten recalled seeing bruised knuckles and bloody noses on Election Day, but the proposition carried.

Because housing was critical in the new town of Crane, several oil companies built outlying camps for their full-time employees, including bunkhouses for the bachelors, complete with mess hall. Typically the houses in these camps were superior to most in town, the rent very reasonable. The school ran buses to bring camp children to town. For those in the sandhills camps west of town, it could be more than a twenty-mile ride each way.

Many years later the companies began closing these camps, often selling the houses to their tenants at a bargain price to get them off their tax rolls. Cliff Newland, facing retirement, bought a house in the Gulf camp from a man who had previously bought it from the oil company. The seller had already tacked on a tidy little profit and sought a bit more. The house had 220-volt wiring to accommodate an electric stove and perhaps other appliances. The seller wanted a substantial extra payment for the special wiring. Cliff said he had no need for it and declined to pay the premium. Rather than see him get it for nothing, the seller climbed up into the attic to tear out the wiring and fell through the Sheetrock ceiling. The only real injury was to his pride.

Oilfields gradually came to cover a significant part of the McElroy Ranch. From an economic standpoint, cattle and oil are highly compatible, because a good oil well can pay for a considerable amount of feed. A standing joke says the best mineral supplement for cattle is a working pump jack. However, there are hazards. Something about the smell of crude oil is attractive to cattle. A broken pipeline or spillage from a well can create small black pools, which draw cattle to drink. It is rarely immediately fatal unless they consume an unusual amount, but it has a cumulative effect. It ruins the digestive system so that the animals waste away and eventually die. An "oiled" cow can be considered lost.

Oil companies usually settled for such cattle rather than expend time and expense on a court case. The McElroy Ranch had a standard set of damage fees, adjusted up or down as the cattle market fluctuated, to ease its dealings with oil operators. On some ranches, however, it was not unusual for an old cull cow to become a valuable registered animal of high pedigree when her demise called for compensation.

The oilfield had its hazards for a cowboy, too. A rider had to keep an eye out for abandoned steel cable and similar obstructions that might trip his horse. Old slush pits, where spilled oil had been allowed to accumulate, could become a trap. Once when wild dogs were killing calves, Tommy Camron came upon one and spurred after it with rope in hand and ready. The dog ran over the lip of an old pit where waste oil had stood long enough to congeal and be covered by blowing sand. The dog's light weight did not disturb the smooth-looking surface, but the horse broke through and plunged headlong into a deep pool of oil. Tommy managed to fight his way out, but the horse drowned.

On hot summer days when we were riding in the oilfield, we youngsters liked to go up to a rig and ask for a drink of water. The oilfielders usually stopped at an icehouse on their way to work each day and filled their water cans with all the ice they could force into them. The water coming out of those cans would be cold enough to freeze our teeth. We found most oilfield workers cordial and willing to share with us. Most of that generation had come from farms and ranches in the first place. Perhaps we reminded them of home.

As a class, they were good, solid people out of pioneer stock. Despite the rowdy reputation most boomtowns acquired, they were likely to have more churches than gin and beer joints. This is not to say there was no violence, for Saturday night was likely to see a few roustabouts mix it up after spending an inordinate part of their wages on what was delicately known as spirituous liquors. Some boomtowns attracted organized crime that could turn vicious. Kilgore was notorious for that, as was Wink. Martial law had to be declared in Borger to gain some control over the thugs who came not to drill for oil but to prey on those who did.

Sometimes a situation called for a visit by the Texas Rangers, who tended to be long on nerve and short on patience. In extreme cases they might act as judge and jury and mete out punishment without waiting for judicial sanction. Nothing struck fear into the heart of a boomtown thug like an announcement that the Rangers had arrived.

To kill a Ranger was tantamount to suicide. The murderer was unlikely ever to face a jury. In those days, long before the American Civil Liberties Union, justice was sometimes meted out swiftly and with a finality that left no chance for appeal.

Crane was mercifully spared most of the extreme violence. What crime it had was usually tied directly or indirectly to bootlegging and occasional highjacking of oilfield equipment. Texas Rangers had little to do in Crane. I dimly remember that they came in once and broke up some slot machines, and they were always on the lookout for bootleggers. The Rangers were awe-inspiring to a youngster. They were usually easy to spot by their neat manner of Western dress, the no-nonsense way they carried themselves, and the pistols worn high on the hip, none of that low-slung holster stuff we saw in the movies.

Bill Allman told me the town's first killing resulted from an argument between the owner of a café and his cook. The cook drove an ice pick into his boss's heart. A brand-new cemetery was established on the far side of a hill just south of town. A woman who worked in the café assumed ownership and operated it for several years without the bother of deed or court order. Nobody in those early days was much concerned about such legalities, for they knew the town might dry up and blow away when the boom played out. Many towns did.

Killing remained almost unheard of in Crane after that early incident. The most notorious was the shooting of several members of a ranch family some miles from town. The crime was committed by one of the family and had nothing to do with the oilfield folk.

Mrs. R. V. Melton told about an early minister who learned the hard way the difference between preaching and meddling. He was outraged by the sin he saw in early Crane. He thought the way to stop it was to condemn it from the pulpit and name names. He got more attention than he expected, for one of the sinners gave him a sound thrashing. The Meltons took him into their tent home, cleansed his wounds, and saw him off to a more hospitable climate where the Lord's word might be received with more grace.

Oilfield justice as practiced in the 1920s and 1930s would make a modern-day defense lawyer break into hives. For a time, the new town had no jail. Lawbreakers were handcuffed to a heavy chain attached to a stout post outdoors.

Mrs. Mary O'Neal was a justice of the peace for several years. When a pair of oilfield workers were brought before her the umpteenth time for fighting, she said, "Each of you take an ax handle, go out in the brush where you won't disturb anybody, and beat each other to death!"

One early Crane sheriff was a fragile old man who knew he could not win in an even fight with miscreants. His method was to ease up on them quietly, hit them on the head with a pistol barrel, then arrest them while they were too stunned to resist. This was sometimes known as a "cowboy shampoo."

In some oil towns a simple method of cleaning house was for peace officers to gather up all the "undesirables," male and female, load them into a boxcar, seal it, and ship them off to be someone else's problem. Any reluctance was met with severe corporal punishment.

Bootlegging was the most common crime in those prohibition days. Riding a pasture, Dad once came across a bootlegger's stash hidden in a thicket. Out of a mischievous desire to see what might happen, he moved the stash. Shortly afterward two bootleggers got into a knock-down-drag-out fight, one certain the other had stolen his goods.

The pervasive gas in the air caused health problems. Several Crane youngsters came down with a mild form of tuberculosis. I was one of them. I missed attending school most of my fifth-grade year because the doctor ordered me to remain in bed all but a short time each day. Teachers sent books and lessons out to me, and Mother saw that I kept up with my classmates.

The experience was not entirely negative. Condemned to remain on my back most of the time, I had to turn inward and entertain myself. This released my creative urges. I wrote stories. I did imaginary radio broadcasts, telling these stories. I made "movies" by drawing pictures on long strips of paper, then pulling them through slots in a large piece of cardboard so that only one drawing was revealed at a time. From behind the cardboard I would voice the dialogue and inflict the stories on my younger brothers. They were sometimes less than enthusiastic, especially on reruns.

DESPITE A LONG EXPOSURE to the oil fields, I never worked in them except for a short-term summer job on a tanking crew. We were dismantling old steel storage tanks in late August. The heat inside such a tank can only be imagined; it cannot be described. The job was not devoid of danger, either. A worker on top of a tank dropped a heavy bucketful of steel rivets, which brushed Bill Lowe as they fell. They would have brained him had they struck him on the head.

The tanking job had a strong impact. It convinced me that whatever it took, I intended to go to the university and become a writer. But how was I ever going to convince Dad?

SIX

THE HAPPIEST SUMMERS OF my youth were spent batching on the Lea Ranch while caretaker Wes Reynolds went off on an extended vacation. They gave me my first feeling of independence and self-sufficiency, helping ease my inferiority complex and also wean me from the apron strings. I stayed most of the summer, while my younger brothers rotated. I did the cooking, such as it was. My brothers would starve out after about a week and plead for relief.

Dad had been leasing the place since the late 1930s for his own growing herd, which he kept separate from the company-owned cattle. The owner, P. J. Lea, had acquired the place after the turn of the last century and had built it up to something more than twenty sections, or twenty-plus square miles. The ranch house was typical of the more ambitious built during that period, large, with tall windows, high ceilings, and screened-in porches front and back. Good circulation kept the house tolerably comfortable even on hot summer days.

Though windmills pumped water for outside use and for livestock, kitchen water came mostly from a cistern which caught rainwater from the roof and strained it through filters. To get the water, we turned a crank and activated an endless chain of metal cups, each tipping forward and dumping its load as it came over the top.

There was no electricity. For light we used kerosene lamps and lanterns. Summer daylight lasted until bedtime anyway.

The cookstove was a heavy cast-iron wood burner, standing on an insulated metal sheet that caught small coals and kept them from the wooden floor. Some ranch houses set their stoves in a box of sand, which served the same purpose. Mesquite wood was plentiful, though somebody—most often me—had to chop it into stove lengths and carry it in.

I loved that old house with its long hallway that connected the two porches, large bedrooms on either side, and a living room next to the back porch. What it lacked in modern conveniences, it made up in comfort and old-fashioned country charm.

Wes was a typical bachelor cowboy, firmly set in his ways, without fear of bosses or bosses's sons. He did not enjoy cooking, so he seemed to survive mostly on boiled black coffee and roll-your-own Bull Durham cigarettes. Wartime rationing made it hard for him to get enough coffee, whereas he had little use for sugar. He would trade his sugar ration stamps to Mother for some of her coffee stamps.

Wherever he went about the place afoot, he carried a cup of coffee with him. When he finished it, whether in the barn, the chicken house, the cistern house, or in the corrals, he set down the cup and left it. Every few days he ran out of cups and had to conduct a coffee-cup roundup.

After Wes left on his vacation, Myrle and I decided to do him a favor and give the house a thorough cleaning. He was not the neatest of housekeepers. We rearranged the place in nice order. We swept and mopped, we washed all the dishes afresh, and we threw out a lot of old, outdated prescriptions that he had let dry up through neglect.

Wes was not pleased. He liked things the way they had been, chaotic. It was a mess, but it was *his* mess. Worst of all by far, we cleaned and scrubbed his crusted old coffeepot. When it became too full of grounds he would simply pitch them out and put in fresh coffee. Our diligent scrubbing had all but ruined the pot, he said. It took months to get the right flavor back into it.

He might not have been half as disturbed if we had shot his horse.

As a matter of fact, we *did* shoot his horse. Wes's favorite was a big *grulla* named Blue Bull that gave us boys a lot of frustration. It was hard to pen. It would come in with the other horses but turn back just before entering the gate. More often than not it spilled the rest of the horses too, taking them with him. Moreover, it was iron-jawed and would not respond to the bit. It went its way regardless of the rider's intentions.

We finally had enough and decided to teach it a lesson. We took a 410-gauge shotgun and stood back far enough not to do any lethal damage. Just as the horse was about to turn at the gate and race away, we let it have a dose of buckshot across the rump. It went through that gate so fast it almost ran into the opposite fence before it could stop. Afterward, all we had to do was start toward the pen, and old Blue Bull would lead the other horses in at a gallop.

Wes probably wondered at the change in his horse's behavior. We never told him.

Wes welcomed any chance for a woman-cooked meal.

Old-timer George Lee was holding down McElroy's Sand Camp. Mrs. Lee was a great cook. When there was special work to be done at Sand Camp, Wes was there, making up for lost time at Mrs. Lee's table. Ironically, despite his wife's wonderful way with a cookstove, Daddy George was so skinny he looked as if a strong wind might carry him away.

Many years later we named a son Stephen Lee in honor of the Lees. They had retired and bought a modest house in Midland. One of the last times I saw them, several of us raised a windmill in their backyard to furnish water for the house.

During my tenure as head cook at the Lea Ranch, the food was nothing to compare with Mrs. Lee's. Dad periodically brought over some beef. The only thing I ever learned to do with it was to slice it into thin steaks, dip it in flour, and fry it in a skillet. I was also fair to middling with french fries. My biscuits tended to be flat and shy on flavor, and not to be dropped on a sore toe. I was afflicted with ingrown toenails, a result probably of wearing narrow-toed cowboy boots from the time I was able to walk. I eventually gave up boots except when they were really needed. I decided that boots were for vanity, and shoes were for feet.

We ate a lot of canned ranch-style beans, which contained a strong flavoring of chili powder. We occasionally set out traps and feasted on quail, illegal but a welcome change from our usual monotonous fare.

Occasionally a school friend named Joe Pearce came out and stayed with us awhile. Joe was always delightful company. What mischief one of the Kelton boys didn't think of, Joe would.

Myrle and Joe decided it was time to try their hand as wage-earning cowboys though they were still in their early teens. They hired out to our great-uncle, Frank Kelton, who operated a large ranch near Pecos. Most cowboys of service age had gone off to serve their country. Uncle Frank had to take what help he could find, including chronic misfits, drunks, and jailbirds.

These men were a revelation to Myrle and Joe. They had never been exposed to characters of that kind. A middle-aged cowboy known for a love of whiskey gave them a note and asked them to deliver it to his estranged wife when they went to town. They knocked on her door and were met by a belligerent dreadnaught of a woman. With a scowl, she demanded, "What do you boys want here?"

Joe handed her the note and stammered, "Y-y-your husband asked us to deliver this."

She glanced at it and boomed, "Is that old son of a bitch still alive?"

The boys decided it was time to return to civilization.

Myrle, still in his first year of high school, had been keen on a schoolgirl of about the same age. He found out that while he had been at Pecos she had begun going with another boy. He sat down and wrote a breakup letter, then handed it to Joe for appraisal.

Joe read it with all the solemnity of a judge, then remarked, "It looks okay to me. But hadn't you ought to leave the cusswords out?"

As brothers will, Myrle and I often disagreed about one thing or another, occasionally to the point of violence. One day we hitched a team to a wagon and set out to repair weak spots in the Lea Ranch's outside fence. We fell into an argument about something trivial. We were carrying a sackful of steeples with which to secure barbed wire to fence posts. In his frustration Myrle began throwing steeples at the mules, agitating them considerably. By the time we got back to the house, they were skittish as jackrabbits.

I decided to carry some trash barrels out to the dump before unhitching the mules. Myrle opened the gate for me to enter the horse pasture. As the mules started through, however, he gave the gate a push, and it struck the nearest mule. Squealing in fright, the pair took off and made a sharp turn going through the gate. The coupling pole broke. The wagon bed bounced up, then flipped over. I landed on my belly in the sand with the reins wrapped around my wrist. The mules took off in a wild stampede, dragging me several yards before I could get loose. I lay there with a mouthful of sand, watching the wagon's front wheels bounce off across the pasture behind the mules, and wondering how in the world I was going to explain this to Dad.

They circled the pasture and came back, still in a run until they reached the corral gate and stopped, shivering and shining with sweat.

I declared my indignation, and Myrle declared total innocence. He said he could not figure out what caused the mules to act that way other than my general ineptitude. Neither of us came up with a plausible story to tell Dad, so we just told him we had a runaway. The old wagon—what was left of it—was retired from service. So far as I know Dad never learned the particulars, but he made it clear that he knew boyish foolishness was in back of it somehow.

I remembered this incident long afterward when I witnessed a rancher's frustration over horseplay by his son and a friend from school. He said, "One boy can be a lot of help. Two boys aren't worth killing."

It was about a quarter mile from the ranch house up to the road. On some Saturday afternoons I walked to the road and hitchhiked to town for a milkshake and a movie, which usually involved a total investment of about fifty cents. I made sure to start hitchhiking back well before dark. Usually some passing oilfield worker would pick me up. I guess they realized a skinny kid in cowboy boots was not likely to be a highjacker.

At least I did not ride my horse to the highway and tie him to a fence post while I thumbed my way to town. I knew a cowboy who did that. He got on a bender and forgot about his horse for a couple or three days. When he returned the horse was still there, though in cowboy parlance it was "a little bit drawed." Dehydrated, in other words.

We had no radio at the Lea Ranch, so my main entertainment was reading and playing records on a small windup phonograph. I had a collection of Gene Autry, Bob Wills, and Roy Acuff music, which I sang to my horse as we worked the pastures, just like Gene but without a guitar.

Eventually Dad decided Wes needed a radio to keep him from being lonely out there all by himself. Wes argued that he had never had a radio, did not need a radio, and would not listen to the damned thing if he had one. Dad brought him one anyway, a battery-powered model. Wes did not accept it in good grace. "You've wasted your money," he declared. "I won't listen to the damned thing."

After Wes had had the radio awhile, Dad made some comment about country music. Wes brightened and said, "That old Uncle Dave Macon can shore play the banjo, can't he?"

A couple of years later Wes showed what stern stuff he was made of. He rode up to a windmill, tied his horse, and climbed up on a wooden ladder to see if the steel tank was full of water. A rung collapsed under his weight. He fell to the ground, breaking his leg. After the initial shock, he crawled toward his horse, but the animal spooked at the sight of Wes inching himself along on his belly. It jerked the reins loose and ran off.

A couple or three hundred yards away was a primitive two-rut road occasionally used by oilfield trucks. Wes crawled painfully through the sand, dragging the broken leg. Then he lay at the roadside until at last a truck came by. He waved it down, and the oilfielders took him to town.

Our principal duty in Wes's absence was general caretaking, making sure the windmills kept pumping so the animals had plenty of water, checking the fences to be sure they didn't leak cattle, and watching out for screwworm cases. The screwworm for years had been a scourge to livestock operators across the Southwest. They hatched in open wounds from eggs deposited by a specific type of blowfly. They ate live flesh and, if left unchecked, would sooner or later kill an animal. They were particularly bad in the navels of newly born calves, in castration cuts, and in wounds cut by barbed wire or lacerations caused by sharp horns. White-faced cattle were especially susceptible to pinkeye, which attracted screwworms. One of the nastiest jobs was treating a bad infestation of screwworms in a cancer-eyed cow. That was another strong incentive for a would-be writer to get serious.

Mature cowboys would rope cattle in the pasture and treat them on the spot. Dad discouraged us boys from doing this, especially to full-grown cattle, unless an adult was with us in case something went wrong. We usually drove the afflicted animals to the nearest pens and put them in a chute. That eliminated the risk of becoming entangled in a rope, though we could still get hooked, stomped, or knocked down.

The year 1941 was one of the wettest on record for West Texas, and screwworms literally exploded. Most days we rode from daylight until dark, looking for and doctoring cases.

Unbeknownst to most people in the industry, a couple of government scientists at Kerrville, Texas, had quietly been studying the screwworm fly and its sex habits for years. Drs. Raymond C. Bushland and Edward F. Knipling were trying to find a way to stop its reproduction cycle. As an agricultural journalist I later got to know these men. The eventual result of their work, starting in the 1950s, was an eradication effort using radiation on laboratory-produced pupae and a massive release of sterile flies to overwhelm the native population.

The idea drew much ridicule at first. Ranchers used to the time-honored animal-castration method wondered how anybody could "cut" millions of male flies. I attended a San Angelo meeting at which T. A. Kincaid Jr. and Dolph Briscoe Jr., presidents of the Texas Sheep and Goat Raisers Association and the Texas and Southwestern Cattle Raisers Association, respectively, signed the first checks to initiate a pilot program in Texas. With the endorsement of those two organizations, even many of the most vocal doubters contributed.

Eradication worked after several years and some disappointing setbacks. The Southwestern states at last were free of the screwworm. A permanent barrier remains in the southern end of Mexico to keep them from coming back.

This was one case in which species annihilation was welcome, at least to livestock operators and wildlife managers. Elimination of this hazard in Texas resulted in far greater survival rates among wild animals such as deer, with the result that overpopulation sometimes became a problem. This required increasing the harvest during the fall hunting season and thinning of does. The alternative was starvation, nature's effective but cruel way of fitting the numbers to the feed.

At the time we were fighting the screwworm problem on the Lea and McElroy ranches, few would have dreamed the pest could ever be eliminated. Earlier, cowboys carried two types of medicine on their saddles, one a chloroform screwworm killer, the other a fly repellant to discourage reinfestation. About the time I was old enough to make some semblance of a hand, a double-purpose treatment was developed, an odorous black liquid known as Smear 62. It was effective but unpleasant to use. It seemed to soak into the skin, so that it took a lot of soap and hard scrubbing to eliminate both the black and the odor. Usually the last vestiges had to be tolerated until they wore off.

A cowboy would carry the medicine in a pouch tied to his saddle. Most often this pouch was the top of an old boot with a wooden bottom nailed to it. On hot days Smear 62 tended to expand. Once a can of it swelled enough to blow the lid off and cover part of my saddle—and my leg—with black. The stain never came out of the leather or my Levi's.

That summer began with something unheard of on the McElroy Ranch, a flood. One of our annual chores was to saw up enough mesquite wood to carry all the ranch houses through the coming year. Dad jerry-rigged a circular saw powered by a pulley that circled the rear wheel of a pickup standing on jacks. This sat on the lip of a drop-off about ten or twelve feet high. A truck was parked at the lower level, just beneath. As it was cut, the wood was pitched down into the truck bed. We spent a goodly amount of time that spring cutting wood and stacking it between the ranch kitchen and the barn.

In early June, just after school was out, we had a record rain. That huge woodpile floated off down the draw. We had to do the whole job over.

Several tires floated away with the wood. Later, when the war brought on tire rationing, a couple of these were found amid the debris and put back into service.

It was those heavy spring rains that brought on the screwworm explosion and kept us on horseback all summer. It reached such proportions that it became impossible to see all the cattle between daylight and dark. We would alternate pastures, trying to cover each one at least every two or three days. Once, riding with Dad and hunting wormies, I saw several cattle shaded up in a mesquite thicket. I asked if we shouldn't go look them over.

The sun was in the west, and we still had a lot of ground to cover. Dad said, "I don't see any of them down. We'd best keep looking for the *bad* ones."

Though Dad was a great cowboy, he was not much of a teacher. He seemed to take it for granted that we should already know everything he did, or that we ought to learn by observation and perhaps osmosis without asking a lot of questions. He could become highly impatient when we demonstrated that we *didn't* know it all, and give us a chewing-out that blistered the hide.

Over the years, talking to people who grew up under similar circumstances, I have found this impatience not uncommon among ranchers trying to raise their sons to follow in their footsteps. Often I found the working cowboys more patient and willing to teach me than Dad was. But of course Dad shouldered the weighty responsibility of running the ranch. Any day a cowboy wanted to, he could quit and move on. Dad was stuck with it. His strong Puritan work ethic would not settle for anything short of the best that could be done, at least by his sons.

He rarely showed his impatience to the grown cowboys, though there were times when he must have struggled to contain himself.

He was critical of the way I mounted and dismounted from a horse. He once made me buckle my saddle on a fence about the height of a horse, then practice getting on and off. I must have done it a hundred times before he let me stop. It was one of the few times I can remember him trying to teach me how to do something instead of assuming I should already know.

Dad often accused me of being "as slow as the seven-year itch." He contended that I moved like an old man and gave me a nickname, Pop, which stuck to me like a cocklebur. Every rancher and cowboy in that part of the country came to know me as Pop. A few old-timers still call me that, though I am not self-conscious about it anymore. My thin gray hair easily qualifies me for the name.

When I was in my senior year of high school Dad cornered me

on the front porch and asked if I had decided what I was going to make of myself. We both agreed, without stating it aloud, that I would never become a real cowboy. Who would pay me for my limited skills?

I had known for years what I wanted to do but had not known how to tell him. I was afraid he would not understand. But I had to answer his question. I told him I wanted to go to the University of Texas, study journalism, and become a writer.

Surely enough, he did not understand. That was when he said, "That's the way with you kids nowadays, you all want to make a living without working for it."

Tom Schreiner was the ranch's Norwegian-born bookkeeper. He lived in a small house a stone's throw from ours. Dad was always amused by his fractured English, but he respected the old man's experience and practical judgment. He sent me to talk to him, hoping he might change my mind and help me decide on a "dependable" occupation.

Schreiner had come to this country as a young man to seek his fortune. He never found his own, but he helped other people make theirs. He had had a wide range of experiences, including a stint once as a clerk in a hotel where the writer William Sydney Porter, known by his pen name O. Henry, was a long-term guest. He told me about having to help sober up Porter so he could meet a story deadline. He told me about several newspapermen he had known, most of them drunkards and ne'er-do-wells.

Seeing that he had not convinced me, he finally said, "Vell, Elmer, if dot is vat you vant, okay. But remember, writers are alvays drunk, and they are alvays broke."

For many years I was convinced that he was half right. About the *broke* part.

Schreiner was in several ways a tragic figure. He was out of place on the ranch, yet there seemed nowhere else left for him. He was highly qualified at his job. He had personally hand-delivered the multimillion-dollar check that Franco-Wyoming paid J. T. McElroy for the ranch soon after the Crane oil discovery. However, he had a drinking habit that got in the way too often. The best anyone at our level could figure, the company did not want to lose him altogether, so they put him into what amounted to exile out in West Texas, far from the main offices in California. He never attempted to be anything other than what he was, an urban and urbane man. He was consistently well dressed, usually even wearing a tie. He never sported boots or a cowboy hat as some did in an effort to "fit in."

He always tried to present a friendly countenance, but a feeling of melancholy often manifested itself. He frequently drank too much. He was among friends, yet alone. He seemed to regret having left Norway as a young man and often expressed a wish to go back to the old country. After World War II he finally did, retiring from the ranch and returning to his boyhood home to live out his days. By then his health was breaking.

He soon discovered the truth of the old adage that you can't go home again. He was a stranger in his homeland. Most of his relatives were gone except the younger generation, who did not know him. Most of his boyhood friends were either aging or dead. He found himself more alone than before and began writing letters to his American friends, expressing a hope that he could return to Texas when his health improved. It never did. He died, as lonely as ever, in a homeland that no longer was home, a *querencia* that lived only in his heart.

SOME DAYS BURN THEMSELVES into the memory so that we can recall tiny, insignificant details even when we cannot remember our wives' birthdays. Such a day was Sunday, December 7, 1941. The Ys was in the midst of its late-fall "works." We Kelton boys had gone out to the wagon after school on Friday afternoon at Red Well, on the southern edge of the ranch. After supper the cowboys sat around a second fire, separate from the one used for cooking. Dad called this the "bullshit" fire, for it was witness to a lot of idle conversation. He had placed a small portable radio on the chuck-box lid, and talking lapsed while everybody listened to *Amos and Andy*.

We rounded up and branded the next day, then were to move to headquarters in the afternoon. The cook loaded the truck with the chuck box on it and headed out. The cowboys were to work another pasture as they moved northward. Dad told me to gather the branding irons and other equipment once they cooled and bring his pickup to headquarters. Soon I was there by myself. I tried to start the pickup, but it was dead. Not a spark could I get from the battery. Afoot, seven or eight miles from home, I decided that all I could do was wait. Perhaps when I did not show up by dark, someone would come looking for me. If not, I would spend a cold night sleeping in the pickup. Before long I was starting to feel lonesome and hungry, wishing the cook had left some cold biscuits behind. Tom Grammer or Hub Castleberry would have, but we had a different cook this time.

Luck was with me. By pure chance a government trapper and his wife happened along, traveling to town on a rarely used two-rut road. Against his wife's protest that they would be late, he tied on and towed me to headquarters.

The next day, Sunday the seventh, was one of the few times I can remember that Dad ever let weather change his work plans. It had begun raining during the night and was still raining hard at daybreak. He decided gathering cattle would be next to impossible, so the roundup crew spent the day loafing around headquarters. The chuck wagon was parked in a hay shed adjacent to the barn, out of the rain.

I went to our house and worked on a poster for a high school play while listening to the New York Philharmonic on the radio. The announcer broke in with first news of the Japanese attack. I had never heard of Pearl Harbor, but I hurried over to the bunkhouse and told the cowboys they should turn on a radio in the lobby. A hush fell over them as they pondered what this meant for all of us. I doubt that anyone realized the extent to which it would change our lives.

The event stirred up a vigorous debate between the wagon cook and one of our neighbors, Harold Smith. A homegrown socialist, the cook argued that the government should confiscate all money in the country and divide it equally among the citizens. Harold maintained that within a couple of years the money would be back in more or less the same hands as before.

The cook's family later came into significant oil money, and he became a Republican. Paul Patterson once remarked that the best cure for a socialist is a dose of capital.

I HAD BARELY TURNED sixteen when I finished high school. We just had eleven grades at the time. The requirement was soon raised to twelve years so that my younger brothers spent a year longer in school than I did. They felt gypped.

All through high school our class had built up a special fund by operating the refreshment stand at dances and football games. The money was to finance the traditional senior trip and the school annual. But after the attack on Pearl Harbor, school trips were drastically curtailed and the annual was canceled. Double L Martin turned our hard-earned fund over to China Relief. I often wondered if he remembered that a decade later when the Chinese were shooting at American troops in Korea. But of course the Chinese were our allies in 1942 and suffering terrible atrocities at the hands of our common enemy. China Relief seemed a worthy place to put our savings.

Dad eventually lost his grazing lease in 1947. Owner Lea's sons had come home from military service and wanted to try their hand at ranching. The area was dry. Dad could not find another suitable place, so with an aching heart he sold the herd he had nursed along at such a financial, physical, and emotional cost.

It turned out to be his salvation. West Texas as a whole had a seven-year drought during the 1950s. The Crane area had the use of it even earlier. For the Lea Ranch the drought lasted about ten years. It would have wiped out Dad's herd long before the rains came again. As it was, those cows endured the long drought on paper, in the bank.

SEVEN

DESPITE MY HAVING JUST turned sixteen, I felt that I was grown when I put high school behind me. It did not take long for Dad to set me straight. He gave me orders just as he had when I was a callow youth of fifteen. My education had barely begun.

He gave in to my wish to major in journalism, but he was dubious about my going off to the University of Texas in Austin. Too far and too big, he said. He favored something smaller, like Texas Tech in Lubbock. But Tech's journalism school had not yet built a reputation. Dad queried several friends and came to the reluctant conclusion that if I went to a smaller school I might never get a job on any newspaper larger than what he called the *Midland Headache*. So the University of Texas it was.

One reason I chose UT, besides its highly rated journalism department, was that Texas' leading folklorist, J. Frank Dobie, taught a course there in Southwestern life and literature. It was said that when he first proposed it to the regents, one declared there was no literature in the Southwest. Dobie was said to have replied, "There is plenty of life, so I'll teach that."

A student had to be a junior to take the course. I frequently saw Dobie around the campus in his floppy old rancher hat and his khaki pants with cuffs tucked into the tops of his black boots, South

Texas–style. I would be tempted to introduce myself, but then I would wonder what a freckle-faced kid from the West Texas sandhills could say to a man of his iconic stature, especially a kid who couldn't earn his beans as a cowboy. Consequently I never actually met him. By the time I came back from service after World War II and had the prerequisites, he was no longer on the faculty. I took the course under another fine Texas folklorist, Mody Boatright, but I always regretted the lost opportunity to know Dobie.

I had been on the UT campus only once before, when Paul Patterson took several students to a journalism workshop in my senior year. When I enrolled in the fall of 1942, the war had taken a drastic toll on male enrollment. The student population was something over six thousand, leaning heavily toward females.

Had I been a little older this might have made me feel like a kid in a candy shop, but I was younger than most of the girls and had but little idea what to do with one even if given the opportunity. I took a couple of dance lessons, hoping to improve my confidence and poise. It did nothing to cure my shyness. The only date I recall having at that time was with a pretty Crane high school senior who had just moved to Austin. Back in Crane, I would not have had the nerve to ask her out. But because she knew hardly anybody in her new school, she asked me to take her to the prom. I was charmed by her company, and she tried to make me feel at ease. Even so, I felt like an awkward country bumpkin.

In those relatively innocent times, young college men spent a lot of time talking about sex, but for most it was still an abstract subject based more on hearsay than on experience.

Anyway, I had my hands full enough without the distraction of pursuing girls. Coming from a ranch and a small-town school, I was ill prepared for the university. Its courses were far more demanding than those in high school. I almost washed out in my first semester before I began to get a grip. Moreover, though I had come for an education in journalism, no journalism courses were offered before the sophomore year. I contented myself with working as a volunteer on the student newspaper, the *Daily Texan,* which taught me several painful lessons in humility. If I turned in a story that measured twenty inches long, the editor was likely to whittle it down to ten and alter the wording so much that I could not recognize it as mine.

Professor Granville Price read each edition thoroughly and scrawled caustic critiques on every page, posting them on the bulletin board for everybody to see. Contributors waited in dread to read his verdict. Dr. DeWitt Reddick's specialty was feature writing, which taught me more about the craft than any other course I took. Like Paul Patterson, he was an amiable teacher but no pushover. Earning a B from Reddick was a cause for dancing down the stairs like James Cagney in *Yankee Doodle Dandy*. Paul Thompson was department head, a journalist of the old school with a strong dedication to high ethics and objectivity. Today's advocacy journalism and political partisanship would have driven him to despair.

Teachers I knew in the English department had no grasp of contemporary fiction writing. They had recognized hardly a change since Shakespeare's time, or at least Thomas Hardy's. The contemporary fiction market was in magazines like *Saturday Evening Post, Collier's,* and a host of pulps. The English teachers were contemptuous of commercial writing. If the average reader could understand it, they considered the work too trivial for serious consideration.

Given an assignment to write a piece on a subject of my own choosing, I wrote about ranch life in West Texas. The teacher gave me a D. She said the writing was acceptable enough, but if I ever wanted to get anywhere as a writer I must learn to choose subjects of importance. In contrast to Dobie, she saw nothing important about life in West Texas. Had I written about New York, London, or Paris, I might have been given an A. I knew little about those places, however. I did know about West Texas.

I lived in a student rooming house operated by Edith Burns, a middle-aged widow, five blocks from the campus. Tall, thin, and eternally watchful, Mrs. Burns considered herself a surrogate mother to her "boys," freely dispensing praise or criticism, whichever she deemed appropriate to the occasion. She called me "Cowboy," which might have evoked a chuckle from those at Crane who knew me better. Few students owned a car, so most traveled on foot or on a city bus. The rent for a shared room was fifteen dollars a month. Another fifteen paid for my meals at a student boarding house a short walk away. Sunday nights we were on our own. I might indulge in a hamburger at the Nighthawk or go for a real treat, a tamale-and-enchilada plate at the Mexican Inn on Red River.

Dad had taught me frugality. Every coin that left my fingers was treated like an old friend leaving home forever. A trip downtown on the bus cost a dime. Usually I walked, figuring by the time I got back I had saved twenty cents. Dad and Mother paid for my upkeep, but extras came from my own meager savings. I could not forget how much work I had put into that twenty cents. I preferred to spend it on a movie ticket, the only reason I went downtown in the first place. I took full advantage of the fact that I could now see films any time I wanted, limited only by time and financial ability.

Two first-run theaters charged thirty cents a ticket, forty at night. Down on scruffy Sixth Street, the Ritz and the Cactus specialized in B Westerns, serials, and last-run features. They charged only twenty cents. The Westerns were like a breath of home to me despite the fact that the heroes' clothes were too fancy and their horses too pretty. Sixth Street smelled of spilled beer and fried onions and was home to the homeless. It was not considered a decent place for UT students, and I seldom recognized any. Going there aroused my sense of adventure and the mystique of forbidden fruit.

In recent years Sixth has become a mecca for students and others bent on having a good time to hard rock and outlaw country music, though it is still a place where the unwary can get clubbed on the head and wake up with empty pockets.

Austin's skyline was dominated by two structures, the state

capitol building and the tower on the university campus. Dobie had opposed construction of the tower, which he described as looking like a toothpick in a pie. He thought the campus should remain flat like the Texas prairie. To the south of the tower, a huge memorial fountain featured heroic-sized Pompeo Coppini sculptures of mythical horses and water creatures. Dobie declared that "nobody but God and Coppini knows what it means."

Dobie was a dedicated "aginner." Dead set against parking meters, he served a stint in jail rather than pay parking fines. It was the principle of the thing, not the money, he said.

He was an outspoken liberal at a time when the board of regents was conservative. Earlier, ultraconservative J. Evetts Haley had been dismissed from the history department by liberal regents for his fiery attacks on the Roosevelt New Deal. A decade later, Dobie was dismissed on the pretext that his addiction to long bouts of hay fever limited his effectiveness in class, but the real reason was his liberal politics. So much for academic freedom, right-wing or left.

I rode the elevator to the top of the tower numerous times for its magnificent view of Austin and the hill country beyond. One year I had a professor who was supposed to teach a course in philosophy and logic but spent most of his time talking about semantics, their use and misuse. To illustrate his contention that words are but sounds with no reality of their own, he shocked a young girl on the front row by turning on her suddenly, pointing his finger in her face, and declaring, "You are a whore!"

When the shock wore off and the girl quit crying, he said, "Do you see? Just because I called you one does not mean you really are."

Some time after that he climbed up high in the tower and dived off. That was his ultimate reality. Even worse, in 1966 a deranged sniper ascended to the top and killed thirteen people before he was stopped. For years afterward the tower was closed to the public.

I would ride the bus home for holidays like Thanksgiving and Christmas, usually getting off in McCamey. There Mother or Dad would pick me up when no bus ran through Crane.

Though Dad never said much, he was concerned about this raw kid being so far from home in a large city neither of us understood. One of the few times he ever became openly sentimental with me was when I was about to return to school after a holiday, probably the first Thanksgiving. Watching for the bus, he sat silently, his face sad. As the bus pulled in he said, "Son, be careful and don't get in any trouble. But if you ever do, I'll be there."

Norman Rockwell did a painting much like that, of a worried father sitting at a bus stop beside his eager son and a suitcase with a college sticker on it. When I see that painting I remember Dad's short farewell lecture. It meant more than any amount of money he might have put in my hand.

I managed to pick up a few extra dollars by working as an usher during football games at Longhorn Stadium. And once I had several months of employment mailing the *Daily Texan*. That involved getting up in the wee hours of the morning, wrapping and addressing papers, and delivering them to the post office. One day I accidentally backed the university vehicle into a car parked across the street. I left a note on the windshield, giving the owner my name and address. It cost me a couple of weeks' earnings to pay for the damage, but I knew Dad would not have approved had I done less.

An old friend of my grandfather's once told me, "The Keltons were always an honorable people."

Dad bent over backward to live up to that image.

EIGHT

NOT YET OF DRAFT age, I began nevertheless to feel guilty about not being a part of the war. Donating blood did not seem enough. At seventeen, I decided to enlist. I chose the Navy, assuming that living conditions on a steel ship would be better than on a muddy battlefield. The Navy rejected me because I had flat feet.

That was no problem for the Army. When I turned eighteen it not only accepted me but after a time placed me in the walking infantry. So much for military logic.

The call came late in the semester. I was to report to Crane for transport to Fort Bliss, El Paso, for my physical. This occurred during one of those rare times that West Texas received heavy rains. I started out on the bus, but the driver received orders to go no farther than Kerrville. High water ahead was stopping traffic. I thought I was obliged to report despite hell or high water. It was the cowboy way. I found a truck driver who decided to chance it because he had a load of oilfield pipe he badly needed to deliver. Other bus passengers told me I was foolish, but I hitched a ride with him.

Fording the high water and feeling its strong tug against the truck, I began to wonder if the passengers were right. There are some horses even a *good* cowboy should not get on. The driver seemed confident that his heavy truck would make it through, however, and it did. I reached Crane on time and went to El Paso with five others. My flat feet seemed to raise no concern among the Army doctors who examined me. I told them about my childhood bout with tuberculosis. They found no sign of scarring in the X-rays. Their skeptical attitude indicated that they thought I was just trying to be rejected.

I finished the semester and had a week or two at home before I was to report back to Fort Bliss for induction. I put in some cowboy time, not knowing how long it might be before I could do it again. Elliott Moore told me about his experiences in the prewar cavalry so I would have some idea about what awaited me.

Chuck Olson, one of the ranch cowboys, was also about to join the military. He had shown up at the ranch a lean and hungry teenager out on his own. He was green but eager to learn, so Dad took a liking to him. He called him "Dogie Chuck," as if he were a motherless calf. We took a camera out on horseback and made pictures to carry with us as a remembrance of cowboy days. We carved our names on a rock outcrop in the Dawson pasture, sort of a substitute tombstone in case we didn't come back. I wonder sometimes if anyone ever came across those names in later years. They would have to be on horseback.

Five of us rode the bus to El Paso to report in. Marion Brunette was given charge of the small detail. Tall and curly-haired, Marion had been a leader in the high school band. He had a beautiful singing voice, which saw good service in the church, and had married one of the prettiest girls in Crane. His younger brother, Norman, a classmate of mine, went down with his plane in the Pacific.

We were told to wait at a downtown hotel for transportation out to Fort Bliss. It was June, and El Paso was already hot. Trainloads of newly inducted troops would arrive at the station downtown and march to the base on foot. Not all would make it. Unused to Texas heat, many wilted and fell by the wayside.

We were luckier. We Texans rode out on a bus, another example of military logic.

The food was good and barracks accommodations comfortable by Army standards. The first few days of orientation gave me the mistaken impression that soldier life would be easy. I was soon to stand corrected.

El Paso is on the Rio Grande, divided from its Mexican sister city, Juárez, only by the river. Juárez during the war was declared off limits to American soldiers because of the many snares it offered to the unwary or reckless. In its zeal to recruit men, the Army enlisted young Mexican nationals, promising them American citizenship in return for their service. A majority spoke little or no English. Special schools were conducted to give them enough vocabulary so that they could understand orders.

The language barrier was difficult for many GIs who came from other parts of the country. A Southern sergeant in my training company found Spanish names impossible to pronounce. Calling the roll in his slow drawl, he shouted, "Ga-WILL-er-mo TRUDGE-ilo."

Hearing no response, he called out a second time. Finally someone nudged Guillermo Trujillo and told him, "That's you."

"Here," Trujillo shouted.

The sergeant glared. "Next time, answer when you hear your name."

Some of the Mexican recruits were musical. It was a pleasure in the evening to listen to them play a guitar and sing "Jalisco" or "*Soy Puro Mejicano.*" I had grown up listening to border stations and had known Mexican exchange students at the university, so the music was familiar.

I was first assigned to Fort Bliss's antiaircraft training mission. The early weeks were similar to infantry basic, first getting used to the M1 Garand rifle. I have a scar on my thumb, acquired while learning to load an ammunition clip and jerk my hand away before the powerful spring could catch it. We practiced with the .50 caliber machine gun, and most chilling of all, the bayonet. The thought of cold steel cutting into my gut made me wish for the Navy. In a while we were introduced to the 40 mm antiaircraft gun. We went out on maneuvers in the Hueco sandhills and dug gun emplacements, then practiced firing at target sleeves towed behind a plane.

We had one recruit who could have been the model for the Sad Sack comic strip in *Stars and Stripes*. He seemed unable to get anything right the first half dozen times. In firing a machine gun at the target sleeve, he froze to the trigger while the weapon kept blazing away. The sergeant tried to get his attention by shouting and beating on his helmet with a wrench. The firing did not cease until the ammunition box was empty.

"Why didn't you stop when I told you to?" the sergeant demanded.

"I couldn't hear you," the soldier said. "Somebody kept hitting me on the head."

It seldom rained while we were at Fort Bliss. Naturally enough, the only time we had a big one was during maneuvers. The blanket I spread over my foxhole caught enough water that the weight brought it down and soaked me.

Camping was new to a lot of recruits, but I had slept outdoors so many times with the chuck wagon that it was old stuff. I probably suffered from homesickness less than most because I had had two summers at the Lea Ranch and two years away from home at the university.

We witnessed one chilling event in the sandhills. We were doing a communications exercise when a bomber from the Biggs Air Corps training base passed low overhead, afire and trailing black smoke. We counted the parachutes and realized there were not enough to account for a whole crew. The plane crashed just out of sight. A soldier who happened to be on the telephone could hardly control his voice. He kept shouting, "Holy balls!" It took him a while to convince whoever was on the receiving end that this was real, and no exercise.

While we were in the sandhills, several cowboys rode by on their way to gather cattle. For a few minutes I felt as if I were back at home.

Probably the hardest day of my life up to that time happened in July when the weather was blazing hot. We were detailed to do a radio-telephone communications exercise on top of Mount Franklin, El Paso's largest landmark. We were hauled around to the back side on trucks, which then returned to the post. We had to carry the equipment up the boulder-strewn mountain's west side, set up on top, do the exercise, then carry everything down the treacherous east side and march all the way back to camp. Then I had to report for KP, kitchen police, though I was almost too exhausted to stand up. I decided I was going to be hard to kill. If it had been easy, I would have died that day.

Partway through the session my training battery was moved to a set of five-man tarpaper shacks on the east edge of the post, against the flying field. By coincidence, none of the five in my shack were smokers. I doubt that any other group on the base could have made that claim. We were proud of it, for it proved that we could still swim against the stream. Military service had not taken away all of our individuality.

The Army had only recently deactivated the horse cavalry and put its troopers into armored vehicles. The stables, just below our shacks, still smelled of horses and hay. Sometimes in the evening I would go down there and make believe I was at the ranch. Certain scents can carry a person back to another time and another place. One day I found a slight, soft-spoken young soldier named Lee Irvine doing the same thing. He said he came from a ranch near Buffalo, Wyoming. After that we crossed trails every day during training.

I had read about Wyoming's Johnson County war in which a force of gunfighters hired by ranchers invaded a group of homesteaders they accused of being cattle thieves. He said, "We never talk about that." He revealed that his grandfathers had been on opposite sides.

Because I had some college experience, I was placed in a special intelligence training school to learn to gather information from enemy transmissions and to interpret aerial reconnaissance photos. About this time our battery captain came down with malaria, which he had contracted during service in the Pacific. He was replaced by a tough first lieutenant named Mergen, a short, barrel-chested man of severe countenance whose deep voice could rattle windows. A top sergeant in the regular army, he had received a commission after the war began. He was an officer now, but he was not a gentleman.

I became convinced that I had never met anyone as mean and mercilessly evil as Mergen. Despite the silver bar on his collar, he was still a top sergeant to the core. He drilled us, he drove us, he cursed us, and in general he made our lives almost unbearable. He seemed determined to find out where our limit was and push us over the edge.

I began to suspect that he was not exactly as he seemed, however, when I received word through the Red Cross that my grandfather was dying in Midland. An incurable melanoma had finally beaten him. The company sergeant explained that emergency leaves were only for situations involving the immediate family. Grandparents did not count. But Mergen interceded and gave me a pass. I reached Midland barely in time to stand at Granddad's bedside with other family members and witness the old cowboy's passing.

Sometimes small decisions have fateful consequences. I hurried back to Fort Bliss immediately after the funeral, not waiting the full week the pass allowed. I had missed only a couple of days' instruction. Had I remained longer I probably would have been required to take the course again, and I might have missed much or all of what was to come afterward. I might have reached Europe after the war was over, or I might have been sent to the Pacific.

As it was, I finished basic along with my friends. On our final day Mergen lined us up for inspection. He looked different than I had seen him before, somber, with tears in his eyes. He said in effect, "I've been hard on you men. I've made you hate me, but I've been where you're going. I wanted to make you tough enough to survive."

Christmas furlough (1944). *From left:* **Myrle Kelton, cowboy Chuck Olson, Elmer Kelton, Bill Kelton, Gene Kelton**

He turned and walked back to his quarters, no longer the heartless tyrant we had thought him to be.

This was just at Christmastime. I was given a holiday leave with orders to report to Camp Howze near Gainesville, Texas, about New Year's. The Army had decided it needed no more antiaircraft trainees, for the German Luftwaffe had been whittled down to a thin remnant. The Battle of the Bulge was on, however, and it needed infantry. Howze was an infantry training post, hastily thrown together at the beginning of the war and destined to be abandoned when the conflict was over. We who went to Howze were to take a short refresher course in infantry basics, then be shipped to Europe.

My Christmas leave was much too short, but at least I had one. Most soldiers didn't. I tried for a few days to be a cowboy but couldn't shake loose from the fact that I was a serviceman due shortly to go into harm's way. I left home with a sackful of Mother's cookies and no appetite to eat them.

Howze was a miserable post. The barracks were of flimsy frame construction, covered by tarpaper and anchored by cables to keep them from blowing down. A potbellied coal-burning stove stood at each end in a futile effort to fight back the damp cold. The camp reeked of coal smoke that burned the eyes and nose. Rainy weather caused deep black mud that tried to suck the boots off our feet.

The only bright spot was the nearby town of Gainesville. I visited it two or three times on a weekend pass. Its people were openhanded and kind to soldiers, knowing that most who left Howze were on their way to combat. At the Methodist church they gave me a New Testament, which I carried overseas and kept in my pocket. In the back were the words to several hymns, including "Just As I Am." The congregation sang it shortly before I shipped out. That hymn burned into my memory and brought me comfort during the weeks that followed.

While at Howze I was assigned to a different company than Lee Irvine. However, I saw him several times. My company included a Sioux Indian named Mountain Bear, who always smelled of beer or hard liquor. Once several men tried to hold him under a cold shower to sober him up for duty. They found he was well named, for a bear could not have fought harder. I don't know what eventually became of him, but with a weapon in his hands he was a danger to himself and to those around him.

Mother came by train to visit one weekend. When we parted, her grieving eyes told me she thought this might well be the last time we would ever see each other. That thought had been heavy on my mind too. I believe most soldiers have it as they move toward the unknown.

Bus and train stations were melancholy places in those times. Some of the most touching words I have ever read were on a memorial plaque affixed to a wall near the San Antonio bus station. It said, in effect, "A few feet from this spot, a loving father said good-bye to his son for the last time on this earth."

After six weeks of hurry-up training we rode a troop train to the East Coast and landed at Camp Kilmer, New Jersey, for embarkation. The last night before we boarded the ferry that took us to the ship's dock, I went with many from our group to a post theater. There, come to wish us well, was the great boxing champion Joe Louis, larger than life. I have revered his memory ever since, for if there had ever been a time when I needed cheering up, that was it. A knot of dread had settled in my stomach like a cold lump of lead. It would remain there until the war was over.

By this time I had lost contact with most of the men I had known in training at Fort Bliss and Camp Howze. We had been scattered like leaves on the wind. One of those on shipboard with me, however, was the Wyoming ranch boy. Another was Mountain Bear, sober at least for a time.

The voyage was even more miserable than Camp Howze. We boarded a wooden-hulled old English tub named the *General Squires*. It had been converted into a troopship, with bunks stacked as tightly as possible down in the hold. I was assigned to a bottom bunk. Each time the ship rolled to one side or the other, odorous bilge water passed beneath me. If I let my hand drop over the edge of the bunk, it came up wet.

We were served only two meals a day, those barely edible. We stood up to eat and held our trays to keep them from sliding away as the boat rocked. Smelly steam from the kitchen seemed to pervade the whole vessel, even down into the hold.

Seasickness hit me like the kick of a mule. I wrote home afterward that I made most of the trip by rail. That was only a small exaggeration. It was probably just as well that I had not been accepted into the Navy. We endured a severe storm in the Atlantic. One consolation was the advanced age of the ship. We rationalized that it must have gone through many storms before, perhaps far worse than this, and had not sunk yet.

We were always conscious that German U-boats might intercept us. Soldiers in the hold would have been particularly vulnerable in case of a torpedo. It never happened. After eleven days at sea, the harbor at Le Havre, France, seemed magnificent to behold despite its wartime shabbiness. We disembarked and were fed a meal where we did not have to stand and hold on to our trays or smell the galley steam.

Afterward, we marched to a train yard and were ordered onto what were known as forty-and-eight boxcars, built for forty men or eight horses. I had heard of these from cowboy veterans of World War I, who at times had had to share them with the horses. Our train rolled across France, starting and stopping frequently, sometimes with a violence that knocked us off our feet. The weather was chilly but not painfully cold, so we endured those drafty cars. The major problem was lack of toilet facilities at a time when many struggled with diarrhea. All we could do was squat with our pants down and our rears hanging out of the open doors. I still wonder what message the French thought we were trying to convey with those bare bottoms.

NINE

WE DISEMBARKED FROM THE forty-and-eights at Metz, France, near the German border. A replacement depot had been set up in a complex of buildings the Germans had used for cadet training. We were issued fresh clothing and had a shower, which turned out to be my last bath for about three weeks. We were given arms and ammunition before being scattered among various infantry companies as replacements. It was the last time I saw Lee Irvine. I had already lost track of the unfortunate Indian.

From Metz I was one of a handful carried by truck to a company of the Massachusetts National Guard's Twenty-sixth Division, known as the Yankee Division. As a descendant of Confederates that name should have bothered me, but it didn't. By then we were proud to be known as Yanks.

I reached the company late in the afternoon. A few hundred yards away, Army engineers were building a pontoon bridge across the Rhine despite German artillery fire and Luftwaffe bombers. A couple of times we hit the ditch because of shrapnel when artillery rounds went astray. We were told we would cross the river after dark. We ate, then sat waiting with our backpacks and rifles ready. In another company someone was playing an accordion as calmly as if at a dance back home. The melody that stuck in my head that evening was "Whispering." I still shiver when I hear it.

The serenade was broken up by the sound and fury of an aerial dogfight between American and German aircraft, one side trying to guard the bridge, the other to destroy it. German searchlights played against the dark sky, trying to pick up the American planes.

In the wee hours of morning we were ordered onto trucks and warned against smoking cigarettes or showing any light that could be a target. I studied the loaded rifles around me and hoped everybody had learned enough to keep the safety on. I had observed in basic training that some men were too reckless to be trusted with a loaded weapon. The bridge bobbed up and down under the weight of the trucks. I kept waiting for German artillery to open up again, but it did not, at least not close enough to do anything more than make us sweat.

On the east bank we got off near a town called Dieburg and dug in for the night. I had been designated to be half of a bazooka team. I carried the ammunition and an M1 carbine. My partner carried the bazooka and a .45 caliber pistol. The two of us dug a foxhole. The sergeant came around to assign guard duty and warned that German troops might be only two or three hundred yards away. We should be ready in case they decided to counterattack.

I stood my guard tour, then returned to the foxhole to turn that duty over to my partner. He took my carbine and left his .45 lying somewhere along the edge of the foxhole. After a while I dropped off into a nervous sleep, only to be awakened by his excited voice shouting, "Halt! Halt!" It was followed by a shot from my carbine.

Fearing we were being overrun, I felt desperately around the edge of the foxhole, trying to find that pistol. Then I sat gripping it in a cold, sweaty hand, awaiting the worst. Nothing happened. The night went eerily quiet. At last my partner finished his guard duty and returned. I asked him, "What happened?"

Curtly he snapped, "Shut up."

At daylight we found that a concrete survey marker had a fresh bullet scar. He did not seem to want to talk about it, so I asked no more questions.

One thing I noticed then, and continued to notice wherever I went in rural Germany's farming regions, was a distinctive odor that arose from the *Misthaufen,* piles of manure and straw accumulated at every farmstead. Most of the older farmhouses and the barns were integrated. During winter the cattle were stabled in the basement or lower floor. The heat arising from their bodies helped take the chill from the floors above. Manure-soaked hay or straw was removed regularly and stacked outdoors to fertilize the fields prior to spring planting. Many barns had drainage systems to catch the cattle's urine and hold it for the same purpose. The so-called honey wagons that distributed this waste to the fields had a pungency that could penetrate the worst sinus infection.

I lived in dread that sooner or later we might actually have to use the bazooka. It was an antitank weapon. Everybody except the upper brass knew our Shermans were not a match for German Tiger tanks. I was not sure the bazooka was either. About the best that could be hoped was that it would knock off a track and immobilize the tank. We occasionally heard Tigers somewhere ahead of us, but we never saw one close up. We never once fired that bazooka.

I always thought it was flimsy, resembling two short sections of stovepipe like we had back home to carry smoke outdoors. When it was triggered, fire belched from both ends. It could fry anyone standing behind it.

I was fortunate in that the war was winding down. Our company never encountered a pitched battle after I joined it, though it had survived some hellish ones earlier. Our squads were considerably under strength. Few of the original members were still around, most having been wounded or killed. The company commander had been wounded and did not get back until the war was over. A lieutenant was acting CO.

The worst we had was sniper fire from rear guards left behind to slow our advance and let the main body of German troops escape ahead of us. One day we fanned out to work our way through some dark woods when two snipers opened up on a squad adjacent to ours. They were quickly shot and wounded. I helped a company medic bandage one of them. The lieutenant assigned two of his least dependable soldiers to stay and guard the prisoners until they could be picked up by troops from the rear echelon. One of these men in particular had made himself obnoxious, a newcomer bragging about how brave he was and how many Germans he was going to kill.

We had not gone more than two or three hundred yards before we heard several shots behind us. The two soldiers came running up, breathless and frightened. They had shot the two prisoners. They claimed one reached for a gun. That was ridiculous because the Germans' weapons had been taken away. Moreover, they were too badly wounded and bandaged too tightly to have moved much. The truth was that the two GIs had been afraid to be left behind in those dark, scary woods.

Angry, the lieutenant made them take the point so they would be the first ones shot at. Unfortunately, it never happened. They lived to go home and brag about killing Germans.

Once we came across the body of an SS officer, shot in the back of the head. He had been dead too long for Americans to have been responsible. It was common knowledge that the German Army sometimes assigned hardened SS men to remain with the regular troops and shoot some of them if necessary to prevent their retreating or surrendering. We figured this officer had been assassinated by German regular Army soldiers eager to get away.

Often in the interest of speed we were ordered to ride atop the Sherman tanks that were always with or near us. In one respect that was good, for we did not have to walk so much. On the other hand it was a precarious perch without enough good handholds. At any sign of trouble we would jump off and take up a fighting position or seek cover, whichever appeared most appropriate. Usually cover seemed a good idea.

One day our tank column was following a narrow country road. I was on the second tank. The leader came to a weak-looking

little wooden bridge and stopped. Our tank pulled up close behind him, and those behind us stopped too. Shortly the battalion
commander came roaring up in a Jeep and demanded, "What's the
holdup here? One German plane could knock out this whole column."

The tank driver pointed to the bridge. "Sir, I'm not sure that
thing can hold up under a tank."

The colonel was a skinny fellow who probably weighed a hundred and thirty pounds in his combat boots. He stepped out onto
that flimsy bridge, jumped up and down a couple of times, then
said, "It'll hold them. Bring them on."

It held them. He would have tolerated no less.

We came once to an open field. Beyond stood a stone farmhouse, and past that a dense patch of woods. We saw several figures running into the house and knew they were German soldiers.
The farm family came out to meet us, their hands up.

Our squad leader was Jewish and spoke a passable German. The
farmer told him the Wehrmacht had left the house on the other
side, out of our view, but the company commander was dubious.
He ordered a tank driver to train his cannon on the house. The
driver took dead aim through the open barrel. The range was
probably only a hundred and fifty yards. While the farmer continued to protest, the cannon blasted a huge hole in the house's stone
wall. More soldiers spilled out on the other side and ran for the
woods.

Our squad's sharpshooter brought down one German, hitting
him in the leg. The rest disappeared into the forest. We quickly
searched the ruined house, then I helped the medic patch up the
prisoner. This one was soon carried away in an ambulance, safe for
the duration. We made a sweep of the woods, but the enemy
troops had gone on.

Our squad leader, Sergeant Mordis, and two other soldiers captured a town by themselves. We were moving up a road when a
young girl appeared on a hilltop and saw us. She vanished immediately. Fearing she might be carrying word to German soldiers on

the other side of the hill, Mordis took two men to investigate. From the hilltop they saw a village below. After watching a few minutes and seeing no sign of enemy soldiers, they walked down toward the town. Several civilians including a priest and the *bürgermeister* came out of the village to meet them, signaling surrender.

The main body of soldiers had abandoned the town but left several of their wounded behind in the church, confident that the Americans would give them care. The sergeant and his men accepted the village's surrender. Shortly afterward, they heard the sound of tanks. An American column appeared, infantrymen crouched low with rifles on the ready, prepared to conquer the town at all costs. I can imagine their chagrin when they found that three foot-slogging GIs from another company had already done it.

One of the most dedicated soldiers I knew was a fellow Texan, Aparicio Rodriguez, from Falfurrias. He had broken broncs for the King Ranch and had driven livestock trucks before going into service. Dark-skinned, he had some of the whitest teeth I ever saw. German women seemed drawn to him, but he was shy and acted embarrassed by their attention. He had seen action in the Aleutians before being sent to Europe, so he was watchful. He saw everything that went on around him and was constantly cleaning his rifle whenever we were at rest. One night we were on guard duty when a shell exploded nearby. He did not even flinch so far as I could see. He never lost his cool.

He did not talk much. He had grown up in a region where racial prejudice against his people made him reticent, but he seemed to find me a kindred spirit. He was a philosopher of sorts. On one of the few quiet afternoons we had, he and I were standing guard and watching a farmer's chickens searching for bugs. A hawk appeared overhead and circled a few times before picking out one fat hen for a target. It dive-bombed the hen and sent her rolling. It repeated the maneuver a couple more times, then settled down to supper.

Rodriguez said, "Just like people. The strong knock over the weak."

Racial attitudes in South Texas have improved a lot since he was growing up.

I was told that after the war he tried civilian life awhile, then went back into service and made a career of it. I named a character for him in *The Smiling Country*.

The nearest I came to kissing myself good-bye was one afternoon when the battalion colonel—the same skinny officer who had passed judgment on the wooden bridge—called our company out into an open field where no one but us could hear. He said, "Men, I have volunteered you for a dangerous mission. I can't tell you what it is. I can only say that we are going to go to meet Uncle Joe."

We were loaded into half-tracks and went speeding off down a country road, scattering chickens and stirring up dogs by the dozen. The colonel's seriousness indicated that this was about to get messy. We went a considerable distance before stopping to bivouac for the night in a town called Fulda, speculating on what we were about to do. Reason told us we were expected to slash through German lines and meet the Russian troops. Hence the reference to Uncle Joe, Joseph Stalin.

To our relief, we awoke next morning to find the mission had been scrubbed. Some other outfit had already cut across and joined the Russians. It would have been a grand publicity stunt if we had done it, but some of us probably would not have been alive to read the papers. We rejoined the battalion without winning any medals but all still breathing.

By this time we were meeting surrendering German soldiers on every road. Also, we were overrunning slave labor and concentration camps. Displaced persons of every nationality in Europe were streaming along the roads, going somewhere, anywhere, to get away from where they had been. Windows sported white flags, usually made of pillowcases and sheets, signaling surrender.

One night our squad stayed in a farmhouse where slave laborers had just been liberated. Not knowing any better, I slept on a straw mat one of them had used. I never considered that it might harbor a form of wildlife too small to see.

At this point I had not had a chance for a bath since leaving Metz. I picked up lice but did not realize it until one night when we stayed in a house that had a bathtub. I grabbed that opportunity to bathe. The lice in my underwear attacked immediately. Rummaging in a chest of drawers, I found a suit of underwear about a size or two too large and several inches too long. I had to cut part of the legs off. But nobody could see it under my uniform, and at least I was rid of the lice.

In the film *Patton* years later, George C. Scott as Patton says he first realized the war was nearly over when he began seeing dead horses. That triggered my memory. I had seen the horses too, along with bombed-out wagons and carts. Patton realized the Germans were running out of fuel and as a last resort were falling back on the old ways of transporting supplies. I doubt that I made that connection at the time. That was why Patton was a general and I was a private first class.

The only time I ever felt that I was singled out for enemy fire, we bivouacked at a farmhouse. Another company was camped on the other side of a field. The sergeant told me to take a liberated bicycle and deliver a message to the other group's CO. I struck off alone, delivered the message, and started back. I became conscious that someone was sniping at me from way off. It was too far for accuracy, but I found out how fast a bicycle could travel when the incentive was strong enough.

It was at this place that several of the men liberated a goose, hoping for brief relief from the monotonous boxed K rations we had been eating. They defeathered the bird as well as they could without boiling water and built a fire to start barbecuing. They had hardly more than singed the goose when we received an order to move out. They carried their prize along until we stopped again, and once more they started to cook. It was a short stop. We moved on, and again they carried the goose. By about the fourth or fifth time, the bird looked as if it had been dead a week. They gave up and left it behind, still only half cooked.

I had been on the line a little less than four weeks when an accident took me out. We had just learned of President Roosevelt's death. I had spent a cold night sleeping beneath an overhanging rock ledge, at one point listening to a Tiger tank prowling about somewhere beyond. We walked awhile, then loaded onto the Shermans to speed our advance. As we passed through a small shell-pocked village, along a narrow street between two stone structures, the tank slid to the right on a pile of rubble and sideswiped one of the buildings. My foot was caught between the tank and the wall. My boot was ground into strips. My ankle was lacerated and badly twisted.

I had never felt pain so intense. The grinding seemed to go on for minutes, but actually it was only a couple or three seconds. In shock, I could think of nothing but getting off of the tank. I worked my foot free, the boot hanging in tatters, and jumped from the rear. When I hit the ground the foot gave way, and I was on hands and knees.

Unaware that anyone was hurt, the tank driver started to back up. A middle-aged German farmer stepped up, grabbed me under the arms, and pulled me out of the way.

A sergeant sitting next to me on the tank was hurt worse. His whole leg was caught. Several GIs carried the two of us into a nearby house and put us on beds. Doc Vitali, our medic, saw to the sergeant first because his injury was more severe. Then he bound my ankle as tightly as he could. Shortly afterward, the tank column moved on, leaving us.

It struck me strange later on, remembering how the German people in the house tried in every way to be hospitable. An old Frau kept offering us buttered black bread. Neither of us was in any condition to eat. In retrospect I wondered often about the man who pulled me out of the way. Had he not done so I might have been run over. At the least my legs might have been crushed. From his viewpoint I was an enemy. He could have left me to my fate and felt justified, but he didn't. Because of my pain and confusion I doubt that I even thanked him.

A soldier brought up a Jeep with a small trailer behind it. A canvas was stretched tightly across the trailer's top. We were both placed on the canvas and hauled over bumpy roads to a point where an ambulance picked us up. In the ambulance were a couple of wounded men. It was my impression through my shock-induced haze that one of them died before we reached the field hospital, but it is possible I imagined that.

The mobile hospital, temporarily set up near Kronach, was a complex of large olive-drab tents well behind the moving front line. Red crosses were prominently painted on the tops.

I was placed on a canvas cot, and after a time a doctor came to examine me. He had an orderly remove my clothes. His eyes widened at sight of the German underwear with the legs awkwardly shortened, definitely not government issue. I tried to explain, but I doubt I was coherent.

Like clockwork almost every night, we had been visited by a German reconnaissance plane we called "Bedcheck Charlie." Usually it was a twin-engine type with a distinctive wavering sound because the two motors were not in sync. On my first night in the hospital he came again, strafing the road beside the tent. I stared apprehensively at the canvas overhead, expecting bullets to come ripping through. They didn't, and the plane went on.

On a cot near mine lay a soldier who had had a hand grenade go off on his chest. We all carried grenades hooked in the buttonholes of our jackets. Somehow the pin was pulled from his, and it went off before he could get rid of it. He was badly hurt, but at least he survived.

The only explanation I heard was that the main force of the grenade must have gone outward, away from him.

Another soldier had a badly swollen upper lip. A bullet had passed just under his nose, grazing the cleft. Death missed him by perhaps an inch.

I remained in the field hospital about a week. After the first night or two I slept on a stretcher, leaving the cots to those hurt worse than I was. A large group of emaciated soldiers arrived, just liberated from a German prisoner of war camp. Captured months earlier during the Battle of the Bulge, they were little more than skin and bone. During much of their imprisonment they had received barely enough food to keep them alive. They said the German soldiers who guarded them were but little better off. Supply lines had broken down as the war went against them. Carts and horses could not do the job.

One said they went to sleep in a Belgian barn, unaware that the Germans had started a concerted counteroffensive. The first they knew of it, the barn doors burst open with a loud crash, and they were staring at a Tiger tank. On it was an 88 mm cannon that looked as big as a tree trunk. A German soldier ordered, "*Raus!*"

"We *raused*," the GI said.

Wounded and injured soldiers were being evacuated back to stationary military hospitals in France as transportation became available. After a week I was told a transport plane was about to land, and I was to gather my gear. I had virtually none because I had not salvaged anything after the accident except what was in my pockets.

For years I had looked forward to taking my first flight, but this was not the way I had expected it to be. The DC-3 cargo plane had stacks of stretchers hinged down from the walls. A wounded French soldier was placed on the stretcher immediately above me. Though I could see nothing of the scenery outside, I was managing all right until the Frenchman began throwing up. Then I lost my breakfast too.

Soon I was in a hospital near Reims. It had obviously been a civilian hospital before the war and had been converted to military use. I shared a ward with half a dozen men. One, a sergeant, had landed at Omaha Beach on D-Day and told us much about that experience. Another was a black soldier, a truck driver on what was called the Red Ball Express. His truck had been hit by a shell, and a large chunk of shrapnel cut through his buttocks. When the nurses came to dress his wound I saw that he was black only on the outside. Underneath, his flesh was the same color as everybody else's. So much for racial prejudice.

He liked to sing the mournful "St. James Infirmary" and did so, over and over.

The war with Germany ended about a week after I was evacuated to France. We listened to Winston Churchill's speech on a nurse's small radio. We wished we were somewhere that we could celebrate properly. Like home.

I found out later how my mother got the news about me. The Crane County sheriff, Jack Young, usually took it upon himself to deliver official telegrams from the war department. He was a broad-shouldered, handsome man with a thin black mustache. He would have been a perfect sheriff for the B Western movies. However, he was not skilled at delivering bad news. When Mother answered his knock on the door and saw him waiting on the front porch, her legs almost went out from under her. She assumed the worst. He stood with his hat in his hand, gravely telling her several times how sorry he was to be bringing such a sad message. She was trembling, dying by degrees. Finally he handed her the telegram which said I had been injured in the line of duty. Injured, not killed.

She didn't know whether to kiss him or to shoot him. I don't think she ever forgave him for the terrible moments he gave her. Dad was spared that because he came in from work after the sheriff was gone.

I was mobile, walking on crutches. On Memorial Day those of us not bedfast were offered an opportunity to attend services. We rode a bus for some distance until we reached a large cemetery, burial place for American servicemen killed on and after D-Day. I soon forgot the speeches, but I have never forgotten the deep melancholy that fell over me as I listened to a bugler play taps and looked up through tears at the American flag flowing gently in the wind. In front of me, row upon row of white Christian crosses and Jewish Stars of David stretched up the hillside and beyond in numbers too great to count. I knew how fortunate I was to be alive.

That scene still comes back to me often when I look upon the flag. I think of those men—most of them much too young—who lay buried in foreign ground far from home and those who loved them. I think of the sixty years of good life I have had since that day, a life that was taken from them before they had a chance to taste how good life could really be. Sometimes I wonder, why them and not me?

I have never found an answer.

Over the years something would occasionally remind me of Lee Irvine. I would wonder if he went back to the family ranch after the war and if, like me, he was raising a family. My work caused me from time to time to be in the company of ranchers from Wyoming. I would ask about my Army friend. Nobody remembered him.

Some thirty years after the war I received a letter at the *Livestock Weekly* from Van Irvine of Casper, Wyoming. He was planning to sell a band of sheep and wanted to know our advertising rates. I wrote back, answering his question, and at the end of the letter casually asked if he knew anything about Lee Irvine.

His answer hit me hard. Lee had been his kid brother, he said. He was killed a few days after reaching Germany.

All those intervening years suddenly fell away. The sense of grief and loss was as strong as if he had died that day.

He and Billy Allman, Norman Brunette, and several others often walk through my memory. They are still young, while those of us who knew them have grown old.

TEN

MY FOOT RECOVERED ENOUGH that I quit the crutches, though I walked with a limp and considerable pain. I had to bind the ankle tightly to prevent its giving way. The Army decided it was time to send me back to the outfit after a three-day pass in Paris. I saw the usual tourist sights, though walking was uncomfortable. I passed up the famous hot spots, for I had been brought up to look askance at honkytonks, beer joints, and the like. I went to a couple of movies instead, seeing Humphrey Bogart's *To Have and Have Not* in English and Errol Flynn's *Captain Blood* in French. My excuse, had anyone asked, would have been that I was studying the art of storytelling. The truth was that I simply loved movies and had not seen one since leaving the States.

During the final days of the war the Twenty-sixth Division had crossed over the border into Czechoslovakia. My company came up against the Russians a few miles outside a town known in German as Budweis, in Czech as České Budějovice.

It took me at least three weeks to work my way back to my company, one replacement depot at a time. Every time the Army moved me it lost my vaccination records, and I had to take the shots over again. Moreover, it seemed that every time I traveled

I was hit by diarrhea. I took prescription codeine and ate a lot of cheese, trying to get regular.

In an ironic accident before my return, a sergeant who had survived the entire conflict was killed by another soldier's carelessness just days after the end of the war. Someone had leaned a Browning automatic rifle against a tree. It slid down and fired a burst as it struck the ground. The sergeant lived just long enough to ask what had happened to him. He may not have heard the answer.

When I reached the company I found that we shared a roadblock with the Russians. They were on one side of a graded road. We were on the other. The Russian soldiers were friendly and joyful for having survived the war, because so many of their comrades had not. The Russian officers, however, were a cold, contemptuous lot, who looked through us as if we did not exist and abused their men shamefully.

The Russian soldiers had received their pay after months of doing without and eagerly looked for something to spend it on. They would pay any price for a Mickey Mouse watch. Unfortunately I did not have one. They were glad to buy anything American. We heard later that when they went home those items were confiscated. The Communist government did not want the men contaminated by American luxuries, nor did it want them to show the poverty-stricken people at home how much better life might be somewhere else.

Supply lines were badly stretched in the weeks after the war. For a time we were fed only two meals a day, and those were meager. At the urging of several soldiers in the company, I wrote a letter about the problem to *Stars and Stripes*. The letter was not published until several weeks later, after the problems had been corrected. My name was not printed. I was away on detached service, standing guard duty near the German border, and missed the explosion of outrage from battalion headquarters. By the time I learned of it, the heat had died down. None of my friends gave me away, or I would probably have been on KP for the rest of my military career. The brass were not as concerned about our short rations as about the word getting out. This taught me a stern lesson regarding the power of the press.

WE LIVED IN A small complex of squad-sized tents. It was a strict rule that we use latrines, slit trenches dug a safe distance from camp. However, it was much easier in the dim light of early morning simply to walk to the edge of a nearby field. The infractions came to light when the vegetation turned yellow from nitrogen burn.

It was pleasant to watch a neighboring farmer at work in his fields each day. That is, until he brought out his honey wagon and began treating the ground with tanked urine and pungent manure produced by his barn-confined cows the previous winter. Camp seemed always to be downwind.

It was a disturbing time to be in Czechoslovakia, especially the Sudetenland, for the Czechs were expelling everyone who had a German surname whether they had been part of the Nazi machine or not. This expulsion had Allied sanction despite its hitting the innocent as well as the guilty. We saw disheartened refugees by the score walking along the roads, taking with them nothing except what they carried on their backs or in carts or wagons. They were offered no compensation and no sympathy, officially at least, though some of their families had lived on that land for centuries.

The war in the Pacific was still going on. We were moved back into Germany and started a refresher course in infantry basics at Delherda. We were being prepared to go to the Pacific for invasion of the Japanese homeland. The atomic bombs dropped on Hiroshima and Nagasaki put an abrupt end to those plans, to our great relief.

In later years Harry Truman and the American military received bitter criticism over the use of the bombs and the frightful toll they took on Japanese civilians. However, those losses were but a corporal's guard compared to the deaths both sides would have suffered had we been compelled to invade Japan by force. The Japanese had already demonstrated on islands all across the Pacific that they would die rather than surrender.

The fighting over, soldiers began being sent home on a point system. We were given points for how long we had been in the service, how long we had been in Europe, points for a Purple Heart, and the like. As a relative newcomer, my point score did not add up to much. I was destined to remain in Europe for almost another year. The Yankee Division went home, and those of us without enough points were reassigned.

I BECAME A MEMBER of the Eighty-third Division, Ohio National Guard. We were sent into Austria for a new kind of duty. My company commander was a good soldier though something of a martinet. He saw my curly hair, not cut since I had reached Europe, and declared that I looked like Elsie Dinsmore. He ordered me to find a barber. We were in a little town, Riedau am Inn, not far from Hitler's birthplace at Braunau. The only barber was a woman. She gave me the shortest trim I ever had.

Shortly we were scattered out on detached service to several different points in Upper Austria. I was dispatched to Ebensee, a town that was to have a pronounced effect on my life.

A strong effort was being made to bring European industries back into production. German prisoners of war were cutting wood in a number of forested areas to fuel many of these industries. Ebensee was at the edge of a magnificent Alpine mountain and lake region known as the Salzkammergut, literally "good chamber of salt." Salt mining had been a mainstay of the economy since Roman times. I was assigned to be a guard for a wood-cutting detail.

Coming from the Crane County sandhills, I had never seen anything that remotely compared with the Austrian Alps. They were overpowering. We soldiers rode in the back of an Army truck as it negotiated a narrow, crooked road between the old salt merchants' city of Gmunden and the salt workers' town of Ebensee. Looking straight up at those massive granite mountainsides took my breath away. To our left lay the bluest lake I had ever seen, the

Traunsee. It is a glacial lake, carved out during the last Ice Age, almost six hundred feet deep in the middle. On its far side towered the forbidding Traunstein, on whose steep slopes many climbers have fallen to their deaths.

We passed a majestic statue of a lion. It faced the lake, its mouth open as if it were roaring. Legend says that by oversight its Italian sculptor neglected to carve a tongue in the lion's mouth. In despair he leaped into the lake and drowned himself.

Despite the magnificent scenery around it, Ebensee is plain compared to its richer neighbors Gmunden and Bad Ischl. Like my hometown of Crane, it is where the working people live. The moneyed merchants and aristocrats choose to remain elsewhere. One of its few claims to fame is a ski facility atop the mountain Feuerkogel, and a cable lift that carries visitors to the top for an extraordinary view of the Salzkammergut mountain and lake chain. On a rare day when there is no haze, one can see Linz, some fifty miles off.

The town has an ugly stain on its history, a blood-drenched camp where Nazis imprisoned slave laborers to work in a quarry. Though it was not a designated extermination camp in the manner of Auschwitz or Buchenwald, the death toll was said to have exceeded six thousand, killed by neglect, undernourishment, overwork, and the dangers inherent in a quarry where safety was considered unimportant. If slave workers were killed in an accident, indifferent officials simply sent for more. There seemed no limit to the supply.

Terrible stories of atrocities came from behind those ugly barbed-wire fences. One involved a Jewish prisoner who by profession had been an architect. The Nazi officers promised that if he would design some structures for them, they would set him free. They gave him a small frame building in which to do his work. When the job was complete their idea of setting him free was to lock him in the shack, set it afire, and burn him alive.

The dead, and sometimes the near dead, were hauled away by a truck that regularly made the rounds of such camps. They were carried to a crematorium in a death camp at Mauthausen, near Linz.

Local Austrians were shunted away from the camp. If they had to pass nearby, SS guards watched to see that they kept their eyes averted.

American troops took over the camp days before the end of the European war, let the inmates out, and locked the remaining German guards in. A local account holds that several freed prisoners came upon one of their tormenters on the main bridge in Ebensee, beat him to death with whatever they could lay their hands on, then tossed him over the railing into the Traun River to be swept down into the lake. Most of the released prisoners wanted to get as far from that hellhole as they could, though some stayed awhile to exact revenge on the residents through assault, burglary, and minor crimes. A few remained and made Ebensee their home.

In an ironic twist, the facility where so many slaves had suffered became a prison camp for captured or surrendered German soldiers. There they awaited the slow process of repatriation. We guarded them while they felled trees in the forests. As a whole they were easy to handle. They were grateful to have survived the war and confident that after a time they would be free to go home. Most welcomed a chance to get out into the countryside for the day and away from the depressing prison camp. It had been constructed with no thought to inmate needs or comfort, and they found none.

By the Geneva Conventions, imprisoned officers were not required to work, but some voluntarily went out with the woodcutting details for the same reason, to get away from the camp. They mostly supervised and avoided heavy lifting.

We GIs were billeted in a large yellow building once headquarters office for the salt works. From ancient times, salt had been mined upriver in the Hallstatt area and floated down the Traun in long, flat-bottomed boats to Ebensee and the lake. Eventually a rudimentary form of hydraulic mining began. The mines were flooded and the brine drained off into a thirty-mile-long pipeline made of hollowed logs. At Ebensee it went into giant cookers to boil off the water, leaving the dry salt. Over a couple of centuries much of the primeval forest was denuded because of the constant demand for firewood to heat the cookers. After World War II, Ebensee was still site of the saltworks, but transport and evaporation methods were modern. The forests had been allowed to regrow.

Well into the nineteenth century, the aristocracy had not allowed natives to travel far from their home areas for fear that they might smuggle salt. In this enforced isolation the mountain and valley people developed a dialect of their own, markedly different from High German. In American terms it might be regarded as a hillbilly dialect, soft and pleasant on the ear compared to the more guttural proper German. Minor local differences evolved, so that natives could often tell what village or town a traveler came from just by the way he or she spoke. In Ebensee, they could sometimes even identify the section of town in which a person had grown up.

I began making it a point to learn as much of the language as I could. I had a small army handbook in rudimentary German and bought a pocket-sized German-English dictionary to expand my vocabulary.

We soldiers had our laundry done by a most obliging elderly Frau who lived a few doors away from our billet. Talkative and friendly, able to speak a little English, she appeared grateful for the work. Not for some time did we learn that she was the widow of a leading Nazi who had committed suicide as American troops entered the town.

Our routine was to eat an early breakfast at the local Hotel Post, a classic old hostelry built in the style of the Empress Maria Theresa era. The army had taken it over and set up a military kitchen. We would go out to the prison camp to pick up workers for the day in liberated German army trucks. Tree cutting was carefully managed in the interests of protecting and maintaining the forests. An aging but still agile government forester in knee-length leather britches

**German prisoners of war taking a break from
cutting detail (Austria, 1945–1946)**

picked the areas where our details would work. He supervised handling of the wood, measuring and marking each stack in an effort to keep it from being misappropriated. Few of the prisoners and none of the guards had any prior experience in forestry.

Axes brought down the trees. As a tree began to sway, a cry of *"Aufpassen!"* would echo down the slope, signaling everyone around to be alert. Two-man crosscut saws divided the logs into short one-meter lengths. Much of this was done on the mountainsides. Through inexperience or a misguided sense of humor, the prisoners occasionally dropped trees on one another. Fortunately no one was badly hurt, though some sensibilities were damaged and an occasional fistfight had to be quelled by the guards.

The short logs would be pushed down to the bottom of the mountain. Typically they might roll fifty or a hundred feet, then stop and have to be started again. Once in a while, however, one would go wild, picking up momentum and tumbling end over end, a hazard to anyone who got in the way. One day I watched an out-of-control log bounce down the mountain, gaining speed as it went. The prisoners shouted in alarm and scattered to be out of its erratic path. At the bottom was a drop-off of twelve or fifteen feet down to a graded road. A prisoner working at the bottom saw the log coming and began dodging first one way, then the other. His last jump was in the wrong direction. The log caught him squarely across the chest and carried him over the ledge to the road below. He was taken to a hospital, badly broken up.

This was the most serious accident that befell our group. However, one of the German trucks used by another unit lost momentum going up a mountain road and rolled backward, went over the edge and landed upside down, killing several men standing in the back.

As winter came on, bringing snow and biting cold, we found getting up the mountain roads trickier and more hazardous, but the Army was in charge, and the Army did not say stop. All too often the lunch brought to us soldiers was lukewarm or even cold. The prisoners, on the other hand, were usually furnished thick, hot soup hauled out from the prison kitchen. On bitterly cold days that steaming green pea soup looked and smelled awfully good. I wished I could join them, for the meal at least.

I had never liked cold weather. Back home there had been winter days when I thought my feet were frozen to the stirrups. Somehow the Austrian winter, bad as it was, never seemed to hurt that much even though we spent days out in the forest. We were dressed for it, with woolen clothing, heavy overcoat, and overshoes to keep our feet dry. We always kept a fire going so we and the prisoners could warm up when we felt the need.

We were supervised by an impatient young lieutenant who had a built-in frown and groused a lot. He usually stood aloof, offering frequent criticism but few kind words for either GIs or the men we guarded. He was one of several I encountered in the service who demonstrated to me that authority can be intoxicating, and some people are ill-fitted ever to be given power over others.

The prisoners scattered enough in their work that it was impossible to keep all of them in sight. Late one afternoon when we counted them boarding the trucks, I came up short. The missing man was a Bulgarian named Baldur, a name I shall never forget. The lieutenant went into a rage. He ordered me to trail the man and bring him back, threatening to file charges against me for negligence. I found tracks in the snow where the prisoner had set out across the mountain. I lost them where he came to a frozen stream and walked on the ice, leaving no trace. Darkness was descending, so I had to abandon the search and go back to face the music.

Knowing this would be a black mark against his record as well as mine, the lieutenant declared that he would have me court-martialed. But before he could take action, he committed an infinitely more serious mistake of his own. While cleaning his rifle in the officers' quarters, he accidentally shot and killed a fellow officer. The Army took him away, and I never heard any more about him or the promised court-martial.

I never heard anything about Baldur, either. I always hoped he managed to make it home, though odds were heavy against him. The Austrian winter could be merciless to a man lost in the woods without tools and without food.

Some people express surprise when I tell them that many of the so-called German soldiers were not Germans at all. Among those we guarded were Bulgarians, Hungarians, Rumanians, and others from conquered Balkan countries, drafted into the Wehrmacht as battlefield attrition whittled away at Germany's military manpower. They even showed up among the dreaded SS. In the first years of the war, the SS was reserved for what the Nazis regarded as the cream of the crop, superior in physical strength and intelligence. Non-Aryans needed not apply. But late in the war the standards had sunk so far that some of the SS we guarded not only were not German but they did not even speak the language with any fluency.

Though it was a violation of Army rules against fraternization, I found it fascinating to talk to the prisoners about their individual war experiences. I had not reached a point that I could hold up my end of the conversation well, but I had learned enough to follow the gist of their stories. One prisoner had been at the siege of Stalingrad. There it was the winter as much as the Russians that defeated the German forces. He said no words in any language could describe how lethal the cold was. The Germans lacked clothing heavy enough to protect them, and their tanks and trucks often froze to the ground, too cold for the engines to start.

We were a relatively small detached military unit in Ebensee, so the Army provided no extras such as recreational facilities. We took breakfast and evening meals from the Army kitchen outdoors or, if the weather was inclement, in an enclosed annex to the hotel. We had noon meals there also if we were off duty. Local children, many left fatherless by the war, would show up at mealtime and beg for scraps. They were pitiably ill-clothed and thin. Most of us informally adopted them, seeing that they did not leave hungry. Many a candy bar and many a pack of chewing gum were delivered into eager young hands.

We had no movies, no enlisted men's club, not even a reading room. However, in neighboring Gmunden, about ten miles across the lake, the Red Cross maintained a modest rest and recreation center in what had been a forestry school. On off days I often rode over on either the train or one of the passenger boats—they were free of charge to servicemen—to take advantage of the superior dining hall and library. The place also had fine swimming facilities, but most of the time it was too chilly to use them.

Less than a hundred yards from the Red Cross center, a picturesque sixteenth-century castle known as the Schloss Ort stood in splendid isolation on a small island near the edge of the lake. It was and is the city's most prominent landmark, a fixture on local postcards. It had been handed down through generations of church nobility until its last individual owner disappeared at sea off South America a century ago.

The forty-second or Rainbow Division had a large contingent in Gmunden. Its soldiers painted rainbows on just about anything that would stand still. There I found a fellow West Texan, James Turner, who remained a friend through the rest of his life. Ruddy-faced and stockily built, he was an imposing figure as a military policeman. We found we had much in common, for his father, Price Turner, was a prominent rancher at Big Lake. James's brother, Stanley, suffered frozen feet in the Battle of the Bulge but survived.

A group of us were treated to a trip to Berchtesgaden, Germany, to view Hitler's high-mountain retreat known as the Eagle's Nest. I had my first view of Salzburg from the back of an open Army truck. That ancient city on the Salzach River is dominated by a thousand-year-old fortress on top of a mountain. I thought then, and have ever since, that it was the most beautiful city I ever saw.

The Eagle's Nest was as spectacular as we had been led to believe. It was easy to see why the dictator liked to go there, high in the Alps, for the view extended across the mountains all the way over into Austria.

Ed Cumbie of Bronte, Texas, told me he was at the Eagle's Nest one day soon after the war when General Eisenhower came to inspect the place. Beside the ground-floor elevator was a sign: OFFICERS ONLY.

Angrily Eisenhower ordered, "Take that damned thing down." He declared that enlisted men had fought and won the war, and they had a right to ride the elevator.

There was a predilection in the Army to post those signs wherever there was anything the brass wanted to reserve for themselves. Wartime cartoonist Bill Mauldin lampooned that tendency with a drawing of two officers staring at a beautiful sunset. One asks, "Is there one for the enlisted men too?"

ELEVEN

THE COURSE OF ONE'S life may hinge on a chance moment, an unanticipated coincidence. It was by pure chance that I happened to be at Ebensee's boat landing the evening of October 14, 1945, and met Anna Lipp.

Autumn evenings in the mountains were still pleasant, cool but not yet cold. After a day in the forest with the wood-cutting crew, I liked to descend a long flight of stone steps from our mountain-side billet and walk along the edge of the tranquil Traunsee. Lakes were scarce where I came from. The sun disappeared behind the Feuerkogel long before full darkness, making for an extended dusk.

I saw a slender, attractive young woman cross the road and come down the steps toward the dock where the passenger boats pulled in. She wore a traditional Austrian dirndl dress, full skirt with apron, white blouse with fringed silk scarf around her neck. I had admired these colorful dresses since coming into the country, and this one seemed especially becoming. She stopped at a bulletin board where the boats' arrival and departure times were posted.

I had felt awkward with most girls, having had no sisters and having been younger than most of my classmates in school. My brain and my voice did not synchronize well when I spoke to

**Anni Lipp, wearing a traditional dirndl,
in front of the Lipp family home**

members of the opposite sex, but I kept trying to force down my natural shyness. I don't remember what I said, probably something trite about the nice evening. Whatever it was, she did not turn and run, though I would not have been surprised if she had. American soldiers did not have a sterling reputation in relationships with local girls.

I felt emboldened to try to expand the conversation with my limited and badly broken German. I think she was amused, or perhaps bemused. We talked long enough that I learned she was checking the boat schedule for her parents, who planned to go across the lake to market in Gmunden the next morning.

As she walked away, I stayed up with her, trying to keep the conversation alive, such as it was. I thought she would probably brush me off. It would not be the first time that happened to me. Instead, she was guardedly polite, distrustful but perhaps a little intrigued. I found that her surname was pronounced LEEP, and that everybody called her Anni (pronounced AH-nee). That was further along than I had expected to get with her.

A couple of blocks of slow walking and fractured conversation brought us up a set of ancient stone steps to a garden gate beside a big, dark old house where she lived. I asked if I might visit her again.

About that time her mother leaned out of an upstairs window, saw her talking to a soldier, and sharply told her to get herself into the house. She walked up the stairs, then turned and smiled before she disappeared through the door. I took that for a "yes."

I was off duty the next day. I was not eager to meet her mother just yet, remembering the sharpness of her voice. I waited until I was confident the boat had left, then returned to the house. Anni seemed surprised but also amused. I saw her more clearly in the daylight and decided she was even prettier than I had thought. Her blue eyes sparkled when she smiled. We talked, though we communicated as much by sign language as with words. One way and another, we made ourselves understood.

Then she baked an apple strudel.

Eve hooked Adam with a forbidden apple. I was hooked by a forbidden apple strudel, for at that point fraternization with local civilians was still contrary to Army regulations. From the beginning the rule had been observed mostly in the breach. No law is strong enough and no wall high enough to prevent soldiers and girls from communicating.

Never had I met a girl who made me feel so much at ease with her from the beginning. I began going to her house almost every evening. She was not one to do things behind her parents' backs, so I very soon met her mother and father. They were suspicious of my intentions, of course. I was unsure of them myself. As days went

**Anni Lipp with her parents and son, Gerhard, on the Traun River
in Ebensee, Austria (1945)**

by, the parents seemed to warm up to me, though they had reservations. So, for that matter, did Anni. It was clear that she enjoyed my
company. It was also clear that she was not altogether trustful.

Her mother was a hausfrau in late middle age, a take-charge
type in complete control of her household. She always wore a traditional dirndl dress like the one that had helped draw my attention to her daughter, though her figure was fuller. She thrived on
gossip. When she went shopping she came back well informed
about everything that had happened in town, and was ready to tell
it. It might take her an hour to walk two blocks because she
stopped to talk to everyone she knew along the way, and she knew
everybody.

I wondered how she felt about the gossip that surely was beginning to circulate about her youngest daughter, being seen with an
American soldier. Anni and I often strolled down to the lake, or
climbed the steep path up the Kalvarienberg, or made a long walk
out to a splendid waterfall at the foot of the Eibenberg.

Frau Lipp always maintained that she was descended from no-
ble blood, and indeed an ancestor had a large tombstone in the

church cemetery, his surname preceded by the prefix Von. In earlier times that denoted nobility. If there had ever been a family fortune, however, it had long since been used up.

A frequent expression of hers was *"Heilige Maria und Josef!"* in English, "Holy Mary and Joseph!"

Anni's father, Alois, was slight of build, no taller than his wife, his hands gnarled by a life of hard work. A veteran of World War I, he was more a listener than a talker, though he was not reluctant to express a contrary opinion. That habit had put him in jeopardy more than once during the Nazi occupation years. Outdoors, he wore a traditional Tyrolian-style narrow-brimmed hat with what looked like a shaving brush clamped to the back of the crown. It was the beard from a chamois, a wild goatlike animal that lived in the mountains. His eyebrows were bushy, his eyes often dancing with mischief as he contemplated a practical joke. He had an old-fashioned German-style mustache, bristly and curled upward at the ends. It was gray with a light brown stain from tobacco smoke. He rolled his own cigarettes out of crushed raw tobacco leaves and smoked them so short that toward the end he sometimes held them with a toothpick. He could have taught Dad a few lessons about frugality.

ONE THING THAT STRUCK me in Ebensee and elsewhere in Austria was the extreme age of so many structures still in constant use. In the neighboring village of Traunkirchen were two churches, the "new" church and the "old" one. The "new" church was built in 1632. The "old" one dated back at least to the 1300s. The house in which the Lipp family lived had stood for some four hundred years. A beam, uncovered in renovation, bore the carved figure 1520.

Hitler's annexation of Austria in 1938 brought difficult times to the family. One of Anni's brothers, Martin, had been a member of an anti-Nazi youth group and was imprisoned for fifteen months in a concentration camp. He was eventually drafted out of there into the German Army. He survived the war, but his health was impaired. He died before his time.

Her older brother, Louis, had a dour expression and a gruff voice that could be offputting to those who did not know him well, but behind the facade was a more notorious trickster than even his father. He, too, had a tendency to speak his mind when silence would have been safer. An electrician, he was deferred from military service because of his skills until he protested an SS officer's mistreatment of prisoners from the labor camp and punctuated his comment by applying the business end of a blowtorch to the officer's rump. He quickly found himself an unwilling soldier, bound for the Russian front.

Anni had been born in her parents' middle age, the last in a large family. She was given the name of an older sister who had died as a girl. She came near dying, too, of diphtheria when she was about ten. Her sister Resi used an accepted home remedy, wrapping a salt herring in cloth and laying it across her throat to draw out fever. In a while the herring was bone dry and falling apart, with a texture like meal. Nevertheless, the fever came back, and Anni spent about a month in the hospital.

Like her siblings, she attended Catholic school and went to work at fifteen, pulling a wooden wagon down the street before breakfast, delivering fresh bread for a bakery. She worked in the kitchen of a *Gasthaus* next door to her home and eventually in a German Army hospital in Gmunden. Once when she balked at an order to change jobs, she was threatened with being sent to a concentration camp. She changed jobs. Her work in the hospital ended abruptly as American forces moved in.

She had a little boy named Gerhard, then four-going-on-five and without a father. That caused me no concern at first because I had no thought that this would be anything more than a short-term friendship for whatever time I was stationed in Ebensee. By the time I began thinking about a permanent relationship, I had become attached to him.

I found that the quickest way to learn a new language was to

Anni Lipp *(front row, second from right)* **and her kindergarten group in Ebensee**

immerse myself in it, hearing and speaking little else for extended periods. No one in the Lipp household spoke English. That, and almost daily exposure to the prisoners of war, improved my German considerably, though I never would have been mistaken for a native.

I found Austrian folksongs intriguing. In some ways they resembled our own. Anni taught me several in the local dialect. She had a good singing voice, as did her sister Laura. She and Laura sang together what became my favorite, the *"Erzherzog Johann Jodeler."* Yodeling was a vital part of the Austrian folk tradition. I had heard it in many cowboy songs, so I felt at home with the Alpine form of mountain music.

I tried to reciprocate by teaching her "Red River Valley" and "You Are My Sunshine," but with limited success.

Anni was a couple of years older than I. Afraid this might make a difference to her, I padded my own age by a like amount. Not until much later did I tell her otherwise.

After a time I was hopelessly smitten. I had had a few minor crushes in the past, but nothing that affected me so deeply as my relationship with Anni. Soon I was spending as much time with her as I could. When she was not with me physically, she was heavy on my mind. I didn't go to Gmunden on my off days as I so often had before. I began thinking seriously about this becoming a lifetime partnership.

The odds were formidable. For one thing, I was in violation of Army regulations by being with her. Many other GIs had local girlfriends, but so far as I knew none contemplated making it permanent. They were marking time until they could go home, where some had wives or sweethearts waiting. Even after the fraternization rule was rescinded, the Army's red tape made it virtually impossible for a soldier to marry an Austrian or German girl. Just asking about it might get a GI transferred elsewhere.

Eleanor Roosevelt was advising soldiers not to become entangled with European girls but to wait for those back home. Some of my GI friends assured me Anni was a passing fancy, that she would seem only a distant dream once I returned home and saw the girls in Texas.

I knew I was probably too young to make such a momentous decision, but time was pressing me. I did not know how much longer I would be in Ebensee, or even in Austria. If truly serious about her, I could not afford to wait too long.

Had I been older and wiser, I might have taken counsel of my doubts, but fortunately I was neither. I was, as an old Austrian saying goes, young, dumb, and overfed. When I looked at her, when I touched her, my doubts evaporated. By Christmas I knew I wanted to spend my life with her. Still, I saw the impossibility of marriage so long as I wore the uniform. Even if it could be done, I foresaw many problems, starting with the language barrier and the thought of uprooting her from everything she had known, taking her to a land far different from her own. How would she be accepted by my parents, my friends? At least, unlike a few GIs I knew, I would not have to explain anything to a girlfriend at home. I didn't have one.

I considered all the negatives, but every time I looked into those shining blue eyes, I melted like butter in the sunshine. Her smile told me she was worth whatever it took. I wanted desperately to

Anni Lipp and Elmer Kelton

marry her, but doing it would involve time and many obstacles. I would almost certainly have to return home and become a civilian so Army regulations no longer applied. Then I would do whatever was necessary either to return to Austria and get her or send for her and the boy to come to Texas and meet me.

Whatever reservations she might have had, she did not tell me. She said she would wait however long it took and endure whatever came.

In Texas, a boy and girl might elope to sidestep parental objections, but in Austria at that time such a thing was rarely considered. The girl's father had to approve. I put a lot of study into constructing the proper way to ask Alois Lipp for his daughter's hand in marriage. It would have been challenge enough in English, but I had to phrase it in German.

I was surprised at his casual response. In effect, he simply said, "If you really want her, take her."

It came to me that he never really expected me to follow through. He thought when I left Ebensee that would be the end of it. But I meant to fool him. I meant to fool them all.

I tried to stay on his good side by bringing him cigarettes and, at Christmastime, some cognac, which I managed to obtain through Army channels, not entirely legally. I celebrated the Christmas of 1945 in Ebensee with Anni's family. They included the two brothers, their wives, four sisters, and three husbands. Anni was closest in age to her sister Laura, quite pretty herself, and as talkative as her mother. In spirit, though, she was closer to an older sister, Resi, who had spent the war years in Germany with her husband, Karl Redl, an electrical technician. Resi was probably the most sophisticated member of the family, having traveled more widely than the rest. She and Karl had smuggled their wartime savings out of Germany, rolling paper currency tightly and hiding it in pot handles and other unlikely places. They converted it into Austrian money while the old currency was still valid. Anni's mother had inherited the family home but owed her sister half of its value. Resi and Karl paid off the debt.

The oldest sister, Mitz, lived in Bad Aussee, thirty-odd miles away in the Steiermark Province. Another sister, Frieda, worked in an Ebensee textile factory. Frieda was inclined to quick criticism. I felt more comfortable with her husband, Karl Loidl, a big man with a big laugh. He was known to dance on tabletops when inspired by wine.

All of Anni's siblings except Mitz had children. Their cheer and anticipation reminded me of Christmases back home with my cousins. The holiday spirit was similar, transcending the language difference. Gifts were sparse, for the long war had left most working people impoverished. They had little to give except love. The Lipps had their share of that despite typical sibling differences that bubbled along beneath the surface. One trait that ran strongly in the family was a susceptibility to diabetes. Another was a stubbornness profound enough that it actually had a name: *Lippschedl*, the Lipp hard skull.

Their Christmas was more structured than ours in Texas, following rituals that went back for generations. It had more religious overtones than the casual observances I had known at home. The warmth of this holiday made me feel I was already a part of the family. From that point I never looked back. Whatever problems lay ahead, I was determined to make this work.

I SENSED THAT THE wood-cutting detail was winding down. Dreading the day we would receive orders to leave Ebensee, I continued to spend as much time with Anni as duties allowed. We rode the cable car up to the top of the Feuerkogel and trudged through the snow. We went out to watch competition at a ski-jumping facility, freezing our feet because each of us thought the other wanted to stay longer. We strolled together along the river and talked of a time when we would no longer have to say auf Wiedersehen.

The order came soon after the holidays. The good-bye was painful, for I did not know where I would be sent. The best I could do was promise to get back when and if I could. Fortunately the new post was not beyond reach. Several of us were transferred to temporary guard duty at a prisoner of war camp a few miles out of Vöcklabruck, about forty miles from Ebensee. I found I could ride a train most of the way, but the camp was several miles north of the nearest railroad station. I set out on foot the first weekend, following the road. A farmer came along with a hay wagon and gave me a ride part of the way. I hiked the rest. The next time I caught a ride on an Army truck. Soldiers almost always stopped and picked up GI hitchhikers.

We were not taking these PWs to the woods but simply keeping them safely inside a barbed-wire enclosure, watching over them from shaky guard towers just outside the fence. The prisoners were being held temporarily, pending their being processed to go home if no war crimes were charged against them.

We were billeted some distance away and trucked to the camp. One of the soldiers had adopted a large dog, part German shepherd. It always rode with us. As we passed a farmhouse each day, out would pop a small dog with a loud and furious bark bigger than it was. The GI dog would respond in kind as the little one chased him and us down the road. They sounded as if they wanted to tear each other to pieces. One day as the big dog stood at the rear of the truck, barking at the one that barreled along behind us, a soldier raised his foot and pushed it off. It landed on top of the little one. Their vicious barking turned into two loud squeals of terror. The big dog came racing after the truck as fast as it could run while the little one tucked its tail and scooted back to the farmhouse. Both yelped as if they were being killed.

I had found that some soldiers were like those dogs. The louder they talked, the faster they retreated.

===== ☀ **CHAPTER** ☀ =====

TWELVE

I WAS AT THE Vöcklabruck camp only about three weeks. My next assignment, in early February, turned out in several ways to be the best of my Army career. Because I had a couple of years of college behind me, I was picked to fill a vacancy in a military government office in Linz, provincial capital of Upper Austria. I was still only a private first class, so mainly I was a gofer, going for whatever some officer wanted. For a week or so I drove a Jeep. Then they moved me to a desk job that involved considerable travel out into the countryside.

My section's principal task was care and repatriation of displaced persons. From all over Europe, they were scattered about the province in several former slave-labor camps. My primary duty was to visit these camps, inventory supplies, and requisition whatever the camp leaders said was needed. In terms of physical effort it was an easy assignment. Emotionally, it was draining.

The camps were dreary places, made the sadder by knowing about the misery and suffering inflicted there upon people whose only crime had been that they were not Aryan. Most of the remaining former prisoners were still drawn and haggard, haunted by the horrors they had managed to survive. Many would crowd eagerly around me, hoping I had brought something for them.

Usually all I had was forms to fill out, listing each camp's needs. I encountered people with hollow, vacant eyes, and realized their ordeals had driven them over the edge into insanity. Now and then I heard wailing as one would lapse into posttraumatic stress and relive the terrors of the past. It sent shivers down my back and made me want to turn away.

To those misguided souls who claim the Holocaust never happened, I can only wish they had been to those places with me. After all these years I occasionally awaken from a nightmare, seeing again what I saw then.

I would make my rounds of the camps, then bring my notes back to the office in Linz and fill out the required requisition forms in quadruplicate or quintuplicate. Two or three weeks later I would return to the same camps and, more often than not, find that nothing had been done. Few of the requisitions had been acted upon. Whatever the people had needed before, they still needed, and more.

It was irritating to me, but it was a brutally real and unnecessary hardship for the inmates of the camps. Finally, in exasperation, I unloaded my frustrations on the lieutenant in charge of my office. He listened patiently, then said, "Son, you'll never make a good soldier. You're taking this seriously."

I realized he was not taking it as seriously as I was, nor was anyone else so far as I could see. Most were weary of war and its aftermath. They were killing time, awaiting orders to return to the United States.

In spite of this, we managed to process hundreds of displaced persons and get them started on their way home. Most were happy about it, but we were surprised to find that some did not want to go. This led to one of the most wrenching scenes I witnessed in Europe.

It was assumed that all these people had been forced into labor camps against their will except the Ukrainians. Those were considered guilty unless they could persuade the authorities of their innocence. The cards were stacked against them. People in the

Ukraine had suffered grievously under Stalin and his Communist regime before the war, and Soviet authorities considered Ukrainians hostile. They contended as a matter of policy that Ukrainians brought out into Germany and the occupied countries to work had come of their own accord. In their eagerness to get along with the Soviets, American authorities accepted this assumption at face value. Therefore, these unfortunate people were automatically regarded as former enemies no matter what hell the Nazis might have put them through.

One day an inspection trip carried me to Braunau on the Inn River. There I witnessed a group of Ukrainians being forced to leave at gunpoint while they pleaded and cried not to be sent back to Russia. They knew—and we knew from reports we had heard—that they stood a strong chance of being shot or at the least sentenced to gulags as political prisoners. But gullible American officials had agreed to a Russian demand that all be repatriated. With a knot in the pit of my stomach, this powerless pfc watched these unfortunate people being shipped off to a dark fate.

I had already formed a low opinion of bureaucrats in general. I was disgusted by the arrogant manner of some Austrian officials with far too much power in their hands, pushing the local people around. That day I lost whatever faith I still had in the infallibility of government authorities.

This green kid from the West Texas sandhills had done a lot of growing up.

Working with these poor people, and my acquaintanceship with the Lipp family, taught me some valuable life lessons. I found that beyond the differences in language, religion, and politics, people everywhere are much the same at the basic human level where we all live. They feel the same emotions, the same fears and hopes. And as I observed with the wounded black soldier in a military hospital, beneath the skin our flesh is the same color.

Some of the stories I heard from refugees were heartbreaking. One vivid in my memory was from a woman who was with a group fleeing ahead of the Russian advance late in the war. Many feared the Russians as much as they feared the Nazis, for stories were rampant about rape and murder by Russian soldiers, even against those who had been enslaved. The group was almost exhausted when it took refuge for the night in a farmer's barn. They expected by the next day to be overtaken. One of the refugees was a terrified young woman with a baby. During the night, the baby made one outcry, then was quiet. The woman who told the story said she heard a faint drip, drip, drip, and assumed it was raining outside.

In the morning it was discovered that the young mother had slit her baby's wrists, then her own.

Whatever my disappointments in the work I was given, the job had some grand perks I would never have expected to enjoy in the Army. We were billeted in a nice old hotel, the Goldene Kanone, a few blocks' walk from the office. Instead of an Army kitchen we were fed in the hotel dining room on white tablecloths, the food prepared by competent Austrian chefs, though the cuisine was mostly American style. We were served draft beer with the evening meal. The highlight was the great variety of tasty German-style breads—white, brown, and the heavy-as-a-rock farmer's bread. I enjoyed the Wiener schnitzels. I was less enthusiastic about the Austrian love for fat pork and sauerkraut.

We had American movies from time to time, and I watched two Italian operas sung in German, *The Barber of Seville* and *La Traviata*. To see an overweight Wagnerian soprano portraying the dying, consumption-ridden Violetta is an experience not soon forgotten.

I got to feeling overconfident about my prowess with the German language. One day I picked up the telephone and told the operator, *"Gib mir Nummer ein-und-zwanzig, fünf-und-dreissig, bitte."*

She probably had me pegged from the first word out of my mouth. She said in perfect English, "Just a moment, sir."

When I went out on inspection trips I did not have to drive. I was given an Austrian driver and chauffeured around in a nice car

that probably had been used by some German officer. One chauf-
feur made me wish I were doing the driving for myself, however.
He drove too fast, not an uncommon failing when Austrians get
behind the wheel. Many know only one speed: flat out, even on
narrow, crooked mountain roads. One day as we passed a farmhouse, he saw a white hen pecking insects in the grass. He swerved
to hit her, braked to a sudden stop, jumped out and grabbed the
injured hen. He took off as a farmer came chasing after us, shak-
ing his fist.

"My supper," the driver said.

Later he was driving one of my colleagues, missed a curve and
smashed into a tree. He survived, but the GI did not.

In addition to other pleasurable aspects of the job, I had every
weekend off. Naturally I spent these in Ebensee. I would travel
fifty- to sixty-miles distance depending upon the route. The easiest
way was to ride the train, though often the schedules made for a
late arrival. I would ride the main line that connected Linz and
Salzburg, changing to a Salzkammergut trunk line at a station called
Attnang-Puchheim. It had been an important switching point during the war and had sustained saturation bombing by Allied planes.
The area around the station and yards was little but rubble, twisted
steel rails, and burned-out railroad cars. The main line had been re-
paired enough so traffic could move.

When weather was favorable I often chose to hitchhike, for
there was always military traffic on the roads, and Army truck drivers would not pass a GI with his thumb up if they had room. Usually this was a faster way to reach Ebensee. No way was ever quite
fast enough for me, of course. I would get as far as Gmunden by
hitchhiking. There I could catch a train or another Army truck for
the last short distance. Or I could ride a passenger boat, which took
about an hour.

Anni would be waiting for me with open arms. I thought I had
no need to fear death anymore, because I knew what heaven was
like.

It seemed a golden spring, though that was due to the time I

spent with Anni. It was not a golden time for the Austrian people. All around lay the debris of war, grim reminders of the bleak years just past. Much of central Linz, especially anywhere around the railroad station and the tracks, was in ruins. Bomb-shattered walls stood naked as tombstones. Food was still in short supply. Relief agencies warned that many people were going hungry, that some faced possible starvation.

The overall postwar mood was dark, almost ominous, very much as reflected in the film *The Third Man*. People otherwise honest participated in the black market as a means of survival in a time of shortages and deprivation.

Linz, an industrial city, was divided both geographically and politically by the Danube River. On the far bank was the Russian occupation zone, stretching to Vienna and beyond. We were beginning to feel postwar tensions rising between Washington and Moscow. We heard speculation that the Russians might suddenly swarm across the Danube and overrun us.

One night I was sitting with several other soldiers in a park near the main bridge across the river, enjoying the cool of the evening, when bullets began striking the stone walls behind us, singing as they ricocheted. The firing came from the Russian side. We ducked, thinking the invasion might have begun and we would be its first victims. We heard the racing of a motor and saw a little Volkswagen beetle streaking toward us on the bridge. GI guards stopped it at a checkpoint just as it came off into the main square. A fat little man crawled out, trembling but overjoyed that he was still alive. He turned out to be a black-market operator. He had the little car loaded with contraband hams.

For that minor infraction, the Russians risked hitting innocent bystanders on our side of the river. Fortunately, no one was hurt.

I never knew what became of the fat man or the hams. Probably very little. The black market was an accepted part of daily life, winked at by most of the authorities. Many were involved in it themselves.

An American officer in Linz committed suicide after he was discovered diverting goods from the military post exchange.

I MAY NOT HAVE been altogether conscious of it, but I was storing up memories against the future. I was haunted by the possibility that all my hopes might fall through under the weight of the many obstacles, and this might be all the time Anni and I would ever have together. The weeks were passing quickly. We kept hearing rumors in the office about going home. I even investigated the possibility of getting a job with some civilian relief agency so I could remain in Austria, but that led nowhere.

The call came at the end of May. Though a faint voice somewhere inside tried to tell me it was good news, I felt as if I had been kicked in the stomach. I had time for one last trip to Ebensee before being shipped to an embarkation point in France. I took an extra day to make it a long weekend and wangled a box of Army ten-in-one rations for Anni and her family. All the way to Ebensee, I dreaded having to tell her. The walk from the railroad station to her house seemed twice as long as it really was.

As she opened the box, I could not contain the bad news. My throat was so tight I could barely speak, but I managed to say, "This is my last time."

Her face fell. Her sister Resi happened to step into the room at that moment. Anni turned to her and began to weep. "He's going away," she cried. She turned back to me, and we clung to each other like lost children. Nobody could say anything more. Though we had known it was coming, there is no way to prepare for a parting that deep down you realize may be forever.

We made the best of the last days. We walked to the familiar places. We rode the train up to Bad Aussee to visit her sister Mitz. A relative there made his living picking up passengers in an open-topped horse-drawn carriage at the railroad station. He frowned when Anni told him we would like to ride to the lake at Altausee. We assured him I intended to pay, and the frown lifted. He had assumed that he was expected to haul kinfolks free of charge. Anni and I walked together along the edge of the lake, arms around one another, using up much of the afternoon while the carriage man waited patiently. He was far from young, but perhaps he had memories of his own. I paid him for his time. Under the circumstances, it was worth far more than that.

For remembrance, we took pictures with a camera for which I had traded my cigarette rations. I still carry a couple of them in my wallet.

We delayed the parting as long as we could. Anni rode the train with me as far as Attnang-Puchheim. All the way, we held on to each other with a quiet desperation. We were still clinging as the main-line train pulled in from Salzburg. It stopped only a couple of minutes, so there was little time for the last good-bye. That was probably merciful. Leaning out the open door of the baggage car, I watched her standing alone on the platform as the train pulled away. I kept watching until she was beyond sight. Then I sat down and wept as if someone close to me had died.

Soon after returning home I heard Roy Acuff sing "Blue Eyes Crying in the Rain," a song Willie Nelson made famous years later. It was not raining in Attnang-Puchheim, but I never forgot the blue eyes crying. They were Anni's. And they were mine.

THIRTEEN

WHEN ANNI RETURNED HOME from Attnang-Puchheim, her father said, "Well, he's gone. You've heard the last from him."

But she hadn't. Back in Linz, I immediately wrote her a letter, trying to reassure her that I meant everything I had said.

We returnees traveled across Germany and France by rail. We had a comfortable passenger train instead of the drafty forty-and-eight boxcars we had endured the year before. I thought I had seen war's devastation at its peak in Linz, but Munich's railroad station and its environs were damaged even more. I remembered what Hitler had promised his people before the war: "Give me five years and you will not recognize Germany." He was right, but not in the way he expected.

We got off the train at Le Havre, France, the same port through which I had come into Europe. It was considerably improved. We were mustered in a tent camp called Phillip Morris while waiting to sail. It disturbed me to see fellow soldiers casually discarding photographs of European girls as they prepared to go home to wives and sweethearts. It seemed a callous thing to do. I could not imagine throwing away any of Anni's pictures.

Our transportation was far better than the last time. Instead of a leaky old English tub, we went aboard an American Victory ship, built for troop transport during the war. I was again assigned a bunk in the hold, but it was roomier, and no bilge water sloshed back and forth.

I dreaded seasickness, vividly remembering how hard it had hit me before. This time, perhaps through anticipation, I became ill before the ship left the dock. I was soon over it and back to normal while many others were leaning over the rail. We were assured that it was all in our heads, but I never accepted that idea. One of the soldiers brought along a German shepherd dog. Nobody told the dog it was supposed to get seasick, but it fell as ill as any man on the ship.

I had mixed emotions. I ached inside, missing Anni. I had written to her just before we sailed from France, though I had little confidence that she would get the letter. On the other hand, I began thinking more and more about home. I rationalized that once there I could start the wheels in motion to reunite us.

We sailed past the Statue of Liberty, a soul-warming sight to one returning from service abroad. The landing in New York was quiet. No brass bands greeted us. The war in Europe had been over for more than a year and the Pacific war almost that long. Returning GIs were no longer a novelty. Life in the States was getting back to normal, or on the surface seemed to be.

I had a short pass in New York. I spent part of it going to a movie, seeing Joel McCrea in a Western, *The Virginian*. It reminded me of the ranch to which I was returning. Many years later I got to meet McCrea at the National Cowboy Hall of Fame.

In Austria, I had become used to civilians speaking only German. An elderly man walked up to me on the street and said something in English. I did not understand him. I told him so in German. He looked as confused as I was. Finally he broke through to me. He said, "I just want to know how to find the railroad station."

Readjusting was going to take time.

Shortly I was on a train bound for Fort Sam Houston in San Antonio to be discharged. There we were given indoctrination to prepare us for a return to civilian life. It was assumed that most of us bore emotional scars from the war and would face difficulties in reentering normal society. Among other things, we were counseled on various occupations we might find compatible with our military service. For instance, a long list of potential jobs was offered for a clerk-typist. A great many possibilities were listed for someone who had worked in the motor pool.

My classification, however, was rifleman, infantry. The list was short. One item was *walrus hunter.*

In later years when I struggled with my writing career, I sometimes wondered if I had missed my true calling.

We were given a strong pitch for remaining in the reserve, but I feared this might keep me entangled in military red tape that had prevented my marrying Anni.

Finally I was handed my discharge, a beautiful document, and a bus ticket to carry me home. The route carried me through Austin, so I stopped off and visited a couple of my teachers in the journalism department at the university. I told them I would be back in class that fall. Dad and Mother were to pick me up in Midland, where my Grandmother Kelton lived. When my grandfather had realized his cancer was terminal, he sold his ranch interests and bought a house in town so Grandmother and young Aunt Clara would have a home after he was gone.

I landed in Midland about daybreak, too early to wake up the family, so I walked to a café to eat breakfast. There sat the cranky old wagon cook, Tom Grammer. He was in a good humor this time. He invited me to sit with him at the counter, and we talked about old times and old friends.

Only then did I fully realize that I was home.

The ranch looked the same as I had left it, though my younger brothers had matured some. Myrle by then was seventeen, Bill a couple of years behind him, Gene close to fourteen. In cowboy terms, they were about grown.

I lost no time in hanging up my uniform and getting back into Levi's and boots. I found that the boots gave me trouble with my injured right ankle. On the surface it had healed, but it still ached, and sometimes it swelled when I stood on it too long. I visited Friday's boot shop in Midland and was measured for a new pair of handmade boots with brown bottoms and green tops. I bought a Western silver belt buckle, trying to get far away from the Army olive drab. I still wear that buckle.

Though I had looked forward to getting back on a horse, I paid a hard price the first two or three days. I was so sore I could barely walk. The best cure for that kind of pain is to get back in the saddle and let it wear itself out, so I did.

I soon had an injured ankle on the left side. Helping Roy Mason, a sheep rancher neighbor, I was trying to head a ewe down a fence when my horse's feet slipped out from under him on soft mud. He landed with his full weight on my ankle. It was not broken, but it swelled up and ached along with the other. They became a matched pair.

A dyed-in-the-wool cowboy might have said I had it coming to me for working sheep.

I don't know what the local post office people must have thought. Hardly a day went by that I did not address a letter to Kalvarienberg 2, Ebensee, Austria. And soon I was receiving a letter a day with exotic-looking Austrian stamps.

So far, I had fooled Herr Lipp and the other doubters.

In my letters home from Europe I had tried to prepare my parents. As always, Mother was supportive. Dad did not argue with me beyond saying, "You're too young to know what love means." Like Anni's father, he probably thought it seemed too unlikely ever to come to pass. Given all that distance, and that strange-sounding land so different from West Texas, he figured I would get over the notion once I had been home awhile.

During my months in the Linz military government office I often had time on my hands, so I took correspondence courses. I did it again that summer after coming home, whittling away at credits I needed to graduate from the University of Texas.

I day-worked as a cowboy when jobs turned up. I earned my first paycheck ever from the McElroy Ranch, where I had grown up and tried to learn to be a cowboy. I made the six-day late-summer "works" at $6.00 a day, all the chuck-wagon grub I could eat, and a place to roll out my blankets on the ground. I received a check for $36.

Years later the company was having a disagreement with the IRS and asked if I could photograph old oilwell locations from the 1920s and 1930s to demonstrate that the damages they left were permanent. For half a day's work I was paid $100.

Though I had been a mediocre mathematics student, I could easily see why it was probably fortunate that I had not remained a cowboy.

My teacher friend, Paul Patterson, had returned from the service earlier and had written a book he called *Sam McGoo and Texas Too*. I drew cartoons to illustrate his Texas tall tales. Except for pieces in the Crane high school newspaper and the university's *Daily Texan*, this was my first time to see my work in print. I drew illustrations for a second Patterson book, which did not find a publisher at the time. When it finally did, as *Crazy Women in the Rafters,* my artwork did not make the cut.

Neither did my career as an artist. I decided it was best to concentrate on becoming a writer.

I made a trip with my brother Myrle and Earl Teague to the Pecos rodeo. I had never been a good enough roper to compete in the arena, but I held their horses. We went up to Clovis, New Mexico, to watch a matched roping featuring a famous old-time steer roper, Bob Crosby. He truly was a legend in his time, along with Jake McClure and Toots Mansfield. I had seen Crosby once before when he competed in a rodeo in Midland. Uncle Ben took Myrle and me to meet him. I could not have been more impressed if I had met the president of the United States. In the ranching community, great ropers were the equivalent of today's rock stars.

Crosby was regarded as a wild roper, prone to taking reckless chances. He was later killed in an accident on a ranch road.

Exploring ways to get back together with Anni, I wrote to Tom Connolly, Texas's senior senator. After a time I heard from one of his staff assistants. The wheels of government grind exceedingly slowly, but eventually I was notified about immigration regulations and what had to be done to get the process underway. There was enough red tape to have wrapped the university tower to the top floor, but at least things had started moving.

I had saved most of my Army pay. There had been little to spend it on in war-weary Austria's empty stores. I was determined to hold on to it and build it up whenever possible. I returned to the university under the GI Bill, which paid for tuition and books and gave me $65 a month for living expenses. I skipped or scrimped on meals, trying to live within that limit, dropping ten or fifteen pounds from my Army weight. I finished one month with ten cents in my pocket, but I did not dip into my savings. I would need them if the immigration log jam ever broke. Neither did I want to call on Dad and Mother for help. They had done enough, getting me this far. They would soon have to send my younger brothers to college.

The deluge of military veterans returning to school swelled the university's enrollment past twenty thousand. Men outnumbered women by a considerable margin, a reversal of the situation I had found before. This did not bother me because I was not in the dating market anyway. Some of the girls looked pretty as an April rainbow, but any momentary temptation was overshadowed by memories of the girl waiting in Ebensee.

I had written a couple of short stories while overseas, though I had not tried to get them published. Back in school, I decided it was time to become serious if I was to be a writer. I bought a grocery sack full of used Western pulp magazines from a secondhand bookstore and studied them, analyzing stories I particularly liked. I dissected them like a frog in a biology lab, trying to unlock the writers' secrets of construction, description, and characterization. I copied segments on a typewriter to get a feeling for tempo and the flow of the language, the ways the authors built word pictures that would transfer their images to the reader. I took the Ezell correspondence course in fiction writing from the University of Oklahoma.

In spare time after classes and lessons, I pounded out short stories on a portable I had bought when I was a junior in high school. Most I sent first to the big slick markets, *Saturday Evening Post* and *Collier's*. These returned from the post office almost as soon as I did. I would repackage them and mail them to various pulp magazines. Those came back, too.

Mark Twain said anybody could quit smoking. He had done it dozens of times. I would become discouraged and decide to quit writing. Sometimes I would stay quit for several hours, even overnight. Then another story idea would strike me, and I would go back to the typewriter.

After I left Austria, Anni began taking English lessons from a tutor. Mother wrote her a letter, in English of course. With help of a dictionary and the tutor, Anni managed to decipher all but one word, which left her puzzled. Mother addressed her several times as "Honey," a common term of endearment in Texas. The dictionary identified the word properly in German as *Honig,* but Anni could not figure out what honey had to do with anything. It was a food.

The immigration front was starting to show signs of life. By this time many war brides were coming over from Europe, so a routine of sorts had been established. After signing umpteen documents, I was instructed to put up bond to ensure that there would be money enough for Anni to return to Austria if for some reason we did not marry. In addition I sent money to pay her expenses in getting the documentation she needed.

I thought I had cut through a lot of red tape, but it was small compared to the bureaucratic ordeal Anni was putting up with. From the time she received the first set of forms to fill out, it was touch and go as to whether all the effort would ever bear fruit. She could do almost nothing in her hometown to move things along. Regulations required that she take her physical examination in far-off Vienna. She had to have all her papers signed and validated in Vienna. She and Gerhard had to take their smallpox vaccinations in Vienna.

The money I had sent to pay travel expenses and fees melted away as the paperwork continued with no end in sight. On one occasion she was sent five different forms to sign and was required to make five copies of each. Altogether she made five or six trips to Vienna, sometimes alone, sometimes accompanied by her father. Each trip took half a day by train, followed by another half day for the return.

To reach Vienna she had to pass through the Russian zone of occupation, ever a scary proposition though she had the proper documentation. She saw soldiers remove several young girls from the trains for no apparent reason. She could only suspect the worst.

It was almost a year after I had returned home before I became confident that all the effort would eventually pay off. Toward the end of the spring semester I received word through official channels that Anni and Gerhard would soon be on their way. I was to send expense money to Paris to be held for her arrival there. I prepaid their passage from France to New York.

I had no idea how much trouble she still faced. It seemed that almost anything that could go wrong did go wrong. Anyone with less determination would have given it up in despair. She had need of that stubborn *Lippschedl,* which ran so strongly in her family's genes.

There was never extra money in the Lipp household, and what I had sent directly to Anni had been used up. Her father went to daughter Mitz's husband in Bad Aussee for a loan. Olivo Grillo was an Italian who had come into Austria after World War I for a job and had remained. Hardworking and frugal to a fault, he distrusted banks. He led Anni's father up into his attic, where he had a small fortune in paper money nailed to the rafters. He took off enough to pay for train fare to Paris. It should have been sufficient, but fate intervened with a train strike in France.

Anni's father accompanied her and Gerhard as far as Salzburg and bid them a melancholy farewell. From Salzburg things went smoothly enough as far as Stuttgart. There they changed to a train still showing the effects of the war, cold and drafty, many of its windows broken out. She encountered an officious inspector who declared that her passport was not properly validated and she would have to get off the train. She put up a strong argument, but he was adamant until she challenged him to examine the document one more time. He had overlooked a stamp in the back pages. He grudgingly gave up but removed another young woman from the train on the same pretext.

Then, at the French border, came a more threatening complication. Because of a strike, French trains were not running. A bus was standing by to carry the offloaded passengers to Paris, but the train tickets were not honored.

Anni told the bus driver she had to reach Paris. He asked, "Do you have money?"

She did not. He said, "Then you can't go."

She could see herself stranded at the French border without means either to go ahead or to return home, and with a five-year-old boy to care for. She sat Gerhard down on the suitcase and said, "You sit right here and wait. Don't you move."

She dogged the bus driver's steps, arguing that she had money waiting in Paris and would pay him when she got there. For a while he stood firm, declaring that it was impossible, but her persistence finally wore him down.

She spoke German with a mountain dialect. He demanded, "Are you from Czechoslovakia?"

She said, "No, I am from Austria."

"If you had said Czechoslovakia, I would leave you right here." He explained that he was Czech, and ethnic Germans in that country had grievously mistreated his people. He said, "Get on the bus."

Somehow in all the shuffle she had misplaced the name of the Paris hotel to which she was supposed to report. When the other passengers had disembarked, the driver asked her, "Where are you going?"

She admitted, "I don't know."

He took her to an international hotel and explained her situation to the receptionist. He wished her well and left, probably relieved to see the last of her. The hotel people found that she was indeed expected at the American consulate and that she was registered at the Europa Hotel. They delivered her to the consulate to get the money that was waiting for her.

The bus driver never showed up at the Europa to be paid. He might have feared that she would have something else to plague him about.

Though she had become acquainted with Vienna, the streets of Paris confused her. The first time she took Gerhard out to the restaurant where they were supposed to receive their meals, she became lost. A policeman gave a curt, ambiguous answer to her question, so she went even farther astray. Realizing she was on the wrong course, she showed an old man a slip of paper with the hotel's name on it. He pointed her right. After that, she was careful not to venture beyond sight of the hotel unless someone was with her who knew the way.

She had to remain in Paris several days. She met two women from Vienna who were to sail to the United States on the same ship. One, an elderly woman who was to join a daughter in New Jersey, took a special interest in Gerhard. They visited the Eiffel Tower and a few other sights, but Anni was always nervous when she could not see the hotel.

From that point things went more smoothly. She and the Viennese pair traveled together to the embarkation port of Le Havre, the same one through which I had passed twice. They were put aboard a former troopship along with a large number of war brides from various European countries. She and Gerhard shared a double bunk. She endured a spell of seasickness, just as I had.

I received word that the ship was to dock on June 26, Anni's birthday. Mother thought it would be more seemly if we were chaperoned on the trip back to Texas inasmuch as we were not yet married. Besides, she wanted to see New York. She invited my Grandmother Kelton and my aunt Clara, who was barely older than I was.

Dad and Mother had acquired a new Hudson automobile,

Anni Lipp and her son, Gerhard (1945 or 1946)

roomy and comfortable, to replace a Terraplane they had managed to keep running during the war years when buying a new car was out of the question. We did some sightseeing along the way, including a visit to the Grand Ole Opry in Nashville's Ryman Auditorium and to the Lincoln Monument in Washington. My mind was not really on music or history, however. It seemed almost beyond belief that after a full year filled with so many difficulties that I was to be with Anni again. But there was no need to rush the journey, for I could not hurry the ship.

Burning with anticipation, I left Mother and the others at the hotel and took a taxi to the appointed dock. I found the ship already in port, but passengers had not begun to disembark. My nervousness kicked up a few notches as I recognized Anni and Gerhard standing on deck, awaiting clearance to proceed down the gangplank. I was sure despite the distance that I saw her bright smile. When the signal came, she hurried down to me on the dock, leading the boy by the hand. We fell into each other's arms, and the year we had been apart seemed to disappear without a trace.

The long wait had one positive aspect. We had plenty of time to have changed our minds, and we didn't. Because of that, my Grandmother Holland said later, "I think it'll last."

The young woman from Vienna struck a snag. Her fiancé had wired her in Austria not to come, but she had done so anyway. She was taken from the boat to Ellis Island because no one was at the dock to meet her. It developed that the man she had come to marry was in jail. She wrote to Anni months later. She was still in the United States and looking for a job.

The older woman joined her daughter in New Jersey. She visited us once and stayed in touch until her death a few years later.

I can only imagine what Mother and the others thought as they saw Anni for the first time at the hotel. She was hardly a fashion plate, for in Austria new clothes were expensive and still in short supply. She wore a dirndl dress she had brought from home. She had stood in line for a ration ticket to buy new shoes, wistfully looking at fashionable high-heeled specimens in the store window, but all the storekeeper would sell her had been an old-fashioned pair of lace-ups of the style worn by nuns.

One of the first things Mother did was to take her shopping for a new outfit. I went along to translate, for the language lessons Anni had taken were in London-style English. Her vocabulary was limited and had no Texas accent at all. Besides, after all that time apart, I didn't want to be separated from her even for a shopping foray.

Gerhard had little to say. He was bewildered by the tall buildings and the traffic, the clamor of the city, and by a language he could not comprehend. He clung to his mother. Clara and my grandmother quickly began to dote on him. By the time we reached Texas he had already picked up some useful English words.

My mother was not one of the world's great drivers. In New York City she wanted to turn left, but a policeman waved her straight on. She made a big circle and came back, hoping this time to turn where she intended, but the policeman was still there, blocking her. The third time she turned anyway. A sharp whistle brought her to a stop. The policeman took out his pad and asked why she had turned left despite his signal. About the best she could say was, "That's where I wanted to go."

He saw our Texas license plate, muttered something about Texas drivers, and waved us on.

We did not take time for sightseeing after we turned westward, though to Anni and Gerhard everything was new and strange. We spent about three days, taking turns driving, getting back to Midland, where we delivered my grandmother and aunt. We headed out the last fifty miles toward the ranch. South of Odessa, in the dark, we turned onto a graded ranch road. It was an unusually big jackrabbit year. Rabbits were everywhere, on the road and in the adjoining pastures. Missing them was impossible. Anni hid her face and tried to cover her ears so she could not hear the frequent thump, thump, knowing we were leaving a trail of dead rabbits behind us. Back home, plump domestic bunnies had been fed and handled with care. These skinny jackrabbits, all ears and hind legs, would have been poor eating.

The day after we reached home, Mother and Anni cleaned house. It had been left to the tender mercies of Dad and my younger brothers for a couple of weeks, and a good cleaning was overdue. Mother kept trying to persuade her to stop and rest awhile, but Anni had the old-country work ethic and would not quit until the job was done. About the time they finished, a sandstorm blew in. Most of their efforts had been in vain, for the doors and windows were not tight. When the wind blew, the curtains billowed even though the windows were closed. Dust settled over everything.

Dad commented, "One good thing, nobody was ever asphyxiated in a McElroy Ranch house."

Anni even shined all the men's and boys' boots, but Mother assured her that was beyond the call of duty. She never did it again. She was quick to catch on to American ways.

I took her to Crane to obtain the marriage license and have a brief practice session with the Reverend J. N. Whetstone so she could handle the I do's in English. I showed her my hometown, which had none of Ebensee's scenery except for flat-topped King Mountain far to the south, and historic Castle Gap. The nearest thing to a lake was a ranch's stock tank. I feared I had oversold the place to her and that she might be disappointed. She was, but she did not admit it to me.

On July 3, Mother and I took Anni and Gerhard to Grandmother Kelton's house in Midland for a quiet wedding. Anni wore a nice aqua dress Mother had bought for her in New York, along with a tiny hat crowned by artificial white flowers. We went to a photographer to have a wedding portrait made. Looking at it after nearly sixty years, it is hard to believe we were ever that young, that thin, or that innocent-looking.

Witnessed by my parents, two of my brothers, my grandmothers, Clara, and cousin George Gilbert, we said our vows in Grandmother's living room. The Reverend Whetstone spoke Anni's words slowly and a few at a time so she could repeat them after him as she had practiced in Crane. She did not know what most of them meant except that this was for keeps. Mother played the piano. It was a simple ceremony, far from the elaborate, highly structured church weddings customary in Austria. It was over so quickly that it hardly seemed real. It was more like walking through a dream. The main thing I remembered afterward was the minister saying, "You may now kiss the bride." I was quite ready to do that. Then we cut the cake.

There was no honeymoon. We felt we should hold on to what was left of my savings for the expenses we would face in starting our life as a married couple. I have often regretted that we did not even rent a room for the night. Instead, we went back to the ranch. Anni and I slept in the front bedroom, my parents in the back bedroom, my brothers on the screened back porch. It was an inhibited wedding night, to say the least. It was the first of many such nights.

Gerhard did not understand why he had to sleep on the porch with my brothers instead of with his mother, as he had done since leaving Ebensee. He thought *I* should sleep with my brothers.

Next day we went to a Fourth of July barbecue in Crane, where Anni saw how hot July could be in Texas. After that, we drove to Pecos, where I thought I could share with her the thrill of a rodeo. It was no less hot there than in Crane, and dusty as well.

She has never been to a Pecos rodeo since.

My concerns that she might not be accepted in the community had been for nothing. It was common knowledge for a year that I was trying to get her into this country, so her arrival was no surprise. My mother's circle of friends embraced her. Ardeth Allman and Louetta Vines hosted a wedding shower. Louetta, my mother's closest friend, took Anni under her wing and coached her on Texas customs she might need to know. Dutch Regan, who had immigrated from Germany as a young man, told her he had learned English by reading the comic pages because even when the words were strange, he could discern their meaning by context. She used that stratagem until she felt comfortable with the language, then quit the funnies.

Gerhard adjusted quickly. My brothers and cowboys Elliott Moore and Son Guin put him on a horse. He was in kid heaven. From the time he was a toddler, he had always run to the garden gate to watch the horses when a beer wagon pulled up to the *Gasthaus* next door. He picked up English with a speed that amazed us, though thanks to his cowboy teachers he learned some terms that would better have been left unspoken.

The boys decided the name Gerhard was too foreign-sounding. They began calling him Gary for short, and Gary it was from then on. It still is.

I was notified that I could redeem the bond I had put up with the immigration service, though I had to appear with Anni and Gary and our marriage license in El Paso. We drove out and went through the process. We had talked about buying Gary a pair of cowboy boots. They were cheaper in Juárez, Mexico, than on the

Elmer, Anni, and Gerhard (Gary) at the McElroy Ranch (1947)

Texas side of the river. Because neither mother nor son were yet citizens, we duly checked in with immigration authorities at the Rio Grande bridge. We were assured that it was all right for us to go across. We signed a form, walked over, and bought the boots. We were probably in Juárez less than two hours. We checked back with the same authorities as we crossed into Texas again. We had no inkling of the trouble this innocent little stroll across the river was to give us in the future.

As a newlywed, I took ribbing from the cowboys and bawdy remarks from wagon cook Tom Grammer. I still had residual doubts about myself because of my shortcomings as a cowboy. The hoorawing got under my skin and made me self-conscious about showing affection to Anni when anyone could see it. She began to feel I was pulling away from her, perhaps having regrets. This compounded the problems she had in becoming accustomed to a strange country and a new way of life. It was natural that she became homesick, though she would not admit it until long afterward.

I began to realize how she felt and tried to make up for my neglect. However, it was difficult, for I still sought approval of the cowboys and tried to uphold my part of the ranchwork though it took me away from her much of the time. Moreover, my ambition to become a writer often kept me at the typewriter late at night while she lay in bed alone.

I still lacked one semester for my journalism degree, so it was taken for granted that we would leave the ranch and go to Austin in September. Apartments there were expensive, if we could find one. We learned of a trailer house for sale in Odessa. The more euphemistic term *mobile home* had not come into common usage. It was barely more than twenty feet long and showed the effects of having been hauled around the oilfields for several years. Still, it would be a roof over our heads, the first home of our own. We bought it for seven hundred dollars and pulled it to the ranch for a thorough cleaning and some patching on the roof. We also began sleeping in it.

Chuck Olson had come back from the service, bringing with him a 1931 Model A Ford he had purchased in California. Dad bought it from him so we would have transportation in Austin. Unfortunately that never came to be. A rear main bearing broke on the rutted ranch road, and the old car wound up in a garage while we used Mother's to pull the trailer to Austin. The Model A would not have handled that job anyway. The repair cost almost as much as the car had, leaving a big hole in our bank account.

Using Mother's car to pull the trailer to Austin, we placed it in a Barton Springs Road trailer park on the city's south side, several miles from the university campus. I usually squandered a dime each morning to ride the bus to school, but most of the time I walked home after classes. Because I was married, my GI Bill allowance was increased to ninety dollars a month, hardly an invitation to lux-urious living. We paid fifteen dollars a month for space in the park.

The trailer had come with a butane gas stove and tank, but Anni was nervous about using them. We bought an electric hot plate with a movable oven that fit over one burner. She could bake bis-cuits in it. She would buy a pound or two of ground beef, mix it with a liberal helping of bread crumbs, then slice it into small pieces and feed us for several days. We ate a lot of canned Austex beef stew. Thanks to her wartime lessons in stretching a little into a lot, we managed to survive on our ninety dollars a month.

The few times we went to the movies, we walked rather than ride a bus. One night Gary went to sleep during the film, and I had to carry him all the way home, about a mile and a half. He never woke up.

Anni was still self-conscious about her English, but she gradu-ally made friends with women in nearby trailers, using a mixture of sign language and words similar to the one that had first brought us together in Ebensee.

We were amazed by Gary's easy grasp of the language. We had expected to hold him back from school for a year, but by Septem-ber he understood well enough that we enrolled him in the first grade in Austin. A sympathetic teacher gave him special attention. Though he struggled, he managed to make a passing grade. Anni walked with him the several blocks to school until he was familiar with the route. After that, he went alone, meeting up with other boys along the way. He was always more self-sufficient than his size and age would indicate.

In addition, he developed a frugality his grandfather in Austria could have appreciated. When he clasped his fingers around a coin, it was his forever.

================== **CHAPTER** ==================

FOURTEEN

MY WRITING CAREER HAD not made a passing grade yet. The stories I wrote kept coming back with rejection slips. However, I began receiving short notes from one editor, Fannie Ellsworth of *Ranch Romances*. That was the same pulp magazine Mother had read to me when I was not yet able to read for myself. Mrs. Ellsworth would tell me briefly what was wrong with the story and encourage me to keep trying.

Finally, late in the semester, she sent me a check for $65, a cent and a quarter a word for five thousand words. The story was entitled *There's Always Another Chance*. I felt as if I had ridden the famous old bucking horse, Midnight, to a standstill. Here I was, not yet out of college, and I had already sold a story. I thought I could see fame and fortune waiting around the corner.

Anni had resigned herself to my sometime neglect in light of the favorable implications for our future. She had observed golf widows and football widows. She once described herself as a typewriter widow.

I realized a writing career was not made overnight but had no idea it would be a full year before I managed to sell a second story. Fortunately, because of my ranch background I was invited to San Angelo to interview for a job on the *Standard-Times* and was hired to be a farm and ranch writer. I did not remain in Austin for graduation ceremonies. As soon as my final test was done, near the end of January, we pulled the trailer to San Angelo and set it up in a camp a couple of blocks from the stockyards. That turned out to be an appropriate location in view of the type of work I was undertaking.

San Angelo was and is a green oasis, especially for travelers approaching from the semidesert west, where annual rainfall takes a sharp drop. The North, South, and Middle Concho rivers join to form one stream that meanders off eastward and merges with the Colorado. At that confluence of three rivers the frontier army in 1867 had established an isolated outpost that became Fort Concho. Tall trees, pecan and other varieties, cast their heavy shade upon grassy riverbanks and outlying residential areas.

At the time we moved there, the population was roughly fifty thousand. As a Boy Scout I had once camped with friends on the river and thought San Angelo the prettiest town I had ever seen. Except for some in Austria, I still felt that way on seeing it again in 1948.

My immediate superior was a veteran newspaperman named Al Sledge, who had been at the *Standard-Times* too long to leave because he had so much at stake in the company's retirement program. Al knew the livestock community and especially the wool- and mohair-buying fraternity. He was particularly devoted to attending wool sales because the buyers as a group knew how to party when the work was done. Al loved to party, and the reddish hue in his face reflected it.

He was a serious newsman, however, out of the old school. He believed in getting it first and getting it right. Farm-raised, he was deeply partisan on the side of the rancher and farmer. Just before I arrived, he became involved in a libel suit involving a horse race. A horse had been disqualified to run, and Al printed the judges' stated reasons. He never apologized for telling the truth. Though fighting the suit cost the newspaper a great deal of money, it backed him and won the judgment.

One of my first days on the job, he sent me out to the local live-stock auction to watch and learn, and to introduce myself to some of the stockmen. The university and the service had diminished but not cured my natural shyness. I had to force myself to approach strangers. I quickly found, however, that most of these people were like the ranching and oil-patch folk I had known while growing up. As soon as they saw that I was not trying to sell them something, they were friendly and openhanded. I felt that I had not strayed far from home.

My first out-of-town assignment was a polled Hereford bull sale at R. A. Halbert's Ranch south of Sonora. Sledge went along, taking a couple of his partying buddies. It was left to me to do the driving, which turned out to be fortunate. I learned a little about salesmanship by watching Halbert. Slight of build and soft of voice, he led the bulls into the ring himself. The higher the bidding went, the sadder the expression on his face, as if he were being forced to give the cattle away. Actually, the prices were near a record, but a good salesman knows how to show a worried face and make buyers believe they are getting off cheap.

Sledge and his two friends had a great time passing a bottle back and forth. When we returned to the office he was in no condition to write up the sale. I had to do it, though I had no previous experience at sale reporting and probably botched some of the figures. Next day he soberly promised me it would never happen again, and it didn't.

I came to know Halbert better in later years. In his physical stature, he was not a large man, but he was a pillar of the Sonora-area ranching community, a conservationist committed to leaving his range in better condition than he had received it. He was also a hard worker. I stopped to visit him once when he was in his late seventies or early eighties and found this little old man shoveling cement into a wooden form for a new water trough. Several husky employees were standing by, and there is hardly any way to go wrong in shoveling cement. Nevertheless, he felt he had to do the job himself to be certain it was done right.

In his eighties he began experiencing heart trouble. A pacemaker was installed to keep his heartbeat regular. Son-in-law Vestel Askew went to the ranch to check on him but did not find him at headquarters. A Hispanic ranch hand told him the *patrón* was out in a far pasture.

Disturbed, Vestel demanded, "Do you mean he's out there with that pacemaker, driving his pickup?"

"Oh no, *señor*. He is just on his horse."

I had taken a news photography course at the university and felt that I knew my way around a camera, but I was disabused of that idea after being on the paper perhaps a week. Not having anyone else handy, the editor assigned me to cover a regional firemen's meeting in Winters, some seventy miles away. Officers were elected, and I lined them up to take their picture with a 4 X 5 Speed Graphic camera. The flash would not fire. I tried everything I knew without success. Finally one of the firemen stepped out of the line and said, "Son, I'll bet if you put this plug into that socket, it'll work." I did, and it did, and I felt about two feet tall.

San Angelo was the hub of the West Texas sheep industry. The city had two livestock auctions, one leaning more heavily toward cattle, the other toward sheep, though both handled anything that walked on four legs. The McElroy Ranch had never run sheep, but many of our neighbors did, so I was somewhat familiar with them. The old rivalry between Texas sheepmen and cattlemen, never as serious as depicted in fiction, had evaporated as ranchers discovered that dollar for dollar, sheep were consistently the more profitable. It was cattle for respectability but sheep for a living.

As my acquaintanceships broadened, I began to see story characters in many of the people I met. I would write stories at night and on Sundays, visualizing real people in fictional roles.

We continued to live in the trailer until early summer. Anni and I slept on a three-quarter bed at one end, a sliding door closing us off from the rest of the room. Gary slept on a couch at the other end. Kitchen and dining room filled a cramped area in the center.

A fold-up table was raised into place at mealtime, then folded back out of the way to provide more space.

My writing career's slowness in taking off convinced me that I had better count on holding my newspaper job for a while. The trailer seemed to get smaller day by day, so we began to consider buying a house. We found a newly built one on San Antonio Street, priced at $6,500. Dad suggested that we wait until houses got cheaper. That seemed unlikely to happen, however, so we took the plunge, making a modest down payment and taking on a mortgage at four and three-quarters percent interest. The house was a plain, box-shaped frame with two bedrooms, a bath, a kitchen, and a living room. It seemed a palace compared to the trailer, though there was no garage. The payment ran $55 a month. I had started at the paper for $45 a week and had soon been raised to fifty.

Soon we wondered how we ever got by on the GI Bill—ninety dollars a month.

I drove the Model A to and from work. It was a curiosity chugging down the San Angelo streets, about the only one of its vintage still in daily use there. It was temperamental, so I had to tinker with it often to keep it running. Its biggest problem was mechanical brakes, which would not stay tight. I never let myself get close to the car in front of me.

Anni was becoming acclimated and was speaking passable English, thanks in particular to neighbor Maxine Howton, who coached her patiently without making fun of her mistakes. Gary was earning good grades in school. I was liking my job more and more as I settled into it. We looked back at all the obstacles we had met and surmounted, and we knew life was good. Whatever all this had cost us, it was worth it.

One seemingly insignificant and almost forgotten incident from the past broadsided us, however. More than a year after we were married, two federal officials showed up at our door to serve a warrant against Gary. They said he had entered the United States illegally when he came back from Mexico after that little walk we made across the Rio Grande to buy him a pair of boots.

We argued that the authorities at the bridge had okayed our crossing, but they said the authorities had been in error. It made no difference whose mistake it had been. Gary had violated the law and was subject to deportation. They said we would probably have to take him to Mexico and apply for a visa under the quota system. They were in earnest, as only federal authorities can be, and scary as hell.

I turned to my boss at the San Angelo *Standard-Times,* publisher Houston Harte. A man of potent political influence, he contacted our Congressman, O. C. Fisher. Even with Fisher's considerable clout, that sword continued to hang over our heads for a year or more until we finally worked our way through the maze.

It was another lesson in my ongoing education about the futility of trying to move the unmovable federal bureaucracy. Process was always more important than people. Even a minor technicality could have serious consequences if it compromised the process. Had we simply crossed the bridge without asking questions, like a thousand other tourists that day, nothing would ever have come of it. But we paid a price for wanting to do it properly.

Harte was a newspaperman to the core. He was frugal in many ways, but he believed that if a story was important, it was worth pursuing regardless of cost. A product of the University of Missouri journalism school, he had bought the local paper in the 1920s from an aging Pat Murphy, who had cofounded it in frontier San Angelo forty-odd years before. Bringing with him a cadre of Missouri graduates like editor Dean Chenoweth, he built it into a strong regional newspaper that dominated an area some three hundred miles wide and two hundred miles deep. While doing so Harte helped found many local business enterprises through partnerships or loans. Many a high school graduate went on to higher education through his quiet philanthropy.

Some of his employees feared him because he often wore a dour expression and could be a sobering presence in the newsroom. A frown from him was dreaded like a visit from the IRS.

Yet he had their respect and loyalty because a handshake from Houston Harte was as good as a bond.

Unlike some bosses who object to employees' outside activities, he encouraged my fiction writing. In my fifteen years of association with him, he never spoke a cross word to me. Praise was not frequent, either, but when it came it was like sunshine on a spring morning.

When I joined the *Standard-Times,* Chenoweth, in his fifties, was recuperating from a heart attack. Old-timers on the staff were trying to take up as much of his workload as they could. "We've got to save poor old Dean," they said. "Poor old Dean" outlived them all, surviving into his early nineties.

As editor he felt it his duty to read a large stack of out-of-town newspapers every day, even taking some home with him at night. From these he gleaned many ideas for local stories, which he assigned to the various reporters. Most were worthy, but some were on the strange side. During a long drought that baked Texas in the 1950s, he suggested that I go to Fairmount Cemetery and ask the grave diggers how far it was down to wet dirt.

To him every story, no matter where from, had a local angle if the reporter was diligent enough to find it. If yaks were reported sick in the Himalayas, their affliction might be something that could infect Texas cattle. "Check on it," he would say.

Dean had a wonderful memory. Often some obscure old-timer would die, and a young reporter could find nothing to write about him or her beyond a few dry, bare-bones facts. But Dean would remember something unusual the person had done or experienced years before and give the story a special human touch. Many an obituary to which he contributed went into family albums to be read and reread over the years.

He liked to tell about his World War I service and the time General Blackjack Pershing spoke to him personally: "He looked straight at me and said, 'Button that tunic, soldier.'"

The paper was to some degree a stopping place for young journalists on their way up. They would gain some experience, learn how to spell Schleicher County, then move on to a larger publication or some other line of work. However, a core group of professionals like Sledge, George Kunkel, Grady Hill, Blondy Cross, and Johnny Brewer stayed on year after year until they retired or died in harness. They gave the publication continuity. Like Dean, they also gave it heart.

Every day when I was not covering a story out in the trade territory, I would visit the livestock auctions or make a round to the three major hotel lobbies, interviewing ranchers and farmers who were in town. I would report on range and field conditions, livestock sales they might have made, or just their opinion on one subject or another.

Now and then these rounds yielded a surprise, like the day I walked into the Cactus Hotel, and Otho Drake beckoned me over to his tiny livestock commission office in the corner of the ornate lobby. He said, "I've got somebody here you'll want to meet."

There sat the famous Frank "Bring 'Em Back Alive" Buck, whose documentary films had taken me vicariously to the jungles of Africa and Asia. I had not realized that Walter Buck, who owned a local automobile agency, was his brother. They had grown up on a ranch not far from San Angelo.

Buck had recently appeared in an Abbott and Costello film, *Africa Screams,* a spoof on a noted documentary entitled *Africa Speaks*. I asked him why, for to me it seemed a bit of a comedown. He replied, "They crossed my palm with a sufficient amount of silver."

The short items I picked up on these outings went into a daily column entitled *From the Top of the Windmill*. The column had been established in the late 1930s by a former football coach named Sam Ashburn. By all accounts he was a genial type with whom strangers felt at ease. They would tell him things they might not ordinarily talk about. His trademarks were a small pad of folded paper and several short pencils which he sharpened with his thumbnail. It was said that when he sensed his note-taking was making someone nervous, he could put his hand in his pocket and write fragmentary notes there with a stub pencil, expanding upon them in fuller detail as soon as he was out of sight.

Wool buyer A. S. Baker told me he once encountered Harte in a hotel lobby and let him know about a large sale of wool. He gave the particulars but warned that the account should be corroborated by the wool warehouseman involved. Harte returned to the office to give Ashburn the information but found he was not in. He sat down at Ashburn's typewriter and wrote out the details of the sale. At the end he added: "Baker says this is on the Q. T."

Ashburn was running late when he returned. He saw the note, assumed it was meant for the Windmill column and spiked it for the typesetter, unread. The next morning it came out in the paper with the final line intact: "Baker says this is on the Q. T."

Ashburn died young. Viewing the body in the funeral home, Harte sensed that something was missing. He returned to the office, gathered several stub pencils from Ashburn's desk, and put them in the columnist's pocket. Ashburn was buried with the tools of his trade.

Though I came along almost ten years after him, I often found myself being compared to him and found wanting. In the eyes of those who remembered him, no one could take his place. Many times I heard, "Sam would've done it differently." Eventually those comments stopped. I didn't do it like Sam, perhaps, but by trial and error I found my own way. As a writer, both in news coverage and in fiction, I learned that each person has to develop his or her own voice rather than be a copy of someone else. A copy will always remain a copy; it will never be an original.

One of my duties was to cover livestock shows, both county level and majors such as those in Fort Worth and San Antonio. I got my baptism at the first Fort Worth show I attended, in 1949, though it was by ice rather than by fire. A winter storm had slashed across Texas. I rode a bus, which on a frozen highway slid sideways down part of the long Brownwood Hill. At the show grounds, power lines broke under the weight of ice and fell to the street, showering sparks. The show barns were like freezers.

There seemed to be an unwritten law that county livestock shows, mostly conducted outdoors at the time, were always scheduled on the coldest days in January. They were miserable for the youngsters as well as for spectators. My worst was probably at Kerrville, on a hillside next to the football field. Sleet and snow were falling together, crusting along the backs of steers and lambs and on the shoulders of the young exhibitors. The wind was frigid, cutting like a knife. As I sat on a bale of hay with a portable typewriter in my lap, trying to warm my stiff fingers, I dreaded having to call in the story from a freezing outdoor telephone booth with windows broken out. I remembered what Dad had said to me once: "You kids all want to make a living without having to work for it."

Since that time most counties have built indoor show facilities so youngsters no longer have to endure the kind of misery their parents and grandparents underwent in their own 4-H Club and Future Farmers of America days.

Over the years I felt rewarded for all those cold days when someone I did not know would tell me that I had taken his or her picture at a stock show long ago. Occasionally I would be shown a yellowed clipping of my article and photograph, kept proudly all that time.

Summers I attended many horse shows and ram and billy sales. There the problem was not ice but June to August heat. Anni accompanied me at times, but she eventually gave it up. Whoever said love conquers all never sat in the thin shade of too many mesquite trees at too many country goat sales.

Though agriculture was my specialty, I would occasionally fall into something unrelated to it, like the one time I covered a Friday-night high school football game. I was much better at covering goat sales. They never asked me to do a sports story again.

Another time I was the only one available to cover a manhunt for two prison escapees. The pair were known to have robbed a ranch house near the small Coleman County town of Talpa, taking a rifle or two. They had tried to steal a pickup, but the battery was dead. They pushed the pickup down a hillside in a vain attempt to get it started and were last seen headed west afoot along the railroad tracks.

I joined a posse at Ballinger and soon wished I were covering a goat sale instead. The sight of all those men eagerly brandishing loaded rifles reminded me of that Rhine River crossing, when I kept hoping everybody knew enough to keep their weapons on "safety." Had these men actually come upon the fugitives, the pair would probably have been shot to pieces, and possibly a posse man or two as well. As it happened, a lone lawman with bloodhounds found them first, and they gave up peacefully.

I knew after that experience, and the one football game, that agricultural journalism was my true calling.

Once my pulp magazine stories began to sell with some regularity, they provided a nice few years' run as a spare-time sideline to my newspaperwork. However, we had acquired a Plymouth automobile that seemed to be possessed of a sixth sense and a grudge. It could pass almost anything except a garage. It appeared to know when I sold a story, for it would immediately break down. Repairing it usually cost about the amount of the check.

I was fortunate to come along a few years before the end of the pulp-magazine era. They were good training for beginning writers as well as bread and butter for many prolific professionals. But television was beginning to replace short stories as an entertainment medium. The fiction magazines were dying. My agent at the time, August Lenniger, warned that I must switch to novels or give up my fiction career. After years of writing shorter material, the thought of doing a full-length novel was daunting.

Nevertheless, I strained hard and wrote my first, *Hot Iron*. By the time I finished it, the Western market was saturated. The manuscript languished for about a year. Finally Ian and Betty Ballantine, with years of experience in publishing, started their own company. They were looking for young writers they might build up, writers not prone to overappraise the value of their work. They bought that book and, over a period of years, a dozen or so more.

With two careers in parallel, I felt like a juggler trying to keep two plates spinning. I was short-changing my growing family by spending so much time at one or the other, but I rationalized that it would be worth the sacrifice in the long run. Our son Steve came along in 1951, daughter Kathy in 1954. They grew up watching me sitting at a typewriter, my back turned to them. Gary had long since become used to it. As an older brother he in many ways filled in for me with Steve and Kathy.

WEST TEXAS BEGAN TURNING dry in 1950 and 1951. That in itself is not unusual, for the region has experienced many more dry years than wet ones. Most people simply regard it as "another dry spell" for the first two or three years. After that they may consider calling it a drought. The 1950s drought was the longest and most severe within the memory of anyone then living.

Rancher and former sheriff Arch Benge was one of those old-timers who could always tell about something bigger or smaller, better or worse. He downplayed the drought its first few years. He said he had seen more severe ones in his long life, which went back to the 1880s. But finally, after four years or so, he admitted to me, "Anybody who says he's seen a worse one than this is either a damn sight older than me, or he's a damned liar."

As a farm and ranch reporter I covered that drought day after day for seven years. I ran out of new ways to say, "It's still dry out there." I witnessed the courage and inventiveness of farmers and ranchers in their desperate efforts to survive. Ranchers kept whittling away at herds and flocks as the forage declined, but most of the time they did not sell off enough. They seemed to fall farther and farther behind. The rains that came were usually light and far between. Many operators were forced to fold. It was a dismal experience, watching people put the last of their livestock across an auction ring's scales.

Prolonged droughts were usually accompanied by depressed prices. A cow trader I knew bought a string of droughty cattle at what he thought was an extremely low price. He shipped them to a partner in Kansas City, asking him to see to their resale and adding, "I stole these cattle."

In due course he received a reply: "Sorry, thieves here too."

I witnessed the futility of most federal efforts to help. The government entered the picture with good intentions but usually managed to foul things up. Even the promise of a federal program had an automatic inflationary effect. One Friday afternoon the Department of Agriculture announced that it would begin a five-dollar-per-ton subsidy on hay for eligible livestock owners beginning the next Monday. On Monday morning hay prices had advanced ten dollars, not only nullifying the subsidy but costing its recipients an extra five dollars. Those people not in the program were ten dollars poorer.

By this time I had written and published several paperback original Western novels with the Ballantines. As the drought progressed, I began to realize it could be a great background someday for a contemporary novel.

In January 1957, President Dwight D. Eisenhower came for a tour of drought-stricken West Texas. Shortly after he left, the area began receiving what people called "nice Republican rains." They continued all spring and summer, culminating with heavy downpours in the fall that filled thirsty reservoirs. After years of terrible deprivation, the land turned green again. I wrote the first version of my long-planned drought novel and sent it to my agent with high hopes. His reaction was a lukewarm "It's a nice little agrarian novel." Editors did not like it even that much. Nobody bought it.

I refused to give it up. I rewrote it from the beginning and tried again. Still, nobody wanted it. I put the novel away in a drawer and went back to writing more conventional Westerns.

I had joined Western Writers of America in its second year after much urging from fictioneers S. Omar Barker and Nelson C. Nye. Barker, who wrote the Mody Hunter stories I had enjoyed so much as a boy, had begun noticing my pulp stories and wrote letters of encouragement. Nye's specialty was rousing action Westerns. I had read a lot of his work in studying the craft.

The Ballantines sold their company to a conglomerate, so I missed the rapport I had enjoyed with them. At WWA conventions Harold Kuebler, Western editor for Doubleday, invited me to write for his DD Western line. Expanding on an idea I had kicked around for several years, I wrote *The Day the Cowboys Quit,* based on an 1883 cowboy strike at Tascosa, Texas. Harold bought it and asked what I was going to write next.

I had never forgotten my aborted drought novel. With ten years' more experience behind me, I wrote it a third time, starting from the first page. I expanded the story and characterization, and by this time was bolder in the treatment of racial relations between Anglos and Hispanics. Published as *The Time It Never Rained,* it eventually became my signature work. After more than thirty years, I am more often than not introduced as the author of that book, though I have written many others since.

For the last dozen or so years, Forge Books has been publishing my new novels as well as reissuing most of my earlier ones.

I have occasionally been asked if I regret the forty-two years I spent in agricultural journalism, for I could have written many more books had I not been tied to a job. I have no such regret. Many of my novels have come partly or wholly from people, places, and situations I observed in my newspaperwork. I could never have written *The Time It Never Rained* had I not covered that story as a reporter for seven years. The two careers complemented each other well. Having a steady income from journalism freed me to write the kind of fiction I wanted rather than be forced to write things I did not like because I needed a quick check for groceries.

One of the first pieces of advice I give to beginning writers is: "Don't give up your day job." Not only does it buy the bacon and beans when the writing doesn't sell, but it can furnish raw material for stories if a writer keeps his or her antenna up.

As a writer of Westerns and historical fiction, I have always tried to keep my stories plausible and true to history. Insofar as possible I like to have a story grow out of some historical reality, an event, a situation, a period of change in which an old order is challenged by something new. Change is a constant in our history. It has always created conflict between those who hold for the status quo and those who want to travel a different path. Neither is always right, and neither is always wrong.

I try to avoid superheroes, for I have never known any. The people I have known have for the most part been common folks struggling to get along, meeting life's obstacles with the best that is in them, or in some cases giving up and going down in defeat. Not all stories have a happy ending. Life is not that kind to us.

I have often been asked how my characters differ from the traditional larger-than-life heroes of the mythical West. Those, I reply, are seven feet tall and invincible. My characters are five-eight and nervous.

FIFTEEN

ONE OF THE GREAT pleasures of life's journey is the people met along the way. Many could write their own book if they were so inclined.

Early in my job at the *Standard-Times,* Al Sledge heard a coffee-shop report that the Irion County agricultural agent, J. T. Davis, had been hired to work in the Mertzon bank. He told me to phone banker Vester Hughes and confirm the story. I had never met Hughes, though I had heard he was a man of plain speech.

"Mr. Hughes," I asked, "is it true that you have hired Mr. Davis to work for the bank?"

Hughes replied, "Yes, son, that is true. I hired him."

"What will be the nature of Mr. Davis's duties?"

There was a long silence, then a sharp reply: "By God, he'll do what I tell him to!"

I knew an old black horseman named Albert Merrill. His skin was dark as a raven's wing, but his teeth shone like ivory when he smiled. He was well into his seventies but was still breaking horses. One day a bronc colt threw him off and broke his leg. A friend chided him as he lay in his hospital bed: "Albert, at your age don't you think you ought to quit riding those bad horses?"

Albert flashed that bright smile. "When a man has got a settin' down job," he said, "he'd better hang on to it."

Hugh Campbell had a similar experience. A cowboy from open range days, he was raising Hereford cattle near Ballinger, Texas, in his later years. He usually introduced himself as "Hugh Campbell, 'Red' better known," for his hair retained a tinge of red to the end of his long and active life. One day when he was about ninety, he jumped on a young mare to head a cow back down a fence. The cow turned, and so did the mare, but Hugh didn't. He lay on the ground with a broken leg.

He told me, "I don't blame that little mare one bit. I ought to've taken time to put a saddle on her."

As a young cowboy, he was working in the sandhills west of Odessa when a cow rammed a sharp horn deeply into his side. He was taken to nearby Monahans, where a doctor cleaned the wound and sewed it up but cautioned that Hugh should remain in town a few days until the danger of blood poisoning was past. He was placed in a boardinghouse.

That was at a time when Texas had opened state-owned lands for homesteading. Ranchers using that land objected, and at least one hired a notorious gunman known as Deacon Jim Miller to run off homesteaders. Miller was dreaded in that part of Texas as a cold-blooded killer.

Hugh lay on his bed in an upstairs room, feverish, hurting from the wound. He tried to sleep, but someone kept firing a pistol from the front porch. At last, anger drove him out of bed and down the stairs. On the porch a man sat shooting birds from a telephone line. Hugh gave him a sound cussing and threatened to whip him. He stood only a little more than five feet tall and in his condition could not have whipped a lame Chihuahua dog.

Still angry, he went back inside and encountered the landlady. He asked her who that thoughtless son of a bitch on the porch was. She said, "Don't you know Jim Miller?"

Hugh said he recovered much more quickly than expected and returned to the ranch.

He and his brother Seth homesteaded land in the Winkler County sandhills near Kermit at about the turn of the last century. Years later that land became a productive oilfield.

As for Jim Miller, he met his final reckoning at the hands of a lynch mob in Oklahoma, far from the West Texas sands.

Late in his life Hugh attended a bull sale where another visitor was John Wayne. Henry Elder, editor of *Texas Hereford,* photographed the two together and used the picture on his magazine's cover. They looked a little like Mutt and Jeff, for Wayne was fully a head and a half the taller.

Hugh admitted, "Mr. Wayne, I never seen one of your movies, but I don't have to go to the picture show to know how things was. I was there."

Wayne represented the myth of the Old West, but Hugh Campbell was the reality.

Leo Richardson was a sheepman who ranched near Iraan, on the Pecos River. He was a fine example of a working cowboy who patiently pulled himself up by his own bootstraps and became a rancher of considerable renown. In his younger years he worked for various ranches which furnished food and housing. Foregoing comforts that most people considered necessities, he took the larger part of his wages in livestock rather than cash. At one point he owned a nice little flock of Angora goats, only to lose most of them in a cold rain. Stunned but not defeated, he started over. He managed eventually to build up a large registered Rambouillet sheep operation known all over the Texas sheep country.

After my novel *The Time It Never Rained* was published, he told me he had read all but the last chapter. The weather was dry at the time. He said he was saving the last chapter until it rained, because he felt sure I would let it rain at the end of the story. I did not have the heart to tell him that the last chapter was based on his experience with the Angora goats, and it was not going to end as he expected it to.

He had his successes, but he had his tragedies, too. One of his two sons, Leonard, died of a sudden heart attack in his twenties, working on an irrigation pump. The family had no idea of his heart trouble until a bottle of nitroglycerine pills was found in his pocket after his death. The surviving son, Rod, partnered with his father. Up in years, Leo suffered a series of strokes, each leaving him worse off than before. Unable to face another, he took his own life. The crowd at his funeral was so large that I could not get into the church. Along with dozens of others who had revered this remarkable man, I listened to the service on a loudspeaker outside.

I had the same experience at the funeral of Fred Earwood, who was a ranchman as well as manager of the wool and mohair warehouse in Sonora, Texas. Fred, like R. A. Halbert and several others in the Sonora area, was an early proponent of sound range management and soil conservation. He also promoted better sheep and finer wool among his warehouse's clients, to a point that Sonora could truthfully claim a major part of its offering comparable to the best of Australia's Merino fleeces. His wife, Mary, kept warehouse books for years without pay until federal wage and hour officials declared the practice illegal. She said she was just trying to keep costs down for the ranch customers, who too often had more costs than returns.

Fred was a thoughtful man who seldom had much to say until he had given a subject thorough study. On many occasions when I phoned him with a question, the line would fall silent. The first few times I thought the connection had been broken and would ask if he was still there. "I'm here," he would say. "I'm just thinking it over." I got used to the long, silent waits. When he finally answered my question, there was seldom anything more to ask.

Walter Britten was a professional auctioneer who specialized in registered cattle sales, primarily Herefords. Like most in the trade, he would often "roll" bids, taking fictitious bids out of the air to get the action started after an animal entered the ring. This usually worked, for someone in the crowd would offer a real bid, and the sale went on from there. But sometimes when things stalled, he would take a chance and roll bids to get the sale moving again. This could become embarrassing if no one took the bait.

For some reason I never understood or agreed with, as a newsman I was expected to help take bids at ringside. Several times I took a legitimate bid, then Walter would roll a few bids to pump the market. When no bona-fide bids followed, he had to back down. He would say to some imaginary person in the stands, "I'm sorry, sir. When you raised your hand I thought you were bidding." Then: "What was your last bid, Elmer?"

More often than not, I no longer remembered.

He once helped a little group of cattle breeders in a Central Texas county to form an association and conduct their first consignment sale. Few had ever sold at a registered auction before. Walter tried hard to get them all the money he could. One farmer was walking a bull around in the ring. The bidding had reached three hundred dollars, and Walter thought he might squeeze out a little more. He stopped his chant and said, "Mr. Smith, you don't sell bulls like this at home for three hundred dollars, do you?"

The farmer shook his head. "No, sir, about two hundred is the best I ever get."

"Sold!" Walter said.

O. H. McAlister was a colorful Hereford breeder at Big Spring. Tall, outgoing, and a master salesman, he took a load of sale bulls to the Fort Worth show every January. One time the show was in its final day, and three bulls remained unsold. He dreaded having to take them home, where he already had more bulls than he needed. A farmer came along and began giving the three animals a serious study.

"Mr. Mac," as he was often called, stepped up and began a snappy sales pitch.

The farmer asked, "How much do you want for them?"

"A thousand dollars apiece," McAlister said.

The farmer shook his head. "I'm afraid three hundred is about all I could afford." He started to walk away, but McAlister caught him.

"They're yours," he said. "Nobody can tell within seven hundred dollars what a bull is worth."

Raisers of registered cattle tend to be highly protective of their chosen breed. President Lyndon B. Johnson was a Hereford man. He tolerated no other breed on his LBJ Ranch. Indeed, his white-faces grazing along the blue Pedernales River made a beautiful scene of which he could justly be proud.

He was particular about other things, too. In 1960, when he was the vice-presidential running mate of John F. Kennedy, I was sent on a four-day farm tour with Johnson to report for the Harte-Hanks newspaper chain. I perceived very soon that his working staff was afraid of him. One secretary was near hysterics when her tape recorder tangled up and she failed to get his speech. The body of the several speeches he made each day was more or less the same, though he always led with something specific to the town or area where he spoke.

Lady Bird Johnson would sit nearby and tap on her wristwatch if she perceived that the speech was stretching too long, signaling for him to wrap it up.

A highlight of the trip for me was meeting Hubert Humphrey and Harry Truman, who saw my Stetson and asked, "Where in the hell did you get that hat?"

I noticed that when Johnson saw a camera aimed at him, he would make a photogenic gesture and hold it until he heard the shutter click. I saw also that he managed at some time during the four days to get each reporter off to one side, put an arm around his shoulder, give him an exclusive quote, and apply a thick layer of molasses, with plenty of butter. He did it to me, assuring me that I must be one of the finest reporters in Texas for an outstanding publisher like Houston Harte to entrust me with such an important assignment.

Shortly afterward I was helping take bids at a Hereford sale in Johnson City, LBJ's hometown. He came in with his entourage and sat down right in front of me, so close I could have shaken his hand if he had offered it. He didn't know me from Adam's off ox.

* * *

IF WE ARE FORTUNATE we may get to know a few people in a life-time who live beyond all our expectations of the term *character*. One such for me was cowboy cartoonist Ace Reid. We were friends for forty years. Ace's work is known to just about every cowboy and rancher from the Mississippi River to the Pacific. As a successor to the earlier J. R. Williams, creator of *Out Our Way,* he carved out a niche uniquely his own with his *Cowpokes* cartoons.

He grew up on his father's small ranch near Electra, Texas, west of Wichita Falls. He claimed he obtained his education at livestock auctions, where he went with his cattle trader dad, "Old Man Ace." As a youngster he liked to draw pictures. Serving in the Navy in World War II, he managed to get some sailor cartoons into a Navy publication. But what he liked best to draw was cowboys.

After the war he tried several occupations. None gave him the satisfaction he obtained from creating cowboy cartoons. He liked to tell about getting his start with Ed Bateman, who published a horse magazine in Fort Worth. Ace would draw a number of "roughs" in pencil, take them to Fort Worth, show them to Bateman, then return to Electra and finish in ink the ones Bateman approved. He would carry those back to Fort Worth. For this he was paid five dollars per cartoon.

"That easy money like to've killed me," he said.

His first real break came when he met Stanley Frank, who had just founded *West Texas Livestock Weekly* in San Angelo. The meeting resulted in a lifelong friendship and provided a steady outlet for Ace's work.

His second big break came from Houston Harte, publisher of the San Angelo *Standard-Times.* Perhaps remembering his own beginnings, Harte sensed an ambition that he admired. He helped Ace begin his own cartoon syndication program.

Like me, Ace was a shy young cowboy from the forks of the creek and found it a challenge to approach strangers. He purposely set about overcoming his reticence and making himself widely known. By strong will, over time he turned himself into a genuine, silver-plated extrovert. When he walked into a room with

a holler and a joke, everybody within hearing knew Ace Reid had
arrived. He and his wife, Madge, worked hard and traveled far to
develop cartoon outlets in country weeklies and several big dailies
across the West. They expanded this operation into cartoon books
and calendars. Ace made humorous after-dinner talks for stockmen's meetings and chambers of commerce, gaining a name recog-
nition that politicians might envy.

When I first met Ace, he drew one cartoon a week and spent the
rest of his time driving a little Volkswagen Beetle around the country, peddling his cartoon books and calendars in Western-wear
stores, saddle shops, auction sales, and the like. Eventually those
cartoons bought him a small ranch near Kerrville, Texas, and gave
him financial security for the first time in his life.

His father, Old Man Ace, was as much a character as his son.
After Ace Jr. bought his ranch and built a home on the edge of
Turtle Creek, he invited his dad to come see what he had. Walking
along the creek, Ace Jr. was called back to the house to answer a
telephone call. On his return, he found his father sitting on the
creekbank with tears in his eyes.

"Old Man Ace," he demanded, "what's the matter with you?"

The old man said, "Son, I've been a cowman all my life. I've
hunted water, I've hauled water, I've pumped water for thirsty
cows as far back as I can remember. And to see all this running to
waste is more than I can stand."

Old Man Ace once offered to take me out to eat at the Wag-
goner Ranch chuck wagon. He said he had worked on that ranch
in his youth, that he knew every cow trail and rabbit hole on the
place. So we drove out there, and he got us lost. He had not
counted on the many new fences and new roads that had been
built since his cowboy days.

On the last day of his life, Ace Sr. was in and out of a coma. He
was a staunch Democrat, and it was a presidential election day. He
would wake up and ask, "How are the Democrats doing, son?"
The Democrats were losing, but Ace Jr. lied to him. "They're winning, old man." Old Man Ace died smiling.

Ace Jr. had a habit of calling up friends in the middle of the night, often with some nutty idea that had just popped into his head. He got me out of bed once to announce that he was going to sponsor a cattle-sorting contest between a champion cutting horse and a helicopter. He added, "We'll do it in the Astrodome."

In his cartoons he developed a set of stock characters like the hapless ranchers Zeb and Jake, Honest Wilbur the horse trader, and tightwad banker Tufernal, sometimes spelled Tufernell. He had the cowboy psychology down pat, for he was one himself.

To launch an hour's conversation in ranch country one need only mention his favorite Ace Reid cartoon. Everybody seems to have several. Mine shows the minister at the church door, greeting his departing congregation at the end of services. To the uncomfortable rancher Jake, he says, "It's good to see you back. What is it this time, a drought or a break in the cattle market?"

A couple of times Ace drew Jake in a jail cell. One of the names scrawled on the wall was mine.

Among his best friends was Charlie Schreiner III, proud owner of the large YO Ranch near Kerrville. Ace delighted in embarrassing Charlie by putting a YO brand on the scrawniest, all-horns-and-hips, prickly pear-eating cows he drew.

Though he presented a carefree, quick-to-joke face to the public, Ace was more sensitive than he would have wanted to admit. He cherished his friends, especially those of long-standing. He was crying one day when he phoned to tell me he had just learned that Slim Pickens, the character actor, was dying. And he was devastated by the death of Hondo Crouch, his partner in countless practical jokes and nonsensical adventures.

As a sailor on a ship in a Japanese port, he had been exposed to radiation soon after the atomic bombs were dropped on Hiroshima and Nagasaki. A dozen years later he was diagnosed with leukemia, but he survived it. Perhaps that gave him his deep appreciation for life and his drive to squeeze as much pleasure as possible from each day that was left to him.

His last months were plagued by health problems. He asked

that after his death he be cremated and his ashes strewn over the ranch so that "any time an old cow reaches down for a bite of grass, I'll be there." His funeral at the ranch featured a cowboy hymn from old friend Cliff Teinert and a riderless horse with Ace's boots turned backward in the stirrups.

Another real character was Ben K. "Doc" Green, horse doctor and raconteur, an author of some renown. He was a likable rogue who never let facts get in the way of a good yarn, the kind of person you enjoy listening to even when you know he is pulling your leg. His credentials as a veterinarian were often questioned, along with his claim to have studied animal medicine in Scotland. Nevertheless, Doc went right on practicing despite the efforts of other veterinarians to get him prosecuted for operating without a valid license.

He was a natural storyteller of the highest rank. I have seen crowds gather around to listen to him hold forth in a hotel lobby. Once, after I had written several Western novels, he came to me for advice about getting a book published. I had some doubt about his ability to read, much less to write, but I told him what I knew. It didn't take long. After that, I went to *him* for advice, for he did indeed publish a book, a dozen or more in fact, starting with *Horse Trading*. He gained an enviable reputation as a literary primitive, like Grandma Moses in the art world.

He did not literally write his books. He told his stories to a stenographer, who took them down in shorthand, then typed them up for revision. That gave them a strong oral flavor that made a reader feel that he was listening to Doc telling the story in his own voice. His yarns had the ring of truth even when they played fast and loose with facts. He subscribed to the theory that if it didn't happen just that way, it should have.

He told me once, "You're writing fiction. You can keep making up stories as long as you live, but I'm going to run out of true facts."

He did not fit the popular image of a literary figure. Short, portly, and red-faced, he dressed like a cowboy and almost always seemed to sport a two- or three-day growth of whiskers. His voice could reach across a football field, especially when he laughed. He gloried in using that voice to embarrass some unlucky victim. He was a master of the insult.

He was doctoring animals in Fort Stockton, Texas, early in World War II. As I heard it, a local woman who considered herself an arbiter of social affairs decided he needed a radio so he could keep up with the war news. Doc lived a bachelor life under the most rustic of circumstances, sleeping on a cot and rolling up his blankets every morning like a cowboy out with a chuck wagon. His less than gracious response to her offer was that she could keep her goddamned radio; he didn't need it. She brought him one anyway and received a blistering lecture about the virtue of minding her own business. Shortly afterward her husband accosted Doc. He said, "Dr. Green, sir, I am given to understand that you have offered insult to my wife."

Doc pleaded innocence. "I don't see where I insulted her none. All I said was that that nosy old woman could make Jesus Christ use God's name in vain."

The husband mulled it over and replied, "I see no quarrel with that."

Doc considered himself a connoisseur of cowboy art. Once at the National Cowboy Hall of Fame in Oklahoma City he was studying a Western scene when the artist announced himself and asked what Doc thought of his painting.

Doc gave him an evil eye—he was accomplished at that—and said, "If you'd chop it up into little bitty pieces, that frame would make good kindling."

He seemed to relish any opportunity to be outrageous. He once told me, "I am not always agreed with, but I am seldom misunderstood."

He wrote a book called *The Color of Horses* and asked Darol Dickinson to illustrate it with paintings of horses in varied colorations. Dickinson was one of the nation's foremost horse painters. He put his heart into the project and felt that it was some of the best work he had ever done. He laid out the paintings for Doc's inspection and was floored by the negative response.

Doc scowled and said, "Anybody who can't do better than that ought to be out painting barns. Take them back and do them over."

Dickinson told me he studied the paintings time and again. The longer he looked at them, the better they seemed. He saw no way to improve them, so he did nothing. He simply waited a few weeks, then called Doc back for another inspection.

Doc snorted. "That's better. You ought to've done them that way the first time."

Dickinson never told him the truth.

Doc had several physical ailments. Once he poured an assortment of pills into the palm of his hand and told me what each was for: one for his heart, one for his liver, one for his diabetes, and one to offset the harmful effects of the others.

The last time I saw him was at a benefit steer roping. Clean-shaven and wearing a new suit, he said he was on his way to Kansas for a series of book signings. About a week later he was found dead in his car on a Kansas roadside, victim of a heart attack.

A month or so afterward I visited a bookstore in Austin. On the wall was a large photo of Doc. The proprietress told me he was to have had a book signing in her store after his return from Kansas. She had not had the heart to take his picture down.

One of my mentors was my high school journalism teacher, Paul Patterson, whose friendship I have continued to cherish. If I had a mentor among professional Western writers, other than those whose work I studied without their knowledge, it was S. Omar Barker of Las Vegas, New Mexico. He was a prolific contributor not only to Western pulp magazines but to slick publications like the *Saturday Evening Post*. His short Western poems showed up in everything from country weeklies and horse magazines to *The Wall Street Journal*. He was known as the "poet lariat" of New Mexico. Perhaps his best-remembered poem is "A Cowboy's Christmas Prayer," reprinted countless times and once recorded by

Jimmy Dean. A member of a pioneer ranching family, he was also known as "the sage of Sapello," pronounced SAPPY-o. Bilingual, he once served a term in the state legislature.

Omar's fiction almost always had a touch of humor, which I found refreshing. Too many traditional Westerns have been gray in mood and humorless. He made a practice of keeping tear sheets of his stories and poems, getting them bound when he accumulated enough to make a book. If the leftover pages contained stories by his friends, he mailed them out as a courtesy. He sent me a number of mine.

We had corresponded, though we had not met. One evening about suppertime I received a telephone call. The voice said, "Elsa and I are on our way home from Kerrville, and we are spending the night here in San Angelo. Would you mind if we came out for a visit?"

Mind? I would have walked halfway to Las Vegas just to meet him.

We spent a long and pleasant evening. He and Elsa—she was a writer, too—gave me several pointers on writing that I still use after more than fifty years. I found him tall and lanky, with a soft voice and friendly eyes. His parents had moved to New Mexico from Texas, so his accent could have passed for Texan with just a tiny inflection of Hispanic. He was a skilled storyteller, on paper or in person. With provocation he would tell slightly shady jokes that did not classify as vulgar, though they would make Elsa frown. He was a crowd favorite at Western Writers of America conventions for his warm personality and his way with a story. Both he and Elsa served terms as WWA presidents, the only husband and wife ever to do so.

Omar claimed that he was trying to finish writing a book entitled *The S.O.B.s of San Miguel County,* but every time he thought it was done, another came to mind.

The Barkers were a literary family. Omar's older brother, Elliott, was for a long time the state game warden and wrote several books on outdoor life. He claimed he had met his wife when as a young game warden he arrested her for fishing without a license. He had her released on probation and in his custody, where she remained ever afterward. He was still leading horseback trail rides into the Sangre de Cristo Mountains when he was well into his eighties.

Glenn Vernam was an Oregon cowboy who discovered he had a knack for writing stories. While working for ranch wages he began selling to Western pulp magazines. He used to ride a bus to the WWA conventions, carrying a suitcase made of cowhide with the tail still attached. He was bowlegged and wore a round-crowned old cowboy hat of a style that had gone out in the 1920s. He wore glasses with lenses that looked as thick as the bottom of a Coca-Cola bottle. Behind those glasses was a story of courage and determination more poignant than any fiction he ever wrote.

He had spent years amassing factual material that enabled him to write a lengthy book entitled *Man on Horseback,* the long history of man's use of the horse for work and in warfare. The writing done, he set out to draw his own illustrations but was plagued by severe cataracts in both eyes. This was at a time when cataract surgery was still new and hazardous. He was told an operation might cure his problem, but there was a fifty-fifty chance that it might blind him instead. On the other hand, if he did nothing the cataracts would soon blind him anyway. Weighing the odds, he decided that at all costs he wanted to complete the book that would be the biggest achievement of his life.

He could no longer see well enough with normal glasses to draw the pictures. He took a cardboard core from a roll of toilet paper and taped a magnifying glass to one end. Holding the other end to one eye, he laboriously completed the drawings.

The project done, he submitted to the operation. It was successful. With help of those thick glasses, he had vision in both eyes.

Nelson C. Nye described himself as "the baron of blood and thunder," and indeed action was the hallmark of his Westerns. He was a scrawny little man who dressed like a professional frontier gambler in a Hollywood movie. He had a black mustache, wore vests that could light up a dark room, and he always seemed to be smoking a pungent black cigar that could kill at twenty paces. He was frequently involved in a scrap with one publisher or another, convinced that he was being cheated out of royalties he was due.

If a WWA convention turned dull, Nels could be counted on to bring it back to life. He loved to stir up an argument, then stand back with a sly grin and hold the coats. He was like a kid who throws a cat and dog together just to see the fight.

He wrote a good Western, too.

James Propp and his wife, Dixie, were regulars at early WWA conventions. Natives of Oklahoma, they were teaching school in California and had to stay on their best behavior to avoid running afoul of a strict school board. At the conventions, far from home, they felt free to relax and enjoy themselves. Eventually, however, they stopped coming to WWA.

After many years, we were having a convention in Springdale, Arkansas, and I spotted James in the hotel lobby. I walked up and visited with him a few minutes, then realized I had not seen Dixie. I asked about her.

His face fell a little. He said, "I regret to tell you that Dixie died the twelfth of this month." He paused, then added, "I've got her out in the car."

Seeing my astonished look, he explained that Dixie had expressed a wish that she be cremated and her ashes buried beside her parents in her hometown, Muskogee, Oklahoma. James complied with her wishes and took her ashes to Muskogee. Unfortunately he arrived on a Sunday and could find no one with whom to make arrangements. So he brought Dixie to the convention, just as he had in the past.

I saw him again the following year and asked if he got Dixie buried all right. He said, "Yes, I buried her on the Fourth of July. Dixie always loved fireworks, so I set off some firecrackers on her grave. Ran everybody out of the cemetery."

*   *   *

IN THE 1950S AND 1960s the federal government had a temporary
worker program to bring Mexican nationals into the country for
agricultural labor. The last year I was with the *Standard-Times,* I
was sent to Mexico to do a series of articles on bracero farm- and
ranch workers, where they came from, and what they did with the
money earned in the United States. The Pecos cotton growers' association lent me their bilingual trouble shooter, Orson Hawkins,
as guide and interpreter. He had grown up in a Mormon colony at
Colonia Dublán, near Casas Grandes in Chihuahua. We spent several days talking to men who had been to the States under the
bracero program.

We visited a labor camp in Chihuahua City where men gathered
in hopes of being chosen to go north. As we drove up to the gate
we met a couple of frustrated men who told us they had been rejected because they did not have money to bribe the officials. We
interviewed the camp's administrator and asked him point-blank
about the bribery charges. He assured us that such a thing was
never done and that nobody had to pay to be sent to the United
States as a bracero.

As we were about to leave, one of his assistants came in with a
stack of papers and, not knowing who we were, said quietly in
Spanish, "These men have all paid."

I can understand why reporters who deal constantly with politics and crime might become cynical. Most ranchers and farmers
I knew were honest, sometimes to a fault. However, exceptions
arose from time to time.

Billy Sol Estes had established himself as a boy wonder of agriculture. I had gotten to know him casually because my reporting
often took me to Pecos, his home base. He had become heavily involved in many aspects of the West Texas irrigated cotton industry, worked his way far up in political circles, and was influential in
church matters as well. He even had a reputation as a lay preacher.

That was all on the surface, for everybody to see. Beneath the
surface, his enterprises had disturbing aspects. He would approach a
successful businessman and propose either to buy into partnership

or to establish a competing firm and squeeze him out. He did this to my cousin, Joe Bob Kelton, who had a thriving cement business, lining irrigation ditches. He did it to a local mortuary. He tried to do it to the local newspaper but thereby set off a chain of events that brought him down.

Publisher Barney Hubbs did not choose to sell. Marj Carpenter, a reporter for Hubbs, began investigating dark rumors about irregularities in courthouse records. She discovered widespread fraud involving mortgages on nonexistent anhydrous ammonia fertilizer tanks. Marj broke the story, and soon Estes was on the national networks' evening news. President Kennedy mentioned him by name at a news conference and promised that federal authorities were "on Mr. Estes's tail."

Because I was the only *Standard-Times* reporter who had known Estes, I became the unofficial "Estes editor." For several weeks I spent more time in Pecos than at home.

A rumor spread that Estes had skipped to South America, and a banner headline in a Dallas newspaper speculated that this was so. Texas attorney general Will Wilson conducted a hearing in Pecos, drawing dozens of reporters including network television personnel to the Reeves County courthouse. I was sitting near the door when Estes's attorney tapped me on the shoulder and beckoned me out into the hall, along with Cope Routh, who was writing for the Midland *Reporter-News*. He said, "If you-all will come with me and bring your cameras, I'd like to show you something."

He led us down the street and up a set of stairs to his office. There sat Billy Sol Estes. The attorney told us, "I just want you to bear witness that Mr. Estes has not gone anywhere."

The lowly San Angelo and Midland papers had a scoop on the national media that day.

The Estes scandal shook the Pecos area like an earthquake, triggering a rash of bankruptcies, at least a couple of violent deaths, the derailing of political careers, and a prison sentence for Estes. It also proved the old adage that the messenger who brings bad news suffers for it. Marj Carpenter certainly did. Many people blamed her more than Estes for the financial turmoil that engulfed Pecos. The pressure became unbearable, and she felt compelled to move away. She eventually became a nationally honored church leader.

A few years ago I attended a book signing in Granbury, Texas, with several other writers. As I finished scrawling my signature I looked up. There stood Billy Sol Estes with his daughter Pam, who lived there. He remembered me, and bought one of my books.

One of the nicest, friendliest old gentlemen I ever met owned a cattle feedlot and grain elevator in South Texas. He had many friends and customers who had done business with him for years and trusted him implicitly. Some of his feedlot clients left it up to him to buy the cattle, feed them, and sell them. They did not even have to look at the cattle if they did not choose to.

But one day two customers came to look at the same time and discovered that they both owned the same pen of cattle. It turned out that most of the cattle in the feedlot had multiple owners, each unaware of the others. Moreover, the elevator held less grain than the books showed. It was not on the scale of the Estes fiasco, but it caused serious financial losses for many of the old fellow's customers.

Soon after I started working at the *Standard-Times,* I covered three registered cattle sales on three consecutive days, each on a different ranch. I noticed the first day that Cadillacs and Lincolns outnumbered pickups, which gave me a quick clue to the clientele. The next day's sale drew the same kind of crowd and many of the same buyers as the day before. Prices looked high for the time, some heifers selling for as much as a thousand dollars. The third day was a repetition of the first two, many of the same people, the same high prices. The couple selling on the final day had bought cattle at the other two sales. I finally worked up the nerve to ask why they were buying cattle from other people when they were selling their own.

I was let in on one of the trade secrets. The answer: "We buy thousand-dollar heifers from them, and they buy thousand-dollar heifers from us. That raises the average for all of us."

It also meant that the uninformed and unwary were persuaded that these were the true market values and paid accordingly. I remembered something I had read about Jack Haley, the comedian who played the tin man in *The Wizard of Oz*. He took a plunge in the registered cattle business and got his fingers burned all the way to the elbow. He declared, "And I thought there were phonies in show business."

He had met the pros.

In contrast, an unusual example of complete though painful honesty was the situation years ago at Barnhart, Texas. A Midwestern farmer had bought a large number of lambs from several ranchers in the Ozona area, planning to feed them on home-grown corn. The lambs were driven afoot some thirty miles along a laned driveway from Ozona to the shipping pens. Unbeknownst to the ranchers, rain had brought up patches of poisonous weeds along the route. The lambs reached Barnhart, were weighed, and considered delivered. Then, while the new owner waited for the train that was to carry them away, they began dropping, dying from delayed effect of the toxic plants.

The farmer was ruined, or thought he was. But the ranchers discussed the situation among themselves and told him, "They were our lambs when they ate the weeds. The dead ones are still ours."

The surviving lambs were reweighed and shipped to the Midwest. The others were buried. The ranchers lost a great deal of money, but they had gained a grateful customer who would keep coming back for years.

SIXTEEN

ANNI HAD TO WORK her way through homesickness after coming
to Texas. Struggling to adjust to a different language, a new life,
and people she had never known before, she stuck to me as closely
as she could. That was not easy for either of us, because I had
work to do and was also trying to learn how to be a writer. The
heat that first summer was severe for her, though Gary seemed to
take it in stride. He rode a horse almost every day, and that kept
him happy. He had a child's adaptability and was a fast learner.
Within a few months he was chattering along with classmates
without a trace of accent.

Anni never lost her accent. People meeting her for the first time
often try to guess its source, for it is a unique combination of Austrian mountain speech and Texas drawl.

In 1954 I took her, Gary, and little Steve to Austria to visit her
family for the first time after seven years. She was pregnant with
Kathy and due in December. We feared if we did not go soon, she
might never see her aging mother and father again. Their only
contact had been by letter. The Lipps had no telephone. Not many
people in small-town and rural Austria did at that time.

Gary had long since become Americanized and did not want to
go. The high point of his life had been summers at the ranch with

An early family picture: Elmer, Anni, Gary and Steve

his Granddad and Grandmother Kelton. He lived for the last day of school and had to be dragged back in from the country the day before it started in fall. At thirteen, he had become one of Dad's top cowboys, a better one than I had been. We insisted that he go, however. His Austrian grandparents would be shattered if he didn't, for he had practically lived with them his first few years.

We flew into Salzburg. Steve, a few months short of three, proved true to family tradition by becoming airsick on the first leg of the trip, though he soon got over it. From Salzburg we took the train to Ebensee. The cars were crowded, so Gary and I stood outside, between them. Inside, Anni sat with Steve in her lap. Opposite her, two chattering middle-aged Fraus stuffed themselves with candy. Ann's clothing and the fact that she spoke English to the youngster marked her as American. Not realizing that she understood, the two women began discussing everything they saw wrong with Americans. After they had run on for a while she broke in, speaking the Austrian dialect: "Is this a through train?"

Their faces reddened. Soon they were sharing their candy with Steve like old friends. He had been unable to comprehend why everybody talked so funny, but he understood how to accept a gift.

The homecoming was joyous though tearful. It was disconcerting to see how much older Anni's parents looked. They were disappointed that Gary could not talk to them at first, for he had forgotten most of his mother tongue. However, he began picking up or remembering enough of the language that the curtain between them soon fell away. Once he got past his initial longing for the ranch, he enjoyed the visit. Unlike Steve, he was old enough to remember it in later years.

Staying with the family, and now considered part of it, I became better acquainted than before. Frequently I accompanied Herr Lipp to one of his favorite haunts, the *Weinhalle,* where wine was dispensed, or to a *Gasthaus*, where beer was the featured beverage. Once the family spent a carefree evening in the *Weinhalle*. Outside in the fresh air, Herr Lipp felt impelled to sing. Frau Lipp tried to hush him up, but to no avail. While he happily serenaded the neighborhood, she walked home ahead of him, hoping no one would recognize that they belonged together.

It seemed perfectly natural to be back in Austria. It was almost as if I had never left, though there had been much change. Seven years had brought a pleasant measure of prosperity to Ebensee. Gone was the dark mood of the immediate postwar period. The drabness had been scrubbed away or painted over. There seemed to be music everywhere, for Austria is the land of Mozart and Strauss and Lehar. Most of the Lipp men are musicians.

We visited with Anni's kin and caught up on seven years' happenings. The family fawned over Gary and Steve and complimented Anni on how well and happy she looked. Though it was

June, Gary had a snowball fight with his Uncle Louis atop the Feuerkogel, and Steve built a little snowman. Anni wore a dirndl dress for the first time in seven years, the kind of dress she wore the evening I met her. It reminded me, as if I needed reminding, of why I had fallen in love with her.

The problem with such a trip is the farewells as it draws to an end. It was a cloudy, dark day, befitting the gloom we all felt as the family gathered at the train station. We knew it was unlikely that Anni would ever see her parents again. Still, we had no way of knowing that it would be twenty-two years before we returned to Austria a second time. Gary and Steve have never been back. Kathy, an invisible member of our little family group at the time, has been twice.

LIKE THE TRAILER BEFORE it, the frame house on San Antonio Street seemed to get smaller and smaller. After several years of having his own room, Gary had to share it when Steve became big enough not to fall off his bunk bed. Kathy's arrival compounded the space problem.

Stretching our credit to the limit and then some, we contracted to have neighbor David Howton build a new house for us. Just as the first had looked like a mansion compared to the trailer, this one in the beginning seemed huge and empty.

It was finished in the spring of 1957, just as the long 1950s drought was breaking. Our front yard sloped downward, and the soil brought in to cover it repeatedly washed into the street. We kept shoveling it back each time the rain fell, always losing some and having to bring in more dirt. Anni worked hard digging shallow ditches and planting Augustine grass runners, some having to be redone several times before they finally took hold and stabilized the soil.

Though my drought novel did not find a publisher at the time, I was having better luck with paperback original Westerns. They helped swing the $111 monthly payments on the new home. We looked forward to the time, twenty-five years down the road, when the house would be free of debt and we would no longer face those high payments.

Eventually the insurance alone would cost more than that.

Mother and Dad were still at the McElroy Ranch, and so was Gary the day after school was out. Dad had become the general manager, but that burdened him with extra work beyond what he already had as foreman. More often than not, he was shorthanded. He had streamlined and mechanized the ranch operation about as much as he could. Physically, he was wearing himself out.

For several years my brother Myrle and his wife, Ann, had been living at Sand Camp, where we had first gone when Dad went to work for the ranch in 1929. It was quietly understood that he would one day take over Dad's place in running the ranch. But that was not to be.

The Franco-Wyoming stockholders decided in the early 1960s to liquidate their holdings and divide the proceeds. Many being of a later generation than the original owners, they had no sentimental attachment to land or to company. For a couple of years Dad patiently showed the ranch to first one prospective buyer, then another. Few remained interested long. It was not a scenic place, nor was it green for more than occasional short periods. In truth, it was at the edge of the Chihuahuan Desert, and showed it.

For a time he entertained the idea of buying the ranch himself. He hoped if we all pooled our resources we might be able to handle an adequate down payment for the surface rights. But our resources did not add up to enough, and he reluctantly abandoned the idea. Physically, it would have been too much for him anyway, though he would not have admitted it. He was ill, ground down by worry and hard labor.

Eventually, in 1965, the corporation sold the underground mineral rights to an oil company and the surface rights to a group of land investors, along with the livestock.

Counting the cattle was a melancholy event. Because of drought, the herd had been cut to about eleven hundred head, a large part of these being young Hereford heifers kept with an eye to the future.

Buck Kelton *(on horseback)* **with French stockholders**
at the McElroy Ranch (1950)

The pastures were worked one by one, the cattle penned and counted. The switch ends of their tails were bobbed off to show they had already been tallied and to avoid their being counted twice. The hair would grow out again.

With the sale of the ranch, all of us who had grown up there felt as if our roots had been severed. We felt like strangers in what had long been home.

Dad felt it even more keenly than we knew. After the ranch was turned over to new owners, he and Mother put their belongings in storage and rented an apartment in San Angelo while they looked for a modest place to buy for their retirement years. Earlier, Dad had always seemed strong enough to survive anything that came at him. His recent illness had shown how vulnerable he really was. For thirty-six years his life had revolved around the McElroy Ranch, and suddenly that anchor was gone.

He was miserable in town. On days when he had nowhere to

go, he paced the floor like a caged lion. I had seen other retired ranchers, accustomed to hard work and heavy responsibilities, try in vain to adjust to a life of idleness. Most did not survive long, and we feared that he would not, either. Fortunately he was able to break the monotony by visiting ranches listed for sale.

One day a local real estate dealer told me, "I've got a place that would be just right for your dad. It's pretty much like the McElroy Ranch. It's sorry as hell, but it's pretty good."

I thought the description apt but didn't feel at his age that Dad should struggle with any more desert country.

He and Mother found a likely little ranch near the small town of May, north of Brownwood. Compared to the Jigger Y it was tiny, less than two square miles, but it had more grass than several McElroy pastures put together. A pretty little creek ran through the middle of it, the water clear and cool. An almost-new frame house, shaded by huge live-oak trees, had large picture windows on the front and side.

Dad was pleased with the land, and Mother was pleased with the house, a better one than she had known in all her married life. I drove him to Dallas to finalize the papers. His eyes were brighter than they had been in a long time. He was like a kid in a candy store.

Sixty-five years old, he had finally achieved every cowboy's dream: a ranch of his own. It was large enough to keep him as busy as he wanted to be but small enough not to become a burden. It gave him a new lease on life. Had he been able to buy the McElroy Ranch, it probably would have killed him, financially as well as physically, for Crane and Upton counties seemed to remain in a perpetual drought.

After fifteen years I had left the *Standard-Times*. I sensed that I had reached a glass ceiling or was close to it. The Texas Sheep and Goat Raisers Association offered me the editorship of their monthly magazine at a salary I doubted I would ever reach on the newspaper.

Dad counseled against the move, arguing among other things that my job at the *Standard-Times* was secure. His bitter experience during the Depression had taught him to value security above most other considerations. Time proved him right about the change in jobs, but not for the reason he thought. I had a pleasant association with the association directors and the membership, but at heart I was a writer, not a salesman. On the magazine I spent most of my time desperately trying to sell enough advertising to pay the printer and cover the payroll. Moreover, the sheep and goat industry was declining because of indifferent wool and mohair markets.

After about four years I began looking for something else to do, for fiction writing had not become lucrative enough to support my family. One day I went with Stanley Frank, publisher of *Livestock Weekly,* to watch a branding demonstration on the Moore Ranch near Eldorado. He offered me an associate editorship. I accepted on the spot. It was one of the happiest career decisions I ever made.

Stanley was almost ten years my elder, short, bespectacled, a former cowboy who had grown up in Wyoming sheep camps and on a ranch near Barnhart, Texas. He had founded his weekly paper in 1949, literally on a shoestring. Earlier, he had worked for livestock publications that catered to registered cattle breeders. The hype and show business aspects pervading that segment of the industry disillusioned him. He decided if he ever had a publication of his own it would be devoted to the bonafide rancher at the forks of the creek. He found several West Texas stockmen who liked his idea and backed him with enough money to buy a carload of paper and set him up with a printer.

He named his publication *West Texas Livestock Weekly* but later eliminated the first part of the name because his circulation had expanded far beyond West Texas. It became simply *Livestock Weekly.* Initially he sold subscriptions for five dollars a year. Because we resembled each other a little, I was often approached by people trying to give me a $5.00 bill for a subscription. I hated to turn them down.

With blood, sweat, and guts, he put that paper on its feet, filling a niche no one else was serving. By the time I joined him the paper was about twenty years old and financially successful, with heavy circulation across the Southwest and Midwest among livestock feeders and sheep, goat, and cattle ranchers.

He no longer had to solicit advertising. It came to him at a rate that astonished me. He told me never to ask for an ad, but not to turn one down if it was offered.

Though he often talked in the easy vernacular of the cowboy, he was a stickler for proper grammar and correct spelling in the newspaper. By the time he finished editing someone else's work, it was likely to have his pencil marks all over it.

He launched cowboy cartoonist Ace Reid's career, and he gave several other promising writers their first consistent outlets in print. They included John Erickson, whose *Hank the Cowdog* books became a sensation with schoolchildren. Erickson once referred to the weekly as "the cowboy's *Wall Street Journal*." Another writer Stanley encouraged was Baxter Black, highly sought-after cowboy poet and humorist. Old friend Monte Noelke has written a weekly column for more than fifty years. I always suspected that Stanley wished for a literary career himself and therefore promoted talent when he saw it in others.

In the twenty-two years that I worked with and for him, he never gave me more than half a dozen specific assignments. He left it to me to ferret out my own stories and feature articles. In that search I could travel anywhere I wanted to go, handy when I needed to visit some specific place for research on a novel.

Stanley was complex and sometimes unpredictable. I sized him up each morning to get a sense of his mood if I intended to broach some new idea. Most days he was agreeable to about anything I suggested, but now and again he had days when he would not give a dime to see an ant pull a freight train.

The newspaper was his baby, his life's blood. He would not have sold it for any amount of money, though there were times when deadline pressure became so intense that I could almost sense an electrical field building around him. He rarely took a vacation except during the two weeks we closed down at Christmas. He almost never missed being on hand to see the paper put to bed on Wednesday afternoon.

He took slowly and reluctantly to computers. To the end, he wrote on an upright typewriter of World War II vintage. Only when illness forced retirement of the last man in town who would repair a linotype machine did he consent to start composing the newspaper on a computer.

He was a traditionalist, though he learned to fly after a couple of close calls on the highway. Most of his years at *Livestock Weekly* he flew his own plane over the Southwest. He was an expert flier, though not as good a driver. There was always a risk that he might kill himself on the way to the airport.

His passions, beyond *Livestock Weekly,* were flying and golf, which helped ease some of his stress. He enjoyed frequent chances to be a cowboy again, working cattle and sheep on a ranch he owned in partnership with genial, business-savvy Fred Ball.

I retired from the newspaper in 1990 because I had so many demands on my time that I could no longer do justice to them all. Stanley worked a few more years but was increasingly handicapped by emphysema resulting from heavy smoking. Tethered to an oxygen tank at home, he nevertheless wrote a column for the weekly just days before he died. Readers still feel his presence because one of his early columns is reprinted in each issue. They still seem topical though they may have been written forty or fifty years ago.

Stanley's son, Robert, manages the paper. Our son, Steve, is editor. Steve has written two nonfiction books, one a history of the century-old Renderbrook-Spade Ranch, the other a history of the Texas Farm Bureau Federation. Gary attended Angelo State University and Texas Tech University, then made a career working in the cattle feedlot industry. Kathy has spent most of her adult life as a loan officer.

All three of my brothers remained close to the livestock industry. Myrle and his wife, Ann, who met in college, bought a stock

Five generations: Martha Barnes, Neta Holland,
Bea Kelton, Elmer Kelton, Steve Kelton

farm at May, near our parents' place. He raised cattle, did commercial welding, and remained a competitive roper. Hardly a weekend passed from spring to fall that he did not haul a horse to an arena somewhere. When he became older and no longer fast enough on his feet to compete with younger cowboys at calf roping, he turned to team roping. It did not require him to leave the saddle. He was in strong demand as a heeler, looping the steer's hind feet.

He kept a dark sense of humor. He was driving home one winter night and lost control on an icy bridge. The pickup and trailer careened against the guardrail on one side, then slid across and struck the other. The trailer turned over and spilled his horse out

The Kelton family, Christmas (1940)

onto the pavement, skinning him. When I asked later how the horse was doing, Myrle said, "He's all right, but he won't get into a trailer anymore until he sees who's driving."

He and Ann have two sons. Shane is an engineer, Joel a mechanic. Neither followed their father into the cowboy profession.

Because most people called my wife Ann rather than Anni, Mother had two daughters-in-law with the same given name. She solved that problem by referring to them as Ann One and Ann Two.

Bill, my second brother, and his wife, Pat, taught school at Monahans, Texas, for more than thirty years. She inherited an East Texas stock farm at Atlanta, near Texarkana. During his years in Monahans, Bill kept a horse or two and pitched in to help rancher friends work cattle on many weekends. He never gave up being a cowboy. He and Pat have three sons. Bill became a lawyer, Sam a dealer in oilfield equipment, Ted a banker.

Gene, the youngest, still is best known by his nickname, Boob. His wife, Peggy, was a hometown girl. Gene ranches between McCamey and Rankin, about thirty miles from the McElroy Ranch where he grew up. He served many years as a county commissioner. He is more likely to work his cattle on a homemade dune buggy than on horseback. He and Peggy have three daughters. Luann raises goats. Barbara and Robin teach school, but they and their husbands live on the land.

Dad had more than ten active years on the little ranch at May, years he might not have survived if he remained at the McElroy or tried to retire in town with nothing to do. Eventually a series of strokes struck him down. He finished his life in a nursing home, most of the time not recognizing his family. Pneumonia came to him as a friend just before his seventy-ninth birthday.

This is a solemn aspect seldom given much attention in books romanticizing the cowboy life. Cowboys do not stay young. They grow old, they get sick, and they die. It is sad to see an old cowboy, too stove up or too ill to continue the active lifestyle he has lived and loved, spending his final days wasting away in the terminal boredom of a rented room or lying helpless in a nursing home.

Mother lived alone in the ranch house for thirteen years after Dad's death. She drove ten miles once a week to play the piano for religious services in a nursing home. Though her eyesight faded, by her own choice she maintained a high level of independence. She went grocery shopping with Shane's wife, Valerie, the day she died, succumbing afterward to a sudden heart attack. She was two weeks short of eighty-nine.

From the time I was a boy, she never wavered in her firm support for whatever life choices her sons made.

With Dad, at least where I was concerned, it was hard to know. Even after the years I had spent as an agricultural reporter and fiction writer, I never was sure what he thought about my career. We talked of many things, especially when illness began to bring him down. After his first stroke my brothers and I took turns spending nights with him in his hospital room. I urged him to retell old stories I had heard in boyhood and recorded many hours on tape. He helped me get the details right on a few scenes where my memory was hazy, like a colt-castration sequence and a windmill raising.

Yet he never said anything to me to indicate whether or not he approved of my life choices. I harbored an uneasy feeling that he might never have gotten over his disappointment in my youthful efforts to become a competent cowboy.

Years after Dad's death, one of his longtime friends said Dad had often told him, though he had never told me, that he was well pleased with what I had done with my life. I wish I could have heard it from Dad himself, but I understand. I can talk to my own sons and daughter about many things, but pride seems hard to articulate.

A horse taken from the place to which he has long been accustomed will often try to go back. At the least he will stand against the fence and stare off in the direction of his former home. Though Dad was contented on the new ranch at May, to the end he longed for the McElroy Ranch despite the hard work and stress that came near killing him there. But he never went back, not even for a visit. I guess it would have been too painful.

I returned not long ago to see the old place. No one lives anymore at the headquarters where we boys grew up and where our parents spent most of thirty-six years. The buildings that have not been demolished are falling into ruin. Loose cattle roam the yard that we worked so hard to keep neat and clean. Remembering how green and bright and new the place appeared when we first went there more than seventy years ago, I felt as if I were watching the slow death of an old friend.

Dad's instincts were right. In many cases it is better not to go back.

OVER THE YEARS, ANNI and I have visited Austria more than a dozen times. Though both of us love that beautiful country, the incentive for returning has diminished. She has outlived her brothers and sisters. Time there has moved on without us so that we no longer feel so much at home. She built a new life in Texas, and here she prefers to be.

We are celebrating sixty years of marriage despite having started as a bookish ranch kid from the Crane County sandhills and a

**Elmer and Anni in traditional
Austrian costume (1981)**

German-speaking Fräulein from the Austrian Alps. From the beginning, we knew we faced unique challenges, including the language problem and the sharp contrast between her home in the old country and the life we were creating together in Texas. To a large extent we met these by ignoring them, hoping they would go away.

Most of them did.

by Anni Lipp Kelton

FEED A STRAY, and you can't get rid of it. I fed an American soldier an apple strudel, and he kept coming back.

Everything started with a simple errand for my parents. I had
no reason to suspect it would change my life. We lived in a salt-
factory town called Ebensee, in the mountain-and-lake region of
Upper Austria. The evening of October 14, 1945, my mother and
father asked me to walk down to the dock and see what time a passenger boat would leave the next morning to carry them across the
lake to market in Gmunden.

He walked up as I read the bulletin board. I paid no attention at
first. He was just another GI, one of many stationed in Ebensee for
a time after the war. When he first spoke to me, I didn't understand what he said. I spoke no English. He spoke only a little broken German.

I didn't trust him. Everybody said don't talk to the soldiers. But
something about him made me listen. He asked my name and told
me his, though the name Elmer Kelton meant nothing to me then.
He asked if he could walk me home. I saw no harm so long as that
was all there would be to it. We talked in a mixture of German and
sign language. When we reached the garden gate he asked what

time I would be up the next day. It would be six, but I told him nine o'clock.

Mother looked out from an upstairs window, saw us standing together, and ordered me into the house. I thought that would be the end of it, but the next morning at nine o'clock he knocked at the door. I don't remember exactly what was in my mind, perhaps just curiosity. I let him in. We talked while I baked an apple strudel.

We were a poor working family. We did not have much before the war, and we had even less during the war. Things were still hard after the war was over. But at least we could afford an apple strudel.

He liked it and kept coming back. Soldiers did not have a good reputation. I didn't trust him, but still I sort of liked him. I had a fatherless five-year-old son, Gerhard. Elmer gave him chewing gum, and the boy became fond of him. I did, too, more and more as time went by.

My parents were suspicious of him but began to be at ease with his visiting me.

I told him about my life. I started to Catholic girls' school when I was six. When I was fifteen I went to work at the *Gasthaus* next door. The boss was a beautiful woman but mean to her employees. She did a lot of complaining and did not pay much. When her father-in-law was sick she told me to bring some holy water, but she did not want me to waste time from work by going all the way to the church for it. She said to get it from the fountain down the street. No one would know the difference.

Germany already had rationing before it annexed Austria in 1938. German tourists would come in with one suitcase and leave with three, loaded with sugar, coffee, flour, and other staples. After annexation, rationing started overnight in Austria. One day you could buy anything you had money for. The next day you could not buy a needle and thread.

The time came when Germany began drafting young women for work camps, where they were expected not only to work but to "entertain" the German soldiers. Having a son saved me from going

The Lipp family. Gerhard *(front row, center)* wears lederhosen that
his grandfather had made as a keepsake of Austria.

because mothers with children under three years old were exempted. Hitler encouraged young women to have babies because the boys would someday grow up to be soldiers. He must have thought he would live forever and would continue to need an army.

I got a job at a military hospital in Gmunden, mostly working in the kitchen, waiting on tables, and things like that. I scrubbed floors so the German officers could have their parties. The longer the war went on, the less we had to work with but the more that was demanded of us. The cook went to another hospital, and I had to start cooking. I knew nothing about it.

It was too far to go home every day, so Mother and Dad took care of my son. I had no bicycle, and a car was out of the question. I went home by train or boat whenever I had the chance.

Mother and Dad raised a couple of pigs, some chickens, and rabbits, but because of them were not given meat ration tickets. Mother used everything from the pig except the hair and toenails.

Almost everybody went to the black market. We had to. We would trade anything we could spare, like toys and outgrown children's clothes. You could always get something for cigarettes. We would ride the train and then maybe hitchhike on a truck to get out to the farmers. Some would shut the door in our faces, but others would trade us bread or an egg or two and maybe some bacon, potatoes, or flour. I would tie a bag around my waist, covered by my skirt, to carry what we traded for.

We had a hard time hiding that stuff. Officers watched the trains. If they found you with contraband they would take it away and either fine you or lock you up. If some suspicious-looking fellow got on the train, we would hide in the toilet. It was the only way I could get something to carry home to Mother and Dad.

I had a radio in the hospital. It was illegal to listen to the wrong broadcasts, so if I heard somebody coming I would turn to music. As the war was coming to an end I listened to reports about the Allies closing in. We hoped the Americans would get to us before the Russians. Where I lived, they did.

The Americans came to the hospital and said anybody who had a gun must turn it in. A male nurse had asked me to keep his pistol for him. I buried it in a flower bed and covered it with flowers. We had a Greek girl one of the German officers had brought in as his mistress. She knew she had no future with the Germans. She decided to play up to the Americans and told them she saw me hide the gun. They searched the flower bed, but I knew they were coming. I had dug up the pistol and tossed it in the lake. It may still be there.

The American Army had a rule against fraternization. Soldiers were not allowed to speak to us, but some did anyway. One pretty day several American soldiers were riding horses in a park. One picked up my son and put him on a horse. He loved it. At that time I did not know anything about Texas, but now I think those soldiers must have been Texans. Gerhard had always like horses. He still does.

The Americans had opened up the concentration-camp gates and let everybody out. They did not know the slave laborers and political prisoners from the criminals. Most of the camp people just wanted to go home, but some of the criminals stayed, stealing and killing. Dad had to nail his windows and doors shut. The roads were full of people and not safe. The trains were so crowded that people were hanging out of the windows. I could not go home right away, so I sat in the garden and enjoyed myself. I finally took a boat across the lake. It was at the boat landing that I first met Elmer.

After I had known him a while, we began walking together to the lake, the ski lift, and other places, or we would pull a sled in the snow to pick up Gerhard at the kindergarten. The cold made my lips and cheeks turn red. He liked that. He said it looked like makeup, but I had never worn any and did not know how to use it. At that time, none of us did.

He came to see me almost every evening after he got in from guarding German prisoners of war working in the forest. I did not quite understand when he said he wanted to become a writer. The idea was foreign to me. More than once I fell asleep watching him sitting at my little kitchen table, writing stories in longhand on Red Cross stationery.

In later years I spent a lot of time watching him write, wondering when he was going to have time for me.

It was hard when he told me the Army was about to send him home. After he left, Dad said I had just as well forget him. I would never see or hear from him again. I could not help feeling that he might be right. He wrote me a letter from Linz, but weeks went by without any more word from him. Finally Elmer sent me a telegram. I was afraid to open it at first. I feared he was going to tell me it was all over. When I finally read it, he just told me he had gotten home to Texas all right, and to wait for more word from him.

Soon I began to receive letters from Texas, sometimes two or three in one day, sometimes none for two or three days. He said he was going to send for me when he could. He had left some money. I spent part of it on English lessons, but they did not help me much because it was London-style English, not American. I had to go to Vienna several times to sign papers and take a physical examination.

It took a year to clear all the paperwork. Gerhard and I sailed to

America with other war brides. The Statue of Liberty was beautiful, but I was disappointed in the New York skyline. It had looked bright and shiny in the newsreels. Up close it looked dark and smoky.

I had not been sure anyone would be waiting for us when we landed. Everything seemed unreal, unbelievable even though it was happening. I was nervous about coming to a new country, not knowing just what I was getting myself and my son into. I had had a year to think about it and change my mind. I was in love, or I would not have come. When they called us to line up on the deck, I was relieved and happy to see Elmer standing on the dock, waiting for us.

We went from the dock to a hotel. Elmer's mother looked at me and said, "You can't wear those shoes in New York." They were awful lace-up shoes but were all I had been able to buy at home. She took me shopping. She bought me a gray pin-striped suit, some shoes, and an aqua dress I was to be married in.

We drove a long, long time, getting to Texas. I didn't know just where we were going and don't remember much of what we saw. I had no idea what Texas looked like. I had seen farms in Austria but had never lived on one. I didn't know what a ranch would be like.

I was used to tall mountains and deep blue lakes. As we drove across Texas and the land got flatter and flatter, drier and drier, I am afraid my impression was that we had reached the jumping-off place to hell. But I was about to be married, and I tried not to think about regrets.

We got to the ranch at one o'clock in the morning. The next day we cleaned house. Mother Kelton took me to a beauty shop and then to the minister's house so he could teach me how to speak the vows. He wrote them out, and I tried to repeat the words the way he said them. I didn't know what they meant.

On July 3 we drove to Midland, to Grandmother Kelton's modest house. We went to a studio and had a wedding photograph made. Then the minister from Crane married us. About all I

Anni and Elmer's wedding photo (July 3, 1947)

understood was "I do." Afterward we had some punch and cake, then Elmer and I sat on the porch a while. I do not remember a lot because the day went by in a sort of blur. It was overpowering. Everybody was kind, but everything was strange to me. I had to stay close to Elmer so he could tell me what they were saying.

People ask me if I felt odd getting married among strangers. I did, though at the time just about everything around me seemed odd, not quite real.

I think we stopped for a hamburger or something on the way home. We slept in the front room of the ranch house with Elmer's parents in the next bedroom and his brothers and Gerhard sleeping on the back porch. It was not very private, and I am afraid it was not very romantic. Neither was the next day, when Elmer took me to a July 4 barbecue in Crane and a rodeo in Pecos. The heat was terrible. But that was all the honeymoon we had.

I have thought often about that barbecue and the rodeo. I have been to a lot of barbecues since, and I enjoy one now and then. I can't say as much for rodeos. I always remember that Pecos dust.

Looking back, I realize the little trailer house we bought was not very pretty, but it was our first home together, and we did just fine even if we did not have much room. We took it to Austin so Elmer could return for one last semester at the university. Often at night he would sit and work on his typewriter while I lay on the bed trying to learn English from reading the comics, puzzling out the meaning of the words from the drawings. I had to share him with his lessons and his work.

I was still shy about the language. The trailer camp had a bathhouse and laundry room, but I tried not to go when anyone else was there. I did not know how to talk to people. I made it a point to do our laundry early in the morning before anyone else was up. Elmer tried to get me to join a women's group at the university, but I was uncomfortable because I could not speak English.

Everybody had started calling my son Gary, so I did too. I walked him to school the first two or three days. He cried when I left him. But soon he became acquainted with some boys his age and started going to school without me. I would meet him in the afternoon to see that he got across a busy street all right. He had a very kind and good teacher.

Our meals were simple and skimpy. If we could eat today like we did then, we could save enough to become millionaires. We were getting by on ninety dollars a month from Elmer's GI Bill allowance.

I did not begin to feel that I was really learning the language until we moved to San Angelo. I had a good neighbor, Maxine Howton, who taught me more than anybody. If I said something wrong, she would say it right, and I would repeat after her until I learned it. She had a world of patience. We laughed and giggled a lot, but she was laughing *with* me, not *at* me. That made all the difference. She also helped me learn how to drive.

I had no concept of cowboy life. I liked horses but never wanted to ride one. And I was afraid of cows. Once when I was a girl, Dad went with several of us on a long walk from Bad Ischl over the mountains to Bad Aussee. We came to some cows resting on both sides of a tunnel. I didn't want to go through, but Dad made me do it. Coming back, he told me to sit on a log and wait while he went off picking raspberries. A cow came up behind me, and I took off. I landed in a raspberry patch with cobwebs all over me.

Another time we stopped to eat and took our shoes off to let our feet rest. A cow came up behind me and sniffed at the back of my neck. I grabbed a pair of shoes and ran. Later one of my feet began to hurt. My sister-in-law, Nanni, complained of the same thing. I had one of her shoes and one of my own.

I got used to the trailer in spite of its being small. I was small in those days myself. Later, when we bought our first house in San Angelo, it looked like a mansion. I had never lived in a one-family house. We didn't have them in Ebensee. There was not space enough. Everybody built up, not out. Our home in Austria housed three families of Lipps, one on each floor.

There were times when I was homesick, but they did not last long. I stayed too busy to think about it much. Everybody around me did the best they could to make me feel at home. Nobody seemed to think less of me because I came from somewhere else.

I was so anxious to learn English that I did not use German much after the first months. I still remembered it when we made our first trip back to Austria in 1954. After that visit, it was twenty-one years before I had much chance to use it again. My sister Resi came to visit us in 1975. I could understand her, but for the first two weeks I couldn't answer her well. I couldn't think of the German words. It was a little easier the next year when Elmer and I went to Austria for our first visit in twenty-two years, though I still stumbled over some words. Once I needed a safety pin and could not think what it was called. Elmer had to draw a picture of it for me. Now I have forgotten the word again.

If you don't use it, you lose it.

I have no regrets. We made a good life for ourselves in Texas. Besides our two sons and a daughter, we have four grandchildren and five great-grandchildren. Now, when we go back to visit in Austria, I enjoy it. It is a beautiful country. But after a little while I am ready to come back to my own home, my own family. I would not choose to live in Austria again. It is not home anymore. I have lived in Texas almost three times more years than I lived in Austria.

I have not ever gotten used to the dust and the heat in West Texas, but on the other hand Austria has dark, gloomy, rainy spells that last a week or more. In the winter it has ice and snow.

My people there have long since recovered from World War II. They have a good life, but I have a good life here. I would not want to change it, or trade it for any other.